1987

MW00359087

$10⁰⁰

1²/94

6⁰⁰

³/6

JANE'S NAVAL REVIEW

edited by Captain John Moore RN

JANE'S NAVAL REVIEW

edited by Captain John Moore RN

Sixth year of issue

JANE'S

Contents

Introduction

THIS year Brendan Gallagher and I have tried to match philosophy with practicality. The first covers a number of aspects of maritime affairs. In the light of Soviet advances, is the West sufficiently forward-thinking? Is Royal Navy Trident a viable programme? Is the Indian naval build-up a threat to peace? These are questions of great significance, not only for people in NATO but also for the huge population surrounding the Indian Ocean and in South-east Asia. From the British point of view, it is a pity that the two main political parties, after a period of procrastination, failed to offer their viewpoints for publication in this *Review*. Perhaps this is not surprising: the Government's naval policy has been one of indecision, while that of the Labour opposition has been based on obfuscation.

In the USA there has been no doubt of that country's naval aims, as set out by Secretary Lehman. But we should remember the extraordinary pull-back of the Carter regime and be prepared for similar retrogression by the next administration. The whole business of political backward thinking is underlined in Antonio Ciampi's article on Italian naval aviation: a ukase produced by a dictator some 60 years ago was mechanically obeyed until independent minds decided that the Italian Navy should have a measure of control over its own airforce.

The result of the return of a democratic government in place of a military dictatorship is apparent in Adrian English's article on Argentina, and the effect of errant political decisions is underlined in the piece on the South-west Pacific. Both articles have one thing in common: there is little point in considering naval forces unless the political background is firmly established.

This is particularly true of the Soviet Union. Two articles deal with Soviet naval programmes, the future of which depends entirely on the outcome of Mr Gorbachev's initiatives. If Soviet resources are to be diverted from military production to civilian industry, what effect will this have on naval procurement? One possible outcome is a curtailment of current series production and a greater emphasis on the more advanced classes which have so far had the benefit of research and development funds rather than production budgets. A case in point is the single Mike-class submarine: could this be the first of a new generation with a totally original form of propulsion?

The question of non-nuclear submarine propulsion is dealt with by Roy Corlett, while Nigel Ling, who was privy to a pivotal meeting on the design of the Royal Navy's new frigates, offers a dispassionate view of the problems facing the naval architect. Outmoded viewpoints may bedevil the designers of future vessels, but whatever the shape and size of these ships, they require the optimum in weaponry. Some say that guns are outmoded; let them read the Spilman/Round view of this subject. Others maintain that helicopters are too costly; Paul Beaver's piece explains why these essential systems are increasingly taking first place in the procurement queue. But none of these elements has any value unless ships are linked by efficient communications, an aspect of naval affairs that is complicated by commercial rivalries. In their article Bob Raggett and John Williamson assess the prospects for money-saving co-operation in the West.

Now more than ever, navies need cost-cutting methods of construction; Geoffrey Wood believes that the MEKO system makes the production-line warship a reality. From 20th-century technology to an age-old problem: Lt-Cdr Miles Chapman's piece on piracy shows that while the modern version of this crime is murderous and despicable, it is yielding ground in the face of concerted and vigorous government action. This success constitutes a single ray of light at a time when the potential for naval confrontation continues to rise.

J E Moore
May 1987

Acknowledgments

I have only two acknowledgments to make: to Brendan Gallagher, without whose powerful drive this book would never have been finished; to Barbara, my wife, without whose encouragement this book would never have been begun.

The Contributors

Beaver, Paul

Has been writing about naval aviation, with particular emphasis on aircraft carriers, for nearly 12 years. He is author of *The British Carrier*, a standard work on the Royal Navy's conventional aircraft carriers, and *Invincible Class*, which details the development of the current British light carriers.

Blake, Bernard

Served in the RAF for over 20 years as a specialist navigator, a large part of his time being spent on navigation and radio systems research and development work at Boscombe Down and Farnborough. After leaving the RAF he joined Marconi, initially in the development laboratory and later in marketing and public relations. He now edits *Jane's Weapon Systems* and is a regular contributor to *Jane's Defence Weekly*.

Braybrook, Ray

Freelance writer and consultant, specialising in military aircraft and various types of armament. As a graduate engineer, his professional experience includes guided-weapon testing in the RAF, and designing and marketing training aircraft and V/STOL fighters for British Aerospace and its predecessors. His last appointment before resigning from BAe in 1980 was as technical marketing adviser to the Kingston-Brough Division.

Chapman, Lt-Cdr Miles, MBE, RN (Retired)

Royal Navy 1938–1971, specialising in torpedoes and ASW. After war service in the Western Approaches and on North Russian convoys, he was posted to the Home Fleet, Far East (in HMS *Black Swan*, taking part in the *Amethyst* incident) and the West Indies. On retirement was for ten years marine director of the oceanology station in Corsica, and commanding officer of the attached research vessel. Joined Carmichael and Sweet/Jane's Information Services Ltd in 1984, initially to research Capt G. R. Villar's book *Piracy Today*, and is now a defence analyst.

Ciampi, Dr Antonio

Freelance journalist, founded the Milpress international press agency in 1982, specialising in defence, the naval and aerospace industries, and transportation. He has contributed, directly or through Milpress, to a wide range of international publications, including *Jane's Defence Weekly* (London), *Navy International* (London), *Conmilit* (Hong Kong), *Defensa* (Madrid), *Arab Defence Journal* (Beirut), *Asian Defence Journal* (Kuala Lumpur) and *Afrique Défense* (Paris).

Corlett, Roy

Joined the Royal Navy as an electrical artificer apprentice in 1935 and subsequently served in submarines in all rates and ranks up to commander. His final RN appointment was as Staff Weapons Officer to Flag Officer Submarines. Following retirement he worked for Vickers Shipbuilding Ltd before setting up his own maritime consultancy business.

English, Adrian

Born in 1939, he has been interested in the Latin American military scene for many years. He has visited most of the countries of the region and is an internationally acknowledged expert on Latin American military affairs. Since 1979 he has annually contributed material to *Jane's Fighting Ships* and *The Military Balance*. He has also written extensively on Latin American military and strategic subjects, including regular contributions to *Jane's Defence Review*, *Jane's Defence Weekly*, *International Defence Review*, *Navy International* and *Technologia Militar*, and was co-author of *Battle for the Falklands: Naval Forces*.

Grazebrook, A. W.

Joined RNR in October 1952 and transferred to RANR in 1963. Author of numerous articles in *Pacific Defence Reporter*. Adviser to *Jane's Fighting Ships*.

Lehman, John F., Jr

Secretary of the Navy (US) since February 5, 1981. Educated at St Joseph's College (BSc); Cambridge

(England) as Earhart Fellow (BA Hons Law, MA International Law and Diplomacy); University of Pennsylvania (PhD International Relations); Johns Hopkins University (Visiting Fellow). Pennsylvania National Guard 1964. Air Force Reserve 1966, Naval Reserve 1968. Four major publications. Before appointment as Secretary of the Navy was president of Abington Corporation, a Washington-based management firm specialising in defence matters.

Ling, Nigel, TEng(CEI)

Served as a Merchant Navy engineer officer, worked on research and development of fishing vessels, including stability investigations, and worked until recently for the British Transport Docks Board, concerned with naval architecture and design.

Moore, Captain J. E., RN

Entered RN 1939. Served most of naval career in HM Submarines. Commanded 7th Submarine Squadron, was Chief of Staff to Commander-in-Chief Naval Home Command and, finally, took charge of Soviet naval intelligence in MoD. Retired at own request 1972. Editor *Jane's Fighting Ships* since November 1972. Author of several books and numbers of articles on naval affairs.

Owen, Dr David, MP

Leader of the Social Democratic Party and Member of Parliament for Plymouth since 1966. After his election he became Parliamentary Private Secretary to the Minister of Defence, Administration. During 1968–70 he was Parliamentary Under-Secretary of State for Defence (Royal Navy). When Labour went into opposition in 1970 he became a frontbench spokesman on defence. In September 1976 he became Minister of State at the Foreign and Commonwealth Office, where he was responsible for European Community affairs. He was appointed Secretary of State for Foreign and Commonwealth Affairs in 1977. Dr Owen has been a member of the Independent Commission on Disarmament and Security Issues since 1980. Publications include *The Politics of Defence* (1976).

Raggett, Bob

Founding editor of *Jane's Military Communications*, now in its eighth edition, and deputy director of corporate affairs for British Telecom. His career in the communications business includes stints with GEC-Marconi, *Electronics Weekly*, Horizon House and *Telephony*. He is author of several books and numerous articles on communications and military technology.

Round, Mike

Worked on the analysis and design of missile instrumentation and fire-control systems before joining Vosper Thornycroft (UK) Ltd. Since then he has worked on all aspects of ship design, in particular the assessment of weapon systems.

Spilman, Brian

Manager of Weapons Systems Engineering Group at Vosper Thornycroft, following previous appointments in weapons design and project management. Worked for Marconi Radar and Bristol Siddeley Engines Ltd before joining Vosper Thornycroft.

Wallace, Jim, MP

Elected MP for Orkney and Shetland in 1983, he is currently Liberal Parliamentary spokesman on defence and fishing.

Williamson, John

Currently works with Bob Raggett on the *Jane's Military Communications* yearbook and is the international editor of the US magazine *Telephony*. He worked previously for GEC-Marconi and a number of publications, including the *Journal of Electronic Defense*, *Telecommunications*, and *Communications Engineering International*. Joint author with Bob Raggett of the *Eurodata Managers' Guide to Teletex*, and edited the first *Middle East Guide to Data Communications*.

Wood, Geoffrey

Went to sea as a deck apprentice in tankers in 1940 and left the merchant service in 1948. Following a period of small craft delivery worldwide, he worked in naval architecture before taking up maritime journalism. He was founding editor of *Maritime Defence* in 1976.

The naval year

Capt John Moore RN

The US cruiser *Ticonderoga*. The first of a planned total of 27, she commissioned in January 1983. This class is the first to be fitted with the Aegis air defence system, which has proved to be the biggest advance in such systems ever known. Their high cost is justified by their ability to probe far enough and give sufficient warning to make it unnecessary to keep aircraft airborne on standing combat air patrol.

AMIDST the welter of projects currently being produced by the world's arms industries, defence commentators are looking for advance, for innovation, for that bright spark of genius that will increase security and deter war at minimum expense. But the past year has seen little to suggest that their search will bear fruit. Leaden-footed bureaucracy has combined with financial stringency to slow progress, and all that is to be seen is conventional and oft-tried. New programmes rely on what the British defence establishment describes as "traditional wisdom," a recipe for dull repetition of past failings in many areas. This can result only in high costs and scant progress at a time when new ideas and capabilities are hanging around the back door waiting to be recognised.

Research and development, it should go without saying, is the key to advance, but those who hold the pursestrings are too little versed in the complexities of modern systems to accept the need for such investment in order to save in the future. In Britain at present there is a brisk controversy about the need for nuclear power stations. While costs are quoted and arguments rage, it has escaped the notice of most people that, because the government failed to invest in research into the handling of high-grade metals, the vital elements of British nuclear reactors have to be cast in Japan and welded in France. British nuclear submarines, according to recent discussions in the House of Commons, owe much to the expertise of several other nations, a fact hitherto with-held from the taxpayer.

What therefore have the West's leading navies managed to achieve over the last twelve months? In the USA the 600-ship Navy came significantly closer to realisation. Outgoing Navy Secretary John Lehman declares in this *Review* that the aim is to produce 15 carrier battle groups, four battleship surface action groups, 100 attack submarines, "an adequate number of ballistic missile submarines," and amphibious lift for the US Marine Corps. He concludes that "when escort, mine warfare, auxiliary and replenishment units are considered, about 600 ships emerge from this accounting." What he doesn't say is that this is probably the most that he and Defence Secretary Weinberger and their staffs reckoned Congress could be persuaded to swallow.

Mr Lehman makes several references to the additional forces that America's NATO allies could deploy in support of the US Navy. Equally, the Western European navies could rely on the USN to return the compliment. But before they become too complacent on this score, Western European politicians should take into account the fact that the USA has a larger trade across the Pacific than she does in the Atlantic. Who knows how long hostilities might last if we were plunged into the horrors of a large-scale war, and if the "arsenal of the West" were to survive, her trade routes across the Pacific would be as important as the resupply routes across the Atlantic.

Below: **US submarine *Seadevil*, one of the class of 37 boats completed in 1967–75. At 4,640 tons, comparatively small by some standards, these nuclear-propelled boats have four torpedo tubes amidships and carry Harpoon and Tomahawk missiles, Subroc and torpedoes. With a dived speed of over 30kt, they have a complement of 129.**

Top right: **Soviet Echo II-class submarine. Although all 29 boats of this class were completed in 1961–67, they continue in service today. At least ten have had the original armament of eight SS-N-3 missiles replaced by more modern SS-N-12s.**

Above right: **Soviet Natya-class minesweeper. The largest class in the Soviet MCM forces, these 790-ton steel-hulled ships are designated "seagoing minesweepers". The Soviet total of MCM vessels (about 380) is greater than the whole MCM resources of NATO.**

The Navy Secretary refers, almost in passing, to "escort and mine warfare" units. These were the two elements of the fleet that kept Britain alive in the Second World War until the entry of America into the war. Churchill's citadel would have collapsed without them, and yet today NATO has far fewer such vessels than did the Commonwealth navies and their allies in 1939–41, while the modern Soviet Navy has many more ships than did the German Navy and possesses submarines of immensely increased capability.

Even though mine warfare, which can throttle both trade and resupply, is a speciality of the Soviet Navy, the USN could clear the entrances to no more than four or five major ports at best, and would be unable to sweep the coastal routes heavily used by merchant shipping serving the United States. In fairness to the USA, this planning blank spot is shared by all her allies and the majority of non-communist navies. There may be some significance in the fact that the USSR and her allies, as well as the People's Republic of China, have allocated large amounts of resources to the problem of mine countermeasures. For their part, the Western powers can between them muster fewer than two-thirds as many MCM vessels as the Soviet Navy.

The reactivation of the four American battleships has caused a certain amount of murmuring about "dinosaurs" and the like. It would be to more purpose if the murmurers added up the following equation:

battleship firepower + range + speed + invulnerability = major requirement answered.

The same stricture applies to the critics of the aircraft carrier. Fresh-faced lads from Congressional staffs are wont to speak of carriers as vulnerable white elephants and to extol the virtues of shore-based air cover. The need for them was originally demonstrated by the Pacific war of 1942–45, and continues to be by the simple mathematics of time and distance. The anti-carrier lobby might face the realities if they ever found themselves needing cover from a nearest friendly air base located 1,000 enemy-dominated miles away.

As a support for the carriers, the Aegis cruisers and, later, destroyers with similar equipment will continue to provide exceptional cover. Though the Aegis ships have come under fire for their high unit price, they represent a bargain if one takes into account the cost of larger numbers of less capable air defence vessels, plus the increased wear and tear and fuel expenditure occasioned by the necessary extra combat air patrols.

What the USN lacks is an adequate MCM force, sufficient "cheap" escorts, and a force of comparatively simple and therefore inexpensive submarines to provide coastal cover against cruise missile submarines. What the British need is a plan of some sort. Orders for new ships are jerked out in a manner reminiscent of the dentist's chair. The totals of operational ships are fudged, and the requirement stated is far below that dictated by government policies. Combined with the continual grind of exercises and examinations and the ever-growing paperwork now afflicting the fleet, this reduction in numbers is having an increasingly bad effect on the lives of the officers and senior rates. The problem of an imbalance between sea and shore time affects all personnel, and is certainly not addressed satisfactorily in the latest Defence White Paper. Though the Royal Navy is hanging on by its fingertips, the quality of its people allows it to do a great job despite the indecision of its political governors and the ignorant interventions of the Treasury.

The French Navy also has its problems, again largely

Top: The US battleship *Iowa*. Completed in 1943–44, this class of four 58,000-ton ships had spent most of their lives in reserve before it was decided to reactivate them in 1981. Capable of 35kt and a range of 15,000 miles at 17kt, these ships carry a missile armament of 32 Tomahawks and 16 Harpoons. Their main battery is nine 16in guns, with 12/20 5in guns and a large number of smaller pieces. There is space on the fantail for four helicopters.

Above: US carrier *Carl Vinson*, the third of the US Navy's 91,500-ton nuclear-propelled carriers. With a length of 1,092ft, she has four steam catapults and an angled deck to cope with her complement of 90+ aircraft. *Vinson* is now in commission, with two more building and requests for additional carriers in future plans.

Top right: *Knox*-class frigate of the USN, one of 46 completed in 1969–74. Of 3,900/4,200 tons with a speed of 27kt, they carry a 127mm gun, eight Harpoon and four Tomahawk missiles, an Asroc launcher and four ASW torpedo tubes.

Centre right: Soviet Grisha III-class frigate. The Soviet ASW force includes ships of many sizes, from 17,500 tons downwards. The Grishas, which first appeared in 1968, are at the lower end of the scale. Of 1,200 tons, with a gas turbine and two diesels giving a speed of 30kt, they carry either 57mm or 76mm guns, four torpedo tubes, two rocket launchers and depth charges.

Right: British Type 23 frigate. HMS *Norfolk* was launched in April 1987 to commission in 1989. Displacing 3,850 tons, she will carry two Lynx helicopters, eight Harpoon SSMs, Sea Wolf vertical-launch SAMs, a 4in Mark 8 gun and two triple ASW torpedo tubes. Her propulsion plant comprises two gas turbines, four diesels and two electric motors for a speed of 28kt and a range of 7,800 miles at 15kt. Three more of this class have been laid down.

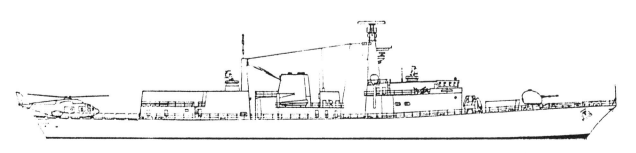

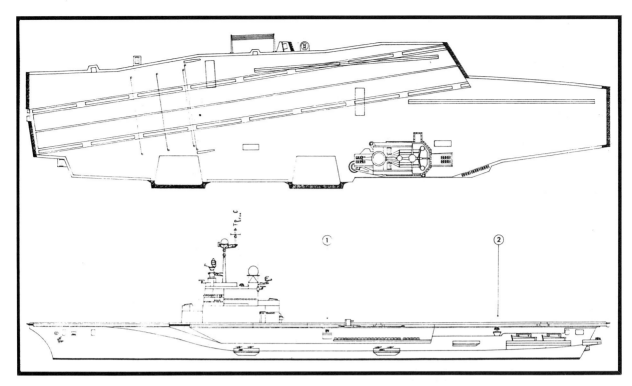

centred on personnel. The transition from a socialist to a right-wing government in early 1986 caused little change to the building programme, and there has been no sign that the ballistic missile submarine building rate is adversely affecting that of other submarines and surface ships. With a nuclear-propelled aircraft carrier, three SSNs, six destroyers and a multitude of amphibious, MCM, survey and auxiliary ships in the building yards, and a programme which is planned into the 21st century, the *Marine Nationale* is in an enviable position.

The other European NATO nations are all embarked on building programmes designed to replace current ships and submarines with vessels of greater capability, though at greatly increased cost. Two problems are of particular interest. The Belgians and the Dutch have found that minehunting in the sandy waters off their coasts is an irksome and difficult task. Their need is for more ships to assist in MCM and they are working in collaboration with other NATO forces to produce a satisfactory ship which could well turn out to be a Quadripartite minesweeper. From international co-operation to inter-service rivalry: Antonio Ciampi writes in this *Review* about the Italian Navy's struggle to acquire its own embarked V/STOL aircraft. In spite of having a carrier capable of embarking such aircraft, the Navy has until now been hog-tied by the antique laws of a long defunct dictator.

Beyond the Mediterranean, India continues to build up a navy of formidable proportions, as Commander A. W. Grazebrook's article makes clear. It is hard to justify such overwhelming force when one considers the abysmal standard of living of the majority of the population of that vast country. Is it part of a plan for hegemony in the Indian Ocean? Perhaps it is prompted by fear of India's Soviet friends, since it surely cannot be seen as necessary to counter the comparatively small naval force of Pakistan. Or is it simply a matter of a big country with a long coastline wanting a proportionately big navy?

Australia and New Zealand are not in the same league as India as far as navies are concerned, despite the huge disparity in GDP in their favour. Elsewhere in the *Review* we deal with the problems of the South Pacific, particularly those facing the Americans in this area. To the north, China has recently demonstrated a surge of interest in naval construction. The resulting ships are not very modern but are adequate for the tasks envisaged and also for export. The Chinese have a long tradition of warship transfers, originally small craft but now, potentially, frigates and submarines. The readiness with which Egypt has taken up such offers when European alternatives have proved too expensive should sound a warning bell in what remains of the West's shipyards.

Japan remains at the top of the world's shipbuilding league despite a recent 25% drop in civilian orders. The fact that the Maritime Self-Defence Force can afford a 1986 programme comprising one destroyer, two frigates, one submarine, two minesweepers/hunters, one support ship and one LCU may well be due to short building times and a rigid adherence to scheduled completion dates. Construction times of less than three years for submarines and destroyers and barely two years for frigates are both highly creditable and a source of real economies. Life is made a great deal easier for the planners when it is possible to forecast some two years in advance the date of commissioning.

The Latin American navies face financial difficulties that could cripple them. Of the 15 countries most in

---

Left: An outline of the first French nuclear-propelled carrier. Of about 40,000 tons full load, the two ships of this class are designed to carry 40 aircraft. Speed is to be 27kt and endurance 45 days. The first is not due to commission before 1995.

Below left: French fleet support ship *Meuse*, one of four 17,800-ton ships completed, with a fifth under construction. She can provide all forms of fuel and stores and can also act as a flagship.

Below: Italian carrier *Guiseppe Garibaldi*. This striking and versatile ship, of 13,500 tons full load, is capable of 30kt on the power of four gas turbines. She can carry 16 Sea King or equivalent helicopters, with 12 in the hangar. The argument between the Italian Air Force and Navy about whether the latter should operate V/STOL aircraft appears to be resolved, so Harriers of some sort should eventually become part of the ship's complement.

Below: Japanese destroyer *Hatakaze*, the first of a new class with a standard displacement of 4,450 tons. She has four gas turbines for a speed of 32kt and carries eight Harpoon SSMs, a SAM system, two 127mm guns, two Phalanx CIWS and an ASW armament of one Asroc and six torpedo tubes. *Hatakaze* commissioned in 1986 and the second of class is due in 1988.

Bottom: Japanese destroyer *Matsuyuki*. One of a class of 12 ships, she carries a helicopter, eight Harpoon missiles, an Asroc ASW missile launcher, six ASW torpedo tubes, one 76mm gun and two Phalanx CIWS. They have four gas turbines for a speed of 30kt.

Right: Brazilian frigate *Constituičao*, one of six British-designed ships commissioned in 1976–80. Four are configured for ASW with an Ikara launcher, six torpedo tubes and a 375mm rocket launcher. The other two carry four Exocets in place of Ikara, and all have a single helicopter. The ASW ships have a single 115mm gun, the others carry two. With two gas turbines and four diesels, all have a speed of 30kt and a range of 5,300nm at 17kt.

Below right: Chilean destroyer *Almirante Latorre*. The Chilean Navy has now taken over four of the British "County" class. Of 6,200 tons, they are armed with 115mm guns, Exocet SSMs and Seacat SAMs.

debt to the World Bank and other financial institutions, ten come from this area. Yet their navies can muster two aircraft carriers, 42 submarines and a large number of destroyers, frigates and amphibious vessels. Brazil, as if oblivious of a national debt of some $110 billion, is talking with assurance about the construction of nuclear submarines. Argentina, with half Brazil's debt burden, is seeking buyers for some of her ships and submarines. Peru, owing one-ninth as much as Brazil, is currently unable to maintain payments on the refit of one of her cruisers in the Netherlands, while Chile is seeking replacements for her deleted ships in the second-hand market. These are all countries with long and distinguished naval histories, and their plight reflects that of most non-communist navies. Prices have risen to such heights that orders cannot be placed when they should be. In consequence, many warship yards would face liquidation if it were not for the support of cartels or governments.

"Towpath Papers" bode ill for the Royal Navy

Dr David Owen MP

THE Royal Navy is facing a crisis of confidence as great as that which occurred between the two world wars. There are ominous signs that we are eroding our maritime strengths. The true state of the Royal Navy is easier to assess because of the accidental finding of the "Towpath Papers," which revealed to the public gaze not just the forward planning of the Navy but, more importantly, gave an insight into the deep concerns of those responsible inside the Ministry of Defence for naval planning. The programmes of the three services are now under considerable pressure. Despite this, a defence review will not take place this side of an election.

What is now beyond dispute is that, in a number of critical areas, there is cause for deep concern about the Royal Navy in the 1990s. When senior naval officers can write about a naval programme alarmingly poor in a wide range of areas, then those who have the best interests of the Navy at heart should be sounding the

Brave, one of the second batch of Type 22 ASW frigates. After the first four an extra 55ft was added to the design, and in Batch 3 (from No 11 onwards) a 4.5in gun was added. The deplorable lack of firepower of the original design resulted from a total dependence on the Exocet surface-to-surface missile and the Sea Wolf SAM. Provision has been made for two helicopters, and six ASW torpedo tubes are fitted. *Brave* is the only one of this class to be powered by four Rolls-Royce Spey gas turbines, the remainder having either Olympus and Tyne or Spey and Tyne.

alarm. Of the many areas of concern noted in the "Towpath Papers," that of submarine warfare, where the future of naval power lies, is the most worrying.

We may never again face limited war at sea with setpiece surface ship battles. Rather, in a period of

Top: Resolution. The first of the Royal Navy's four nuclear-propelled Polaris submarines, she was laid down only 15 months after the Macmillan/Kennedy agreement at Nassau in December 1962. This was a magnificent example of the planning and execution of a set programme which could well be emulated today.

Above: Avenger. One of the six survivors of the *Amazon* class, two of which were sunk in the Falklands War. They carry a helicopter, four Exocet missiles, a 4.5in gun, six torpedo tubes and 132 tons of ballast. The streak beneath the funnel on the hull is a strengthening piece necessitated by severe cracking around the upper deck.

political tension, an undeclared war of stealth could be played out under the sea. The growing Soviet capacity for submarine warfare can hardly be exaggerated. It is over the future of NATO's submarine navy, not its surface navy, that the alliance faces one of its most critical challenges. Britain's contribution is of the greatest importance to NATO in this area, and its expertise must not be lost. Yet that is what is in prospect if NATO remains afraid to ask us to concentrate our resources, or if we are too locked into inter-service rivalry to seek permission to increase the selectivity of our defence effort. What is needed is not a purely British defence review, but a review explicitly conducted with our NATO partners.

Service commanders are also well aware that if

"Fortresss Falklands" continues, it will add financial, logistic and manpower constraints, preventing us from keeping our existing NATO commitments. It is likely to be impossible to persuade the Falkland Islanders to accept a transfer of sovereignty to Argentina, whereas a shared-sovereignty arrangement – or the vesting of sovereignty in the United Nations Security Council through the trust provisions in the UN Charter – offers a possible way forward. Negotiations to settle the long-term future of the Falklands with Argentina are fully compatible with the sacrifices our servicemen made in retaking the islands and defeating aggression.

The Towpath Papers have punctured the Government's repeated claims that it is planning for a 50-strong surface fleet. Now we know that under Naval planning the destroyer/frigate force from 1987 to 1997 will at no time reach the figure of 50 ships but instead will average 48. In 1981 John Nott's mistaken defence review contained at least a readiness to confront the admirals with the reality that they had given too much attention to the size of the surface fleet and insufficient attention to the weapons on the ships. It would be better for the admirals to insist on a navy with a smaller number of ships than a navy with ill equipped ships. If the numbers are then insufficient for the tasks, the politicians will either have to cut the tasks or find resources for more hulls. But they should not be given service support to do this at the expense of weapon effectiveness. The Conservatives have sought to camouflage the fact that much of the Nott analysis, giving absolute priority to the needs of the Central Front and rejected in the post-Falklands euphoria, has now become the accepted wisdom in the harsher economic climate within the Ministry of Defence. The Navy is therefore in danger of losing out unless there is a readjustment of the balance of the UK's existing commitments to NATO.

The Nott review held out the prospect of an increase in the fleet submarine (SSN) build rate to compensate in part for a reduced surface fleet. Perhaps the most serious problem revealed by the Towpath Papers is the fact that extra provision will not now be made for building hunter-killer submarines during the Trident submarine construction programme. The proposal for a second building stream has not been supported on grounds of cost, even though the ideal order rate for hunter-killer submarines would be one every 12 to 18 months. The hunter-killer fleet, which is equivalent in firepower and effectiveness to the battleships of the past, will therefore be one of the many casualties of the continued Trident programme if the Conservatives win the next election.

The defence budget makes it clear that on current plans the cost of Trident will be particularly damaging for the Navy. In 1985–86 Trident absorbed 2.8% of the defence budget. In 1986–87 it will absorb 3.6% – an increase of 0.8%. In 1987–88 it is likely to take 3.9% at present exchange rates. The House of Commons Select Committee on Defence has estimated that at its peak Trident will absorb 12.3% of the Naval

Below: Manchester. The first of the third batch of Type 42 destroyers, *Manchester* and her three sisters are 50ft longer than the previous Type 42s, resulting in improved speed and seaworthiness. The armament has remained the same throughout, although all ships have had extra close-range weapons fitted since the Falklands War.

Right: Renown. Like all the Polaris submarines she has two 143-man crews which take her on alternate 60-day patrols. The Polaris missiles are fitted with Chevaline warheads, each carrying three 60kT MIRVs.

Below right: Ark Royal. The third of the three light aircraft carriers which commissioned in 1980–85, *Ark Royal* is slightly larger than her sisters and was built with a 12° ski-jump. She is currently fitted to carry 20 aircraft (eight Harriers and nine ASW and three AEW helicopters). Four gas turbines give a speed of 28kt.

equipment budget. This expenditure was bad enough when the defence budget was increasing; it is even more grave in its implications when the Government is cutting defence spending by 7% in real terms between 1986–87 and 1988–89. This amounts to a total reduction of £1.1 billion at current prices.

On the basis of these estimates, Trident will represent nearly 9% of total military spending, and 17–20% of capital spending on defence, by 1989–90. The squeeze is well illustrated by the fact that in 1986–87 the naval general-purposes combat forces will get 0.6% less in real terms than was committed in 1985–86. Like the cuckoo in the nest, Trident is on course to take more and more from other parts of our conventional defence effort.

We were told in December 1986 that the amphibious forces are to be retained. But the cost implications of this decision cannot be fully assessed until the announced studies – whether to build new or refit *Fearless* and *Intrepid* – have been completed. The build-up of Soviet ships and maritime air and infantry units in the Kola Peninsula on NATO's northern flank is a major new factor to which, as yet, NATO has made no fully considered response. The other worries are political: the disputed demarcation line in the Barents Sea, disagreements over the Continental Shelf, and the fact that the Soviets are still refusing to accept the median principle in the Baltic off Gotland. Coupled with Soviet eavesdropping incidents, these factors represent tinder which could be ignited at any moment.

On the Northern Flank the Royal Marines can, with the Dutch amphibious forces, make an important contribution to NATO's reinforcement. A refusal to contribute here would make the United States very anxious about the readiness of Europe to take its share of the responsibility for guarding this vulnerable area. To date insufficient provision has been made for the Northern Region in NATO's naval forward planning. But if that gap is to be filled by Britain, then other NATO countries will have to pick up some of our responsibilities on the Central Front.

Surface ship design is a controversial question, and one for experts rather than politicians. But it is to be hoped that the inadequacy of Sea Dart, as exposed in the Falklands War, will not be forgotten, and missile defence as well as missile attack given a far higher priority.

It is doubtful that the search for a cheaper frigate will be any more successful in the future than it has been in the past. With the introduction of towed-array sonar and other ASW innovations, absolute costs are likely to continue to increase. This raises the question of whether it would not be better to put more emphasis

on performing the ASW role with submarines rather than surface ships.

The Government has done so much damage to the naval dockyards that the Royal Navy will come to regret supporting agency management, which, against all logic and sense, separates the capital assets of the dockyards from their management. We know from the Towpath Papers that in 1985 the Navy Board made an "act of faith" in pursuing agency management on unproven grounds of economy and an unquantified increase in the availability of ships. Predictions from the all-party Parliamentary Public Accounts Committee and Defence Committee that the Government was acting without sufficient evidence, and that the navy was likely to suffer from ministerial prejudices over the dockyards, looks likely to be confirmed. From Samuel Pepys onwards, the pursuit of efficiency in the dockyards has always fallen foul of the ambivalence of the Navy Board itself. The Board wants instant refits but, like a car owner using a 24-hour-a-day, seven-days-a-week garage facility, resents the cost. Privatisation of the Dockyards will prove a great mistake.

The search for economies in the naval budget must of course continue, from the dockyards to the doctors in the naval medical services. But there is less and less room for cuts. The most devastating blow to the naval budget fell a few years ago when the Trident programme, against previous assurances, was attributed to the naval budget. Predictably, the Polaris deterrent, instead of being seen as an inviolate addition to the three services' budgets, has been funded increasingly from the naval budget. It is now clear that the combination of a Trident deterrent system and a large fleet of SSNs in a conventional role is something

that Britain cannot afford. While refusing to face up to the need to choose, we are allowing decisions to be made by default and disguising their consequences. We pretend to have a larger surface fleet than we have. We refuse to acknowledge that we are cutting back on our SSN fleet. We risk not having a merchant navy that can support us when tension is rising. We are likely to have insufficient civilian ferries to reinforce the Central Front in times of tension.

Serious individuals within and outside the navy are questioning the present strategy. In doing so they run into the old conspiracy between Labour and Conservative politicians. It suits both parties to pretend for example that the choice that Britain faces is "Trident or nothing". The task of the SDP/Liberal Alliance is to convince the country that this choice is a false one, that we can and should retain a minimum deterrent but at a lower cost than Trident.

The Conservatives, in favour of Britain sticking with a ballistic missile system to replace Polaris, will increasingly point to the large sums of money already committed to the submarine hulls being built at Vickers Barrow. But cancellation costs would be minimal if we continued with building the hull of the first and probably the second submarine, as SDP/Liberal Alliance spokesmen have assured workers at Vickers and Cammell Laird that we would. That would leave open the choice of whether to purchase the French M4/5 ballistic missile or fit a vertical-launched non-ballistic missile system in these hulls. The unwanted Trident missiles and fire-control mechanisms could then be used on Trident submarines in the United States, where the D5 system is not due to be deployed until 1989. This would substantially reduce any claim for compensation by the American manufacturers.

In Government the SDP/Liberal Alliance would maintain our minimum nuclear deterrent with whatever modernisation proved necessary until it could be negotiated away, as part of a global arms negotiation process, in return for worthwhile concessions by the USSR which would enhance British and European

Sir Lancelot. Of 5,674 tons full load, *Sir Lancelot* is one of an original six ships. *Sir Galahad* was lost in the Falklands War. Manned by the Royal Fleet Auxiliary, these ships can carry 16 main battle tanks, 34 other vehicles, 120 tons of fuel and 30 tons of ammunition. They carry a crew of only 68.

Phoebe. A survivor of the rapidly dwindling *Leander* class, which is being paid off in spite of having plenty of hull life left. One was transferred to New Zealand with only 13 years on the clock. Vast sums have been spent on various forms of conversion for these ships. *Phoebe* is one of four which have had their main radar removed – amongst other topweight reductions – to allow the fitting of a towed-array sonar.

security. But increasingly a more fundamental question is being asked: would a UK Trident force be truly independent? It is little short of incredible that a US President as close to a British Prime Minister as Reagan could, as he did at the Reykjavik Summit, agree without any consultation whatsoever to attempt to negotiate the total abolition of all ballistic missiles, Trident included. It brings back memories of the 1962 cancellation of Skybolt, and reminds us of how dependent on the US we are with Polaris and will increasingly be with Trident. Whatever President Reagan may say now, a new US President in the 1990s could well decide not to sell us Trident missiles. If SDI was even part successful and deployed in the mid-1990s, that would raise the question of how viable a UK ballistic system would be in an era of defence in space.

The quickest and neatest way of cutting the cost of any submarine-launched ballistic missile programme would be to build three submarines rather than four. The arguments against this relate to the supposed need to have at all times a British Polaris submarine available and ready to fire within minutes. In fact it is only NATO that needs this capability, not Britain in normal times. And even the NATO requirement is ripe for re-examination. At times of low political tension, and particularly if we can add to the limited confidence-building measures just agreed at Stockholm, NATO (and more particularly the US) could maintain far fewer submarines at instant readiness. Any potential conflict would be preceded by a warning period of increased political tension during which it would be possible to deploy more deterrent submarines.

In the event of the US nuclear guarantee no longer being credible, there would again be ample warning. Under such circumstances the British deterrent would form part of a minimum European deterrent. Whereas in 1962 it was just possible to talk of the British nuclear force being independent in action if the US guarantee weakened, in 1987 it is much harder to conceive of any such circumstances in which Britain would act independently of France. As a member now of the European Community, Britain could not conceivably use its nuclear forces without consulting France and, as far as time would allow, the other European nations. In the last analysis, control would lie with the British Prime Minister and the French President.

Greater Anglo-French co-operation thus makes the utmost sense, not as an exclusive partnership but as part of an inclusive European relationship. Such an arrangement would build on existing Franco-German co-operation over nuclear strategy on the Continent, something made increasingly necessary by the entry into service of the French Hades missile, which could be fired from French territory, over West Germany and into East Germany. There is no doubt that co-operation with France over submarine refitting cycles and joint targeting strategies is necessary now, regardless of what is decided for a British deterrent in the future. Such co-operation would also raise the question of whether it was desirable to buy the French M4 or M5 missile rather than Trident in the event of Britain keeping a ballistic missile system.

Those who currently scoff at the concept of a European minimum deterrent are trying to have it both ways. They are arguing for British independence while locking themselves irrevocably for the next 30 years into American hardware and strategic concepts. Yet Britain would only ever use that hardware independently if the American nuclear guarantee was weakened or did not exist. And when one considers the USA's ability to interfere with the working of Trident in the event of its guarantee being withdrawn, one must question how independent a UK system really would be. The same must apply to a British purchase of US Tomahawk cruise missiles, and forms a strong argument for a European capacity to build cruise missiles.

Above: **Turbulent.** **The second of the *Trafalgar* class of nuclear-propelled fleet submarines, *Turbulent* was commissioned in April 1984. She carries Harpoon missiles and wire-guided torpedoes, and has a complement of 130.**

Left: **Spartan,** **one of the six submarines of the *Swiftsure* class. Shorter and with more beam than their predecessors, these boats have five instead of six torpedo tubes in the bow but are faster and have a greater diving depth.**

There is no doubt that a non-ballistic missile system like Tomahawk deployed in a British hunter-killer nuclear submarine would be far cheaper than any ballistic system, American or French. It would be cheaper than Britain building only three nuclear ballistic missile submarines (SSBNs). Cruise missiles could also be deployed from aircraft or surface ships. They can also be dual-capable, fitted with conventional as well as nuclear warheads. There is too the likelihood of a longer-range, more accurate version embodying stealth technology, the radar image of which would be minute and very hard to detect.

The extent of the deployment of Tomahawk in the US Navy's submarines is not well enough known. A total of 36 *Los Angeles*-class SSNs will each be equipped with 12 vertical-launched cruise missiles, with a capacity for eight more tube-launched. A further 31 *Los Angeles*-class boats will each have eight torpedo tube-launched rounds, and 37 *Sturgeon*-class SSNs will each be equipped with eight torpedo tube-launched rounds. In fact, the maximum possible Tomahawk loading per submarine torpedo room is 24 tube-launched rounds. But because the US Navy wishes to retain a dual-purpose capacity for its submarines, some Tomahawk space is normally given over to the torpedoes needed for the anti-submarine and anti-ship roles. With all submarines carrying a normal Tomahawk load, close on 1,000 such missiles will be available by the mid 1990s, and even now the total is about 600.

The Soviet Navy has an extensive deployment of submarine-launched cruise missiles. It is probable that the Soviet Navy sees its cruise missiles as having a role similar to that of the US Navy's. The US Navy has described its own cruise missiles as being both a "strategic reserve," to be used after a general exchange of nuclear weapons, and a contribution to the non-strategic nuclear forces of the United States.

If Britain was to opt for cruise missiles as part of the minimum deterrent, in any period of tension characterised by doubt about the US commitment a significant number of hunter-killer submarines would have to be fully loaded with cruise missiles and deployed in a way that was not necessarily the best for the purely ASW role. But before it is argued that this would seriously degrade our conventional capacity, it should be recognised that if the US nuclear guarantee was not operating, nor would the whole weight of US naval forces be fully deployed against the Soviet Navy. In such a situation the European navies alone could not possibly match Soviet naval strength, making the transfer of a significant part of our SSN fleet to the strategic role a logical development.

An incoming SDP/Liberal Alliance Government, or a government in which we participated, would look at all of these options on how to modernise our deterrent in the light of available intelligence, the views of the Chiefs of Staff, and the prevailing arms-control environment. Our decision to maintain the deterrent after Polaris is clear. How we do that must be settled in the context of a European-orientated defence review that balances our conventional and nuclear contributions in a way which strengthens the European pillar of NATO.

The Trident threat to Britain's conventional defences

Jim Wallace MP*

Type 42 *Nottingham*, one of the 14 destroyers in the Royal Navy's active fleet in 1987, compared with 28 in 1962. All 12 Type 42s were completed between 1976 and 1985. The design underwent a radical change for the last four, which were lengthened by 50ft in the hope of improving their speed and seakeeping.

THE FACTS of economic life facing the British government which inherits office after the next election will scarcely bring joy to the incoming Chancellor of the Exchequer. North Sea oil revenue will have peaked and be declining. If the new government is ill-disposed to further rounds of privatisation it will have to cope with a loss of receipts following the current "sale of the family silver." It all points to an increase in the public-sector borrowing requirements, making the longed-for and promised increases in public spending all the more difficult to achieve.

Spare a particular thought then for the incoming Secretary of State for Defence. His predecessor will have agreed to a departmental budget which is decreasing in real terms. The total reduction over the period 1985–86 to 1988–89 will amount to approximately 6.5% (4.5% if expenditure on the Falklands is

* Liberal Member of Parliament for Orkney and Shetland.

excluded). Given the many competing claims on the Exchequer for higher expenditure, it would be a brave man who on this occasion would predict any major victories for the Ministry of Defence. A review of our defence commitments must surely then take place. Indeed, the Defence Secretary of a Liberal/SDP Alliance Government would already have been electorally committed to such a scheme.

A defence review is already long overdue. It is not only those of us who sit on the Opposition benches of Westminster who have been critical of the Government as it has tried to squeeze a quart's worth of defence commitments into a pint pot. Some of the Government's usual friends in the media have been making a similar point. As long ago as October 1985, a *Sunday Times* editorial criticised the Government thus:

". . . He [Mr Heseltine] has responded to the imbalance between resources and commitments by dodging the real issues . . . salami-slicing of the armed forces is the worst way of matching defence policy with budgetary constraints . . . any Government which regards the nation as its primary responsibility cannot delay a defence review any longer."

It was perhaps too much to expect implementation of the NATO requirement for an annual increase of 3% to continue indefinitely, but the difficulties of managing the budget might have been reduced if spending had levelled off rather than go into a swift reverse. As a result, and as an alternative to a thoroughgoing review, ploys have been introduced to cut expenditure, delay contracts and postpone decisions. The Ministry of Defence is not unaware that a problem exists:

"Some difficult decisions will have to be taken. . . ." (Statement on Defence Estimates 1986, para 503)

But there does seem to be a reluctance to appreciate the scale of the problem and the long-term consequences for all the services of tackling it in a piecemeal manner.

There have been assurances, both in the Statement on the Defence Estimates and from the Secretary of State (Second Report from the Defence Committee 1985–86, Evidence HC 399, page 3), that the "recosting" of the defence programme would not lead to the abandonment of any major role or commitment. But the budgetary constraints must raise doubts as to whether these roles will be performed as efficiently as they might have been.

The future of the Royal Navy's amphibious capability is an important example of the potential dangers of *ad hoc* cost-cutting. There is broad acceptance of the vital role of the Marines in defence of NATO's Northern Flank. The availability of specialist amphibious ships is essential if they are to be able to properly deploy their expertise. Yet there has been lengthy procrastina-

Above: **The Rt Hon Jim Wallace MP, defence spokesman for the Liberal Party.**

Below: **The Rt Hon David Steel MP, leader of the Liberal Party.**

Hauled back from reserve pending disposal under the 1981 Defence Review, *Intrepid* and her sister *Fearless* were essential to the reoccupation of the Falkland Islands in 1982. But procrastination over the future of the Royal Navy's amphibious forces has continued ever since. Now the plan is to see whether these two ships can be run on or, failing that, replaced with converted merchant hulls.

tion in announcing what, if anything, will replace *Fearless* and *Intrepid*. There is no question of us withdrawing from the commitment to defend the Northern Flank, but the quality of that defence might be materially affected by the outcome of a decision-making process in which cost, and particularly cost-cutting, will be so much to the fore. Apart from anything else, the delays can scarcely be conducive to high morale.

A defence review would undoubtedly be easier to institute than to implement. Each service would make every effort to justify its own projects and operations. The Royal Navy's experience in the last major review, undertaken by John Nott in 1981, would understandably give it cause to be sensitive about any future one.

There is however little point in conducting a review if one reaches conclusions in advance of it. But one question is sure to arise: can Britain afford a 50-strong frigate/destroyer fleet in the final decade of this century. After all, it is argued by some that in any future conflict the role assigned to the surface fleet (protecting convoys carrying reinforcements across the Atlantic and to Europe) would quickly become impossible, as a result of vulnerability to enemy missiles, or redundant, because the conventional battle would be over too quickly. To follow that line of thinking must surely be a high-risk strategy, and one doubts whether any Defence Secretary would weaken our surface fleet to the extent that no attempt could be made to safeguard the reinforcement convoys.

In one important respect the Royal Navy is better placed today than at the time of the Nott review to argue for keeping up the strength of the surface fleet. The basis of its case is the increasing role it is playing in anti-submarine warfare. The rate of submarine building achieved in recent years by the Soviet Union makes ASW capability critical to our defence. The towed-array sonar, probably the most important means of detecting and locating enemy submarines, is now being fitted extensively to surface vessels. Attempts to cut back here would undoubtedly meet staunch opposition, well armed with good arguments.

However, in trying to retain a frigate/destroyer fleet "of about fifty" (Mr Younger's words), the need to order three new vessels a year may not be as imperative as it seems when boldly asserted in House of Commons debates. Analysis of the age profile of the fleet, expected lengths of service of different classes of frigate, and the effect of mid-life refits has led Malcolm Chalmers of Bradford University to conclude

Avenger is one of the six remaining Type 21 frigates, two having been lost in the Falklands campaign. Designed commercially but with a significant input from the Ministry of Defence, they have had their problems over the years – 130 tons of ballast has been added to improve stability, and long strengthening members have been welded amidships to prevent cracking of the hull and upper deck. The RN currently has 34 frigates in service, with nine building. In 1962 there were 76 frigates in the Royal Navy, with six building.

that an average order rate of around 2.5 ships a year would permit the Secretary of State's minimum to be maintained into the late 1990s, while an average of just under two ships a year would not have any consequences until after 1995. It is certainly to be hoped that by that date negotiations will have taken place with Argentina to establish an equitable solution to the Falklands problem, thus allowing redeployment of resources currently committed to the South Atlantic.

A defence review might well establish whether savings could be achieved by reducing the ordering rate while still maintaining numerical strength into the 1990s and allowing for a reassessment of needs in the light of Falklands developments. With the one major exception of Trident, the scope for other significant savings is not obvious, although there must surely be potential for future savings through international co-operation.

The Liberal/SDP Alliance is of course firmly committed to NATO. But we also believe that NATO can be strengthened by building up its European pillar and by fostering co-operation in the development, manufacture and procurement of defence equipment. The Senior Service has possibly been the slowest to engage in such co-operation, although the NATO Frigate Replacement for the 1990s does offer possibilities, both transatlantic and intra-European. No-one should underestimate the difficulties which attend such collaborative projects, not least the conflict between national desires to retain an independent capacity on the one hand, and the advantages of greater cohesion among allies and cost savings through shared R&D and longer production runs on the other.

In pursuit of greater co-operation within Europe on defence matters, the SDP/Liberal Alliance is prepared to open a dialogue with France on possible defence co-operation. This would include the current nuclear capabilities of the two countries. The visit to Paris by David Steel and David Owen in September 1986 demonstrated that there were options to be explored – something that can be taken much further by Government than by two Opposition leaders. Certainly, the much caricatured notion of 12 fingers on the button of some mythical Eurobomb misrepresents the thinking of the two Alliance leaders. Rather, it seems to make eminent sense that the two nuclear-armed states in Western Europe should actually start talking to each other. Even without examining the possibilities of co-operation over future developments (which would be unlikely as long as France refused to sign the Non-Proliferation and Partial Test Ban treaties), it must be possible to explore whether targeting strategies and the cycle of submarine refits can be co-ordinated, as a means of both cutting costs and contributing to arms reductions.

While the savings to be achieved through co-operation are limited, there is one obvious source of very large economies: cutting the Trident programme. The Alliance parties have been unequivocal in their opposition to Trident, not solely on grounds of cost but also because in our view it represents an unacceptable escalation in Britain's nuclear capacity to a level greater than that required for minimal deterrence.

Let us examine the cost argument. Trident was ordered at a time when the defence budget was expanding in real terms. It will have to be paid for at a time when that budget is contracting. Its estimated cost has risen sharply since the first announcement was made, and now stands at £10 billion. The Government likes to talk in soothing terms about 3% of the total budget and 6% of the capital equipment budget "over the period of its procurement." Such an averaging out obscures the fact that when payments peak, probably between 1988 and 1993, they will represent up to 9% of the defence budget and account for one pound out of every six spent on equipment. That must have an impact on spending on conventional equipment. Indeed, the warning signs are already appearing.

There can be little doubt about the importance of maintaining and improving our conventional defence contribution to NATO, if for no other reason than the fact that a vigilant US Congressional eye will continue to be kept on Europe's contribution to its own defence. It would be wrong if Trident expenditure crowded out the conventional defence budget and called into question our continuing ability to contribute effectively.

There is an obligation to find a less costly alternative on that ground alone, but the argument against Trident goes beyond that. At a time when the two superpowers have come within an ace of agreeing 50% reductions in their strategic arsenals, and the Soviet Union has made positive moves towards a reduction in medium-range nuclear weapons, it cannot possibly make sense for Britain to set about increasing its nuclear capacity. The theoretical complement of the Polaris force is 64 missiles, and although one can only estimate the total number of warheads, most discussions assume that 64 warheads are available on station at a given time. The full Trident D5 programme would provide for the possibility of 64 missiles, each capable of carrying up to 16 warheads, although the USA has indicated that it will deploy only 14 per missile. On the basis of the latter figure, there would be 896 British warheads in all. The Government has never said how many warheads each missile would carry, not indeed whether every missile tube would be loaded. But even a conservative estimate would suggest a possible 256 warheads, assuming two submarines on station at any one time in a crisis, each with 16 eight-warhead missiles. A fourfold increase over Polaris is escalation in anyone's book.

Nor is it simply a question of warhead numbers. Trident is significantly more accurate than Polaris and is fully equipped with multiple independently targeted re-entry vehicles (MIRVs), greatly magnifying its capability. These factors, combined with the possible number of warheads, raises the possibility of Trident being used in a counterforce role. Denials by British politicians are not likely to convince Soviet strategists, who would plan for the worst case. Trident, I would argue, offers far more than what is needed for minimum deterrence.

Those who claim that Trident is the only option for

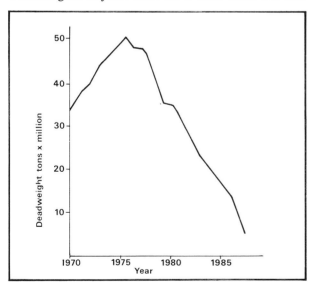

Showing the tonnage of British-owned and registered ships over 500 gross registered tons, this graph is based on figures prepared by the General Council of British Shipping. What is virtually a straight line from 1980 onwards could reach zero before 1990.

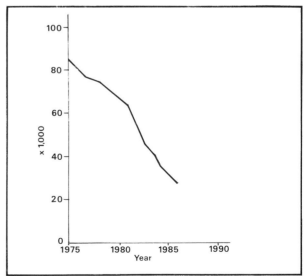

At the present rate of decline the number of British qualified seafarers could reach zero by 1991. Though this is unlikely, the actual total may be only a few thousand unless corrective action is taken.

The British shipbuilding industry, which in 1900 supplied 80% of the world's tonnage, is shrinking even more quickly than UK maritime manpower.

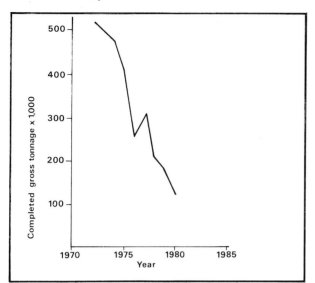

The merchant navies of the rest of Western Europe are going the same way as that of Britain. Significantly, the Comecon fleets are holding their own.

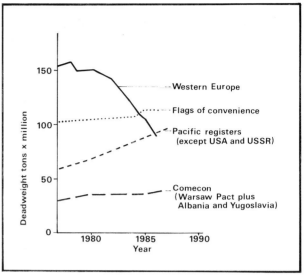

Britain may be right if what we need is the ability to destroy missile silos and penetrate the anti-ballistic missile defence system around Moscow. But if we seek only to deter by being able to threaten unacceptable damage to the Soviet Union, a different set of options is available. These include (as the present Defence Secretary admitted in a recent TV discussion) a longer lifetime for Polaris than has generally been assumed.

As long as it remains in opposition no party is equipped to commit itself to a particular option. We would require access to classified information and the advice of the Chiefs of Staff before a judgement could be made. The Liberal/SDP Alliance would however put our deterrent on the table in arms-control discussions and negotiate it away in exchange for worthwhile Soviet concessions which would enhance our security. If negotiations were successful, we would be ready to maintain a British deterrent capacity at a level no greater than Polaris. Such a policy stresses a commitment to negotiated disarmament while taking no risks with our security.

And one final thought on maritime policy. It is worth recalling a historic role of the Royal Navy: safeguarding our merchant fleet. But how much longer will we have a merchant fleet for the Navy to protect. The existence of a strong merchant navy is important to Britain, both economically and in defence terms, yet it has been allowed to decline from 1,600 ships to less than 600 in ten years. Apart from the dangers of having a diminishing number of vessels

available for requisition in emergency, a shrinking fleet has a peacetime impact on shipbuilding, ship-repairing, marine engineering and other marine-related industries. Perhaps the most serious consequence is the reduction in manpower. Qualified British seafarers now number about one-third of the 1976 total. We have lost men and with them valuable skills and expertise.

A co-ordinated approach to maritime policy is required. The Alliance would propose that this be entrusted to a Minister of Cabinet rank, rather than the most junior member of the Department of Transport, as at present. There is no doubt that worldwide factors have contributed to British shipping's difficulties. To help the industry survive the current recession, we would give it fiscal assistance and institute countermeasures to combat the covert and not so covert protectionist measures adopted elsewhere.

My Parliamentary colleagues of all parties would do well to remember the address of the Commons to Queen Anne in what must have been the first Parliament of the United Kingdom: "Other nations which were formerly great and powerful at sea have, by negligence and mismanagement, lost their trade and seen their maritime strength entirely ruined. Therefore we do, in the most earnest manner, beseech Your Majesty that the Sea Affair may always be your first and most peculiar interest."

Piracy: can the ancient plague be cured?

Lt-Cdr Miles Chapman

MODERN piracy gets the occasional mention in small paragraphs in the daily press. From time to time there may be a feature article, enlarging perhaps on the experience of some unfortunate person and usually rounded off by a few generalities and some statistics culled from the library. This may cause a brief flurry of public interest which soon dies down. But for shipowners, shipmasters and others more intimately concerned, it is an ever-present and probably growing menace.

It is difficult to be more precise about the rate of growth in this type of crime because statistics are extremely difficult to come by, for obvious reasons. The pirates themselves have no wish to publicise their work, and frequently the same applies to the victims. Shipowners, for example, would wish to avoid bad publicity for the company, trouble with unions, increased insurance premiums, and the risk of offending the countries with which they trade. It has been possible to document over 400 cases during the years 1980–1984. This means that on average about two or three ships were being pirated every week. Press reports alone for the time since then indicate that this frequency has not greatly altered, while informed sources suggest that the actual incidence of piracy is probably four times as great.

The Singaporean patrol craft *Justice* belongs to a sizeable force of naval and police vessels controlled by a single shore station working to eradicate the boarding of merchant ships at anchor or proceeding at low speed in the southern entrance to the Malacca Strait.

Piracy today seems to arise most often when the people of poorer countries are confronted and tempted by ships from the wealthier countries. It is a far cry from the rollicking adventures attributed to Sir Henry Morgan, Captain Kidd and others of that era in the Caribbean. Today's piracy is completely unromantic, always terrifying, sometimes fatal. The objective is personal gain, with the possible exception of drug-related incidents in the Caribbean. The pirates have different methods of achieving their goals. Off West Africa, providing they get what they want, there is usually relatively little violence. In the Gulf or Thailand and further south in the Sulu Sea, ferocity and callous violence accompany every incident. Other areas fall between these two extremes, except perhaps for the Singapore Strait, where the pirates prefer to work undetected.

The Boat People

Of the various types of piracy, possibly the most vicious is that practised as a sideline by the Thai fishermen against the Vietnamese Boat People. These refugees leave Vietnam for one reason or another to seek a new life in Thailand or, even better, Malaysia. Whole families or groups of families join forces and acquire a boat of sorts. This is usually barely seaworthy, as the demand greatly exceeds the supply. They then convert their wealth into a portable form such as gold bars or precious stones and set off. Apart from the perils of the sea, they then have to contend with the Thai pirates.

Usually just ordinary fishermen motivated by greed and a traditional hatred of the Vietnamese people, these pirates appear to be highly organised. They are also especially difficult to detect or identify, as the Thai markings on their boats are unfamiliar to the Vietnamese. The percentage of boats attacked seems to have diminished since the early 1980s, but it is still safe to say that at present at least a third of them will be attacked at least once, and usually several times, during their passage. The first attackers, who may strike as little as 50 miles from the Vietnamese coast, may well be content to take all the money and valuables and let them go on their way. Subsequent assailants will take what is left, if anything, and as a matter of course rape the women or even abduct them to be passed around other boats. The men may be killed or allowed to continue their journey. Any subsequent attackers, frustrated at finding nothing left, will probably ram and sink the boat and kill any survivors.

How many times such events have occurred will never be established, though it is known that from 1980 to April 1986 some 1,500 persons perished in this way, possibly because there is less wealth now leaving Vietnam; recent reports speak of an increase in the numbers of rapes and abductions. A total of 18 women are said to have been abducted from a single boat, never to be seen again. Torture of the victims for amusement is another increasing tendency.

The Far East

A somewhat similar pattern of cruelty is seen in the Sulu Sea, where the pirates are based in the Tawi Tawi group of islands or further east. Their traditions go back some 1,500 years, and they are notorious for great ferocity and extreme cruelty. Although any type of vessel is at risk, they tend to operate close to land rather than in open waters, so that the normal ocean-going ship is only endangered when it approaches the coast. Yachtsmen, coasters and ferries make up the greater part of their targets, and there have been many cases of ferries being attacked and the passengers robbed of everything and probably killed in large numbers. Yachts are attacked, their crews murdered and the vessel stripped of everything, including the inboard auxiliary engine. Even large merchant ships at anchor are attacked and robbed. In recent times the pirates have come ashore and raided villages in Sabah, and have been known to hold yachtsmen to ransom.

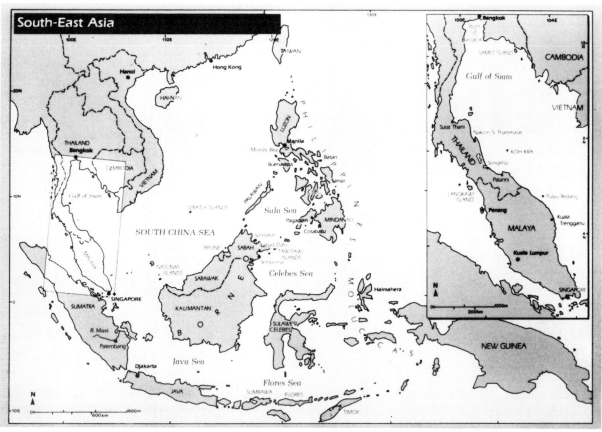

South-East Asia

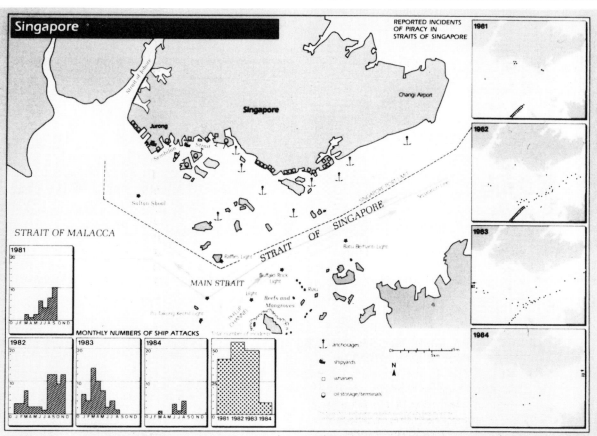

Singapore

REPORTED INCIDENTS
OF PIRACY IN
STRAITS OF SINGAPORE

1981

1982

1983

1984

STRAIT OF MALACCA

STRAIT OF SINGAPORE

MAIN STRAIT

Reefs and
Mangroves

1981

MONTHLY NUMBERS OF SHIP ATTACKS

1982   1983   1984

Total number of incidents

1981 1982 1983 1984

anchorages

shipyards

wharves

oil storage/terminals

The 101,700-ton Norwegian bulk carrier *Viscaya* was attacked off Singapore in July 1980.

Piracy is particularly prevalent in the Singapore Strait and, to a lesser extent, the Malacca Strait, where the traffic to and from two great oceans is funnelled into a narrow channel. The majority of the pirates operating in this area are Indonesian fishermen from the Riau Archipelago on the south side of the channel, but Singaporeans are also involved.

The Indonesians' task is made easier by the Traffic Separation Scheme, which obliges the eastbound (and usually deeply laden) ships to take the southern half of the Strait, through the narrow, hazard-strewn Philip Channel. This is a tricky navigational exercise, demanding maximum concentration from the master and the bridge team. The pirates are well aware of this and, using fast boats, board the ship from astern by means of a thrown grapnel and line. They prefer to operate in darkness, which allows them to mingle with legitimate fishing boats to avoid detection. Once aboard, they frequently prepare their getaway by chopping off a length of berthing rope and hanging it over the stern. They then make quietly for the master's cabin, where they know they will find the safe. They will try to open the safe or, if the master is in the cabin, to "persuade" him to open it. If this is impractical they may remove it bodily, as it is rarely secured to the ship's structure. They prefer to operate unseen, but seem prepared to use weapons if disturbed. The same pirates used to enjoy rich pickings from ships in Singapore's anchorages, but their activities have since been much curtailed by vigorous action on the part of the maritime authorities.

West Africa

The pirates of West Africa almost merit a book to themselves. There has always been piracy in this area but the modern version began to flourish during the Nigerian trade boom in the late 1970s and early 1980s. This resulted in large numbers of ships visiting Nigeria and other West African nations. Harbour and unloading facilities proved inadequate, however, leading to queues of ships anchored off or steaming slowly up and down until berths became available. Apart from being systematically looted in harbour, the ships were thus exposed to the attentions of offshore pirate gangs. These consisted of anything between 10 and 40 men in dug-out canoes powered by large

Below: Balticland, a Swedish motor vessel of 10,899 tons deadweight, was boarded while at anchor in Lagos Roads in May 1981. The master foiled the attack by working his engines and rudder, threatening to capsize the pirates' boat. Although this attack failed, the ship was later attacked at Abidjan.

Bottom: The Swedish Ro-Ro ship *Vegaland* was attacked 20 miles south of Lagos while lying off. The gang, numbering about ten men, arrived in a 10m boat powered by two outboard motors. The crew were locked up, the second officer was shot in the leg (eight shots were fired in all), and cargo was stolen.

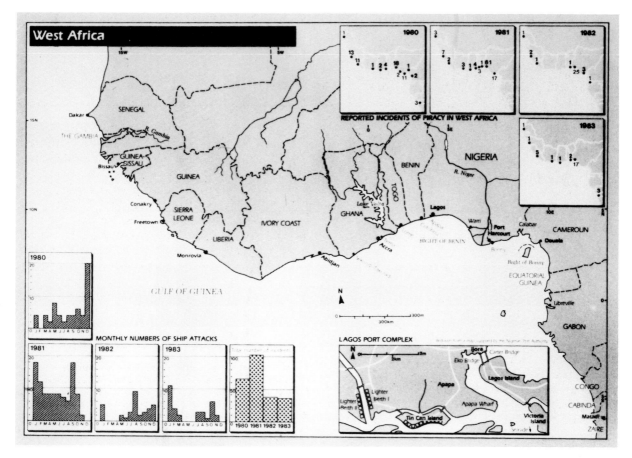

West Africa

REPORTED INCIDENTS OF PIRACY IN WEST AFRICA

1980 1981 1982 1983

MONTHLY NUMBERS OF SHIP ATTACKS

LAGOS PORT COMPLEX

The roadstead off Lagos in Nigeria *(inset)* was particularly dangerous for ships at anchor during the early 1980s. The subsequent fall-off in trade and the efforts of the local authorities have since combined to reduce the risks to merchant shipping.

outboard motors. They would board the ship armed with knives and sometimes handguns, rifle the cargo and take anything else of value. With anything up to 30 ships at a time off Lagos, 12 attacks a night were not unusual. Neither the navy, coastguard nor police seemed able or willing to cope with the situation. Since 1983 the diminishing fortunes of West Africa in general and Nigeria in particular have resulted in a reduction in the numbers of ships attacked. But even going by press reports alone, which probably reflect only a small fraction of the actual total, an average of one attack a week appears to be the current norm.

Brazil

Piracy is generally agreed to be robbery committed on the high seas for personal gain. This eliminates terrorist attacks (such as the *Achille Lauro* hijacking) and, strictly speaking, robbery committed on ships in harbour. However, the latter should be mentioned since it constitutes piracy in spirit if not according to the letter of the law. Possibly the most notorious location for this type of crime is the port of Santos in Brazil, and to a lesser extent Rio de Janeiro. Ships alongside or in the roads are boarded by gangs armed with anything from iron bars to handguns. They take anything movable, and woe betide anyone who opposes them. Many masters have experienced such attacks, and some have evolved their own methods of self-protection.

Although Brazilian patrol ships such as *Solimoes* operate continuously around the country's huge coastline, they provide little protection for ships in harbour.

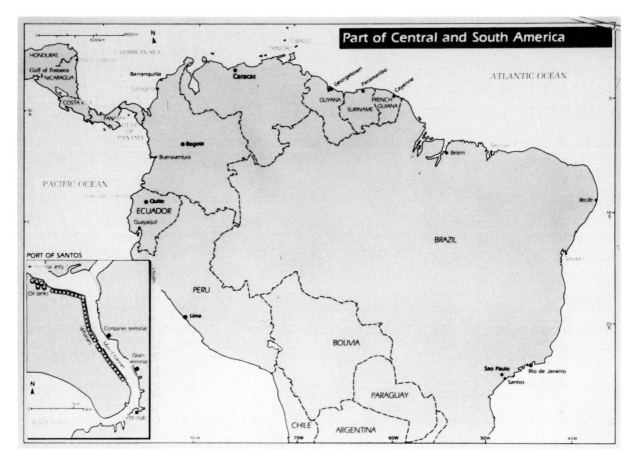

Part of Central and South America

The boarding of ships in harbour is a common form of piracy in several South American ports, particularly the Brazilian harbour of Santos.

The Caribbean

The drug-running chain of supply through the Caribbean runs from Colombia up the length of the Caribbean islands to the USA. Small craft and their crews are pirated or may disappear for three main reasons. First, a yacht may chance unwittingly on a drug transfer or similar operation and is eliminated to preserve secrecy. Second, the drugs may leave Colombia in a relatively large ship, making it necessary to acquire a number of smaller craft nearer the point of landing to distribute the cargo. Third, the sight of a rich yacht close to shore may simply be too great a temptation for a poor native.

There is no record of how many craft have disappeared in this area, but the number is certainly large. The high stakes in the drug trade inspire the traffickers to go to almost any length to preserve their anonymity and to further their activities. Happily, the US authorities are making significant strides in

Above: **This large patrol craft, operated by Trinidad and Tobago, has the size and power needed to discourage piracy in the eastern end of the Caribbean.**

Below: George McIntosh **is one of the small number of craft operated by the Caribbean island communities, in this case St Vincent. They are too few for the task now that the major countries have reduced their warship presence in the region.**

Above: **The US Coast Guard cutter *Alert* is typical of the ships being deployed in the Caribbean in a bid to cut down drug smuggling and the attendant piracy. The Coast Guard acts in close concert with the US Navy, and recent results have been encouraging.**

Below: **The Caribbean is one of the main areas for drug smuggling, with the centre of the trade lying in Colombia. The main threat here is to passing yachts, which can stumble on a drug transfer or be seized for use by the traffickers.**

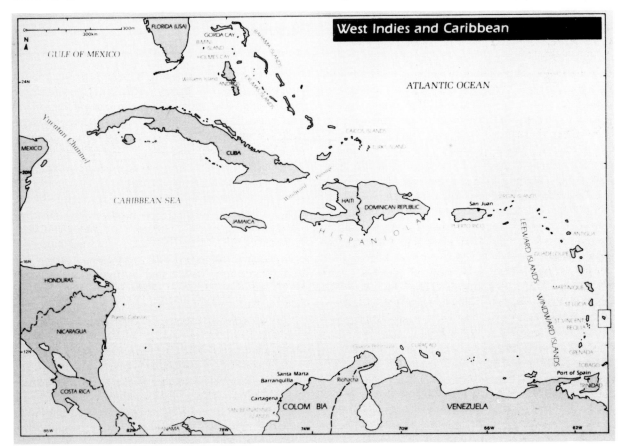

suppressing drug smuggling, but there is a long way to go before the Caribbean can be considered a safe area for yachtsmen. In this connection, before the Second World War, when France and Britain maintained fleets or at least naval squadrons in the West Indies, pirates in the Caribbean had to contend with the possibility of a warship turning up. Nowadays, unfortunately, warships are few and far between.

Apart from the areas mentioned above, pockets of pirate activity exist in other regions. Incidents occur from time to time off the Central American coast; some of these are connected with guerrilla campaigns. The Red Sea has long had its quota of piracy and the Indian Ocean is occasionally affected. An area being mentioned more and more frequently is the approach to Bangkok. In February 1986, for example, at least three ships were attacked by armed gangs who boarded from speedboats and broke open containers. It is reported that there was no reaction to calls for assistance.

Anti-piracy measures

What is being done to combat piracy? The Singapore Government is in the vanguard of the fight, having instituted augmented patrols and special VHF radio reporting frequencies. As a result incidents in the anchorages have decreased in frequency. Discouraging night transits of the Traffic Separation Scheme has had some effect, but is not the complete answer. Ships are encouraged to make it difficult for marauders to get aboard; this is particularly relevant when the vessel is deep-laden, with a small freeboard. Even if attackers are surprised by patrol craft, they have a ready refuge in the Riau Archipelago on the south side of the channel. Here the pirates may easily elude pursuit, either by taking advantage of the natural features (overgrown swamps and jungly inlets) or simply by mingling with the fishermen. Effective pursuit would call for Indonesia to maintain an effective anti-piracy force. But that nation's enormous length of coastline and numerous islands make this an impossibility.

In the Gulf of Thailand a vast sea area has to be policed by a single relatively poor country. The United Nations High Commission for Refugees does its best in the area, and a group of 11 nations contribute a not over-generous $2.57 million a year to help Thailand with the task. Australia has donated four Nomad N24A aircraft to the Royal Thai Navy for patrol duties. There used to be several rescue ships to aid Vietnamese refugees in distress but now there is only one, the West German-financed *Cap Anamur II*, which does sterling work. But rescuing survivors, however humanitarian, is fraught with administrative

problems. The number of countries willing to accept Boat People, and the quotas that they have imposed, are both shrinking almost daily. For this reason many shipmasters pretend not to notice survivors, such are the delays and difficulties in disembarking them at their next port of arrival. One feeble excuse for this conduct is that it is difficult to distinguish between pirate and refugee boats. The best that can be said is that the situation appears marginally better than it was a few years ago, though it must still give cause for concern.

Of all the West African countries, Nigeria has made the greatest effort to counter the problem. This is due in part to outside pressure and in part to a desire to improve the national image. There has undoubtedly been a reduction in the number of incidents compared with the peak in 1982–83. But is is difficult to determine how much of this is due to fewer ships visiting and how much to Nigeria's efforts. Much was made in July 1985 of the execution of six Nigerians for piracy. It is nevertheless still a fact that in 1987 Nigeria and other West African countries continue to have piracy problems. Indeed, they may even be on the increase, incidents having been reported from as far afield as Sierra Leone. In late 1985, for example, it was reported that the armed guard aboard the West German ship *Vanellus* actually ran out of ammunition while beating off a pirate gang.

Terrorism

What was the *Achille Lauro* hijacking if not piracy? The answer is that it was terrorism, committed for political gain and therefore strictly not piracy, which is for personal gain. However, a brief mention must be made of terrorism, if only because it has recently begun to make itself felt at sea. In certain areas – the Philippines is one – groups with political pretensions commit the most awful atrocities in the name of freedom, and seem to be motivated as much by greed as by political concerns. War areas such as the Red Sea, Persian Gulf, the Lebanon and Central America, are also bound to have their dangers. Small ships are particularly at risk off the Western Sahara, where the Polisario guerillas have preyed on trawlers and coasters for several years. In 1985 they attacked a Spanish naval patrol vessel, killing one crew member and wounding others, and in 1986 they are reported to have attacked a Soviet factory ship, which fired back, wounding three. Finally, there is the IRA in Britain. In February 1981, disguised as pilots, an IRA squad boarded the 500-ton coaster *Nellie M* as she entered Lough Foyle in Ulster. The crew were forced to take to the boats, after which the terrorists placed explosives and sank the ship. A year later they repeated the operation on the *Saint Bedan*.

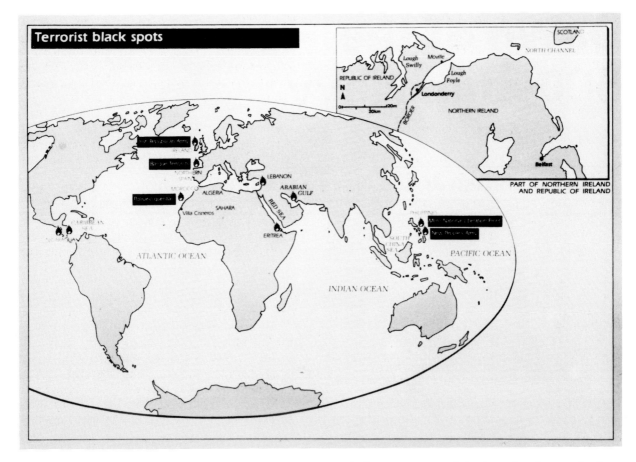

Terrorist black spots

The customary activities of pirates have been compounded in the last 20 years by the depredations of various groups of terrorists, which have either seized ships for their own gain or destroyed them as part of their campaigns.

Conclusion

What then is the future of the fight against piracy? It is certain that unless concerted multi-national efforts are made, piracy is here to stay and even to increase. But even if such a programme were launched with enthusiasm and dedication, the path is a thorny one. To begin with, the definition of piracy is still nebulous. It was largely clarified in the United Nations Committee on the Law of the Sea 1981, but the resulting definition has not been ratified by a number of nations. To many it is not clear whether a 200-mile economic exclusion zone is part of the high seas. If, as appears probable, it is not, then the country claiming the privilege of the zone must also accept the responsibility for policing it. This includes anti-piracy measures. It is also a fact that much piracy occurs off the coasts of countries that do not have the means to maintain naval or police forces capable of suppressing piracy in territorial waters, let alone a 200-mile economic exclusion zone.

Even if the difficulties outlined above were overcome, there remains the problem that in order to combat a menace one must have a clear idea of its size. At the moment no single authority has a comprehensive statistical picture of the situation. Interested bodies such as the International Maritime Organisation must use reports from governments and shipowners as the basis of their statistics. But, as has been pointed out, these are the very people who may be most reluctant to advertise the fact that their ships have been attacked.

Even the probably incomplete reports of the press suggest that since 1984 there has been an average of two attacks a week. The true number is anyone's guess, but is almost certain to be much greater. Piracy today is a fact of life, and one that won't go away until the seagoing nations take effective concerted action.

(For further reading see *Piracy Today* by Capt Roger Villar, Conway Maritime Press).

Dawn of the 600-ship Navy *

John F. Lehman Jr, US Navy Secretary

CLEMENCEAU once declared that war was too important to be left to the generals. But if that is so, it is also too important to be left to the civilian experts. In the United States, with our constitutionally mandated civilian control of the armed forces, we sometimes forget that hard-earned military experience must leaven the theories of civilians if our system is to work.

USS *Yorktown* is the second of what is intended to be a large class of Aegis cruisers. A number of Congressional members chose to criticise this design and were only silenced by the extraordinary performance of the Aegis weapon system under operational conditions.

* Reprinted from *The Maritime Strategy*, US Naval Institute Press.

We would do well to keep this in mind as we near our goal of a 600-ship Navy. Media-anointed experts have raised questions about the size, character, and complexity of the Navy. Do we really need so many ships? Are the Navy and Marine Corps effective in helping to deter Soviet aggression across the full spectrum of violence, from terrorism to nuclear war? Do we have a strategy that guides the planning and training of our forces? Is it the correct strategy? If it is, are we building the right types and numbers of ships to execute it? Finally, can the United States afford to sustain a 600-ship fleet – not only well equipped but also properly manned – in the long term? With defence restrictions becoming law in the zero-growth 1986 budget, and retrenchment the theme of the hour, the answers to these questions take on added significance.

Why 600 ships?

To understand how we arrived at the size of our planned fleet, we must begin by discarding the idea that this number has sprung, fully formed, from the brow of some would-be Napoleon of the high seas. Since the Second World War maritime force planners have found themselves at the mercy of three enduring elements. First is geography: water covers three-quarters of the world, and the United States is an "island continent" washed by the Atlantic and Pacific oceans. Second are the vital interests of the United States, expressed in the web of more than 40 treaty relationships that bind us to mutual defence coalitions around the world. These relationships, together with the energy and commercial dependencies that support our economy in peace and war, shape our national security requirements. Third is the Soviet threat. Whatever its original rationale, the Soviet Navy's postwar expansion has created an offence-oriented blue-water force, a major element in the USSR's global military reach that supports expanding influence from Nicaragua to Ethiopia and Vietnam. From the Baltic to the Caribbean and the South China Sea, our ships and men pass within yards of Soviet naval forces every day. But in this case familiarity is breeding a well deserved respect.

The Navy's recently updated *Understanding Soviet Naval Developments* provides the facts about the Soviet Navy. Every American should be aware, for example, that Soviet nuclear submarines operate continuously off our coasts. Victor-class nuclear attack submarines are routinely found lurking near many of our principal naval ports. Soviet surface units are now making regular deployments to the contentious

---

The *Ohio*-class ballistic missile submarines are designed to take full advantage of the huge water surface of the world. Their Trident I missiles have a range of 4,350nm, while the newer Trident II can carry up to 6,000nm. Such performance opens up immense ocean areas to the launch submarines. Trident II could reach Moscow from the Caribbean, the South Atlantic, the Southern Indian Ocean or the Western Pacific.

and vulnerable chokepoints of the Caribbean Sea and Gulf of Mexico. Worldwide, we find the Soviet Navy astride the vital sea lanes and navigational chokepoints, through which most of the Western world's international trade must pass.

This is the new reality. The pattern of Soviet naval deployments has revealed itself only in the last several years. These deployments constitute a post-Second World War change in the global military balance of power that has been surpassed only by the advent of thermonuclear weapons. No planner, civilian or military, can ignore the growing dimensions of Soviet maritime power.

Geography, alliances and the Soviet threat combine to dictate the number of ships needed to meet our commitments in each of our maritime theatres. Before reviewing these forces in detail, some observations are in order:

● The US Navy often deploys in peacetime very much as it would in wartime. For purposes of deterrence, crisis management and diplomacy, we must be present where we would have to fight if war broke out. Of course, the operational tempo is different, with the wartime rate likely to be three times that maintained in peacetime. We also train as we intend to fight. A carrier battle group would rarely work alone in a full-scale general war at sea. So we often train with multiple carrier battle forces in exercises such as Fleetex and Readex, and in NATO exercises like Northern Wedding, which we conduct in the North Atlantic and the Norwegian Sea.

● Our maritime security depends on significant assistance from allies. Fortunately, we count among our friends all of the world's great navies, save one. In areas such as diesel submarines, frigates, coastal patrol craft, minesweepers and maritime patrol aircraft the allies of the United States have assets absolutely essential to us for sea control in war and peace. In some regions, such as the Eastern Atlantic and the waters surrounding the United Kingdom, our allies

supply a significant portion of the anti-submarine capability. In fact, if we could not count on our allies, we would require a US fleet much larger than 600 ships to deal with the 1,700 ships and submarines that the Soviets can deploy against us. But the world's greatest navies are on our side, and this gives a tremendous advantage to the US Navy and significant cost savings to the US taxpayer.

● America's increasing commercial and energy interdependence with Asia and the growth of the Soviet Pacific Fleet – now the largest of the four Soviet fleets – have negated the so-called "swing strategy" of the 1960s and 1970s, which postulated reinforcement of the Atlantic Fleet with combatants from the Pacific in time of crisis. Today the United States has an Asian orientation at least equal to its historic engagement in Europe. Existing treaty relationships in the Pacific have been augmented by growing commercial connections. For example, in 1980 the value of US trade with the Pacific Rim nations was roughly equal to that with the country's Atlantic partners. Four years later, Pacific trade exceeded that with Western Europe by $26 billion.

Similarly, oil dependencies have shifted tremendously in the last five years. This has forced us to

Above right: **The reincarnation of the four battleships of the** *Iowa* **class as modern missile-carrying ships with a main gun armament outranging any in the world was greeted in the USA with a mixture of derision and opposition. Both have died away as these ships have proved their value.** *New Jersey* **was the first to recommission, in December 1982. The following year she served continuously in the Pacific, then off Central America, and finally in the Mediterranean.**

Below: **At a time when ill-informed Congressional members and staff are hounding the US carrier programme, no fewer than nine naval staffs around the world see carriers as essential. The 91,500-ton** *Theodore Roosevelt* **was commissioned in October 1986.**

reconsider the priorities of naval deployments in the Northern Pacific and Caribbean. The shifting of US sources of crude oil has gone largely unnoticed. Western dependence on Middle Eastern oil is still debated at length, such is its impact on our military thinking and force planning. But in 1985 the United States imported eight times as much oil by sea from the Western Hemisphere as it received from the entire Middle East. Mexico supplies almost 25% of our imports, compared with only 2.6% from Saudi Arabia. We no longer depend primarily on the Middle East and Persian Gulf for our vital energy needs. Instead, the locus of our oil trade is in the Western Hemisphere: Alaska, Canada, Mexico, Venezuela and the Caribbean.

Against this background, let us review our forces in the main geographic areas: the Atlantic, the Mediterranean, the Pacific, and the Indian Ocean-Persian Gulf. The numbers used are notional, illustrating the forces assembled for current peacetime tasks. But they are capable of expansion or contraction should war break out, such is the characteristic flexibility of naval power.

The Atlantic

The Atlantic theatre encompasses the North Atlantic, the Norwegian Sea, the Northern Flank of NATO including the Baltic throat, the South Atlantic, the Caribbean and the Gulf of Mexico. It includes the coasts of South America and the west coast of Africa, all vital sea lanes of communication. And it involves the Mediterranean and the Middle East.

The US Navy has two fleets in the Atlantic, the Sixth and the Second. The Sixth Fleet in the Mediterranean is the principal fighting formation of NATO's Southern Europe Command and provides strike air-superiority, anti-submarine, and close air support forces for the entire Southern Flank of NATO. It is thus a major contribution to the balance on the Central Front.

In addition, the Sixth Fleet is the principal naval force to be tasked with supporting our friends and allies in the Middle East. The threat there is significant. The Soviets maintain a fleet in the Black Sea and a deployed squadron in the Mediterranean. In wartime we would probably also see Soviet naval strike aircraft, aircraft carriers, a formidable number of diesel and nuclear submarines, and a full range of strike cruisers, destroyers and other, smaller, combatants.

To deal with this threat, we start with a base of allied forces in the areas under consideration. The navies of our allies are good. For example, we count on them to provide about 140 diesel submarines, which are effective for coastal and area defence, for the establishment and maintenance of barriers, and for certain other missions.

In wartime the purely US forces of the Sixth Fleet would have to include three or four carrier battle groups committed to NATO. We would also need to deploy a battleship surface action group and two underway replenishment groups. In peacetime we average over the year 1.3 carrier battle groups deployed in the Mediterranean.

The Second Fleet is the heart of the NATO Atlantic strike fleet. It is responsible for naval operations in the North Atlantic, the Eastern Atlantic, Iceland, the Norwegian Sea, off Norway, and the entire Northern Flank including the North Sea and Baltic throat. At the same time it must be able to handle missions in the Caribbean, where we now face a very large Soviet and

Cuban naval presence; in the South Atlantic, where we have vital sea lanes; and along the West African sea lanes, where the Soviets now deploy naval forces continuously.

In wartime the Second Fleet would comprise four or five carrier battle groups, one battleship surface action group, and three underway replenishment groups. The carrier groups alone are equivalent in firepower to 40 Second World War carriers, and could accurately deliver a weapon tonnage equivalent to that of 800 B-17s every day. In peacetime, because most of the Navy's principal training occurs in the Second Fleet operating areas, strength is even higher, six carrier battle groups operating in the Second Fleet at one time or another. We also have exercises under way with our NATO allies, with our South American and Central American allies, and with other nations on an *ad hoc* basis during every season of the year.

The Pacific

Our increasing commercial interests and historic security ties in the Pacific are significantly affecting our naval planning for the area. If we are to protect our vital interests we must have forces available to deploy not only to the Atlantic theatre and the Sixth and the Second fleets, but also to the Pacific simultaneously, to the Seventh and Third fleets, and to the Middle East Force of the Central Command. We cannot abandon one theatre in order to deal with another. The great paradox of the 1970s was the reduction of the fleet's size so that it could be employed only in a swing strategy – just as that strategy was being rendered obsolete by trade, geopolitics and the growth of the Soviet Navy.

The Seventh Fleet is our forward Western Pacific fleet, meeting our commitments to Japan, Korea, the Philippines, Australia, New Zealand and Thailand, and operating in the critical straits of South-east Asia and in the Indian Ocean. In wartime we would need to

Top: **Enterprise** was the largest warship ever built when she commissioned in November 1961. She was also the first nuclear-powered carrier. Her design was a modification of that of the steam-powered **Forrestal** class, and both classes carry the same number of aircraft, about 90. But **Enterprise**'s powerplant means that her range, endurance and flexibility greatly exceed those of her conventionally powered half-sister.

Above: **Vincennes** belongs to the **Ticonderoga** class of cruisers, which have a hull similar to that of the **Spruance**-class destroyers. Four gas turbines give them a speed of over 30kt and they carry a heavy armament of eight Harpoon SSMs, 88 Standard/Asroc surface-to-air and anti-submarine missiles, two 5in guns, two six-barrelled close-in weapon systems, six torpedo tubes and two helicopters.

deploy five carrier battle groups, two battleship surface action groups and four underway replenishment groups to the Seventh Fleet. In peacetime we average over the year the equivalent of 1.3 carrier battle groups in the Western Pacific. That permits a fleetwide operational tempo which gives our people and their families 50% of their time in home port.

We do not have a separate fleet in the critical area of South-west Asia, the Indian Ocean and the Persian Gulf, although some have proposed the re-establishment of the Fifth Fleet for that purpose. In peacetime we

Above: *Chandler* is one of the four *Kidd*-class destroyers. These ships are slightly smaller than the *Ticonderoga* class and carry fewer Standard/Asroc weapons, but are in some respects just as capable.

Below: *Pittsburgh* is the 33rd *Los Angeles*-class nuclear-powered attack submarine. Although it is impossible to forecast how future programmes will fare, the present plan is to build 67 of these boats. They displace 6,927 tons dived and can carry Subroc, Mk 48 torpedoes, and Harpoon and Tomahawk missiles. Vertical-launch tubes are being fitted outside the pressure hull from boat No 32 onwards.

have the Middle East Force of the Central Command and elements of the Seventh Fleet, normally a carrier battle group.

In wartime two of the Seventh Fleet carrier battle groups would meet our commitments in the Indian Ocean, South-west Asia, East Africa, the Persian Gulf and South-east Asia. A Seventh Fleet battleship surface

Bottom: The first of the FFG-7 class was authorised in 1973. Fifty have been completed, with one to come. Two gas turbines driving a single propeller give a speed of 29kt and a range of 4,500 miles at 20kt. With two helicopters, surface-to-surface and surface-to-air missiles a 76mm gun and a Phalanx close-in weapon system, these are valuable ships but nevertheless lack the punch needed for sustained action with battle groups. *Jarrett*, shown here, has the extended transom needed to operate the new Seahawk helicopter.

Above: **Belleau Wood** is one of the most important elements in the USN's amphibious forces. Of 39,300 tons full load, she and her four sisters of the *Tarawa* class can carry four LCUs in the landing dock, 19–26 helicopters (depending on size) in the hangar, the vehicles for a reinforced battalion in the garage, six LCMs on the upper deck, 10,000gal of vehicle petrol, 400,000gal of helicopter fuel, and 1,703 troops.

Left: **First Lieutenant Jack Lummus** is one of 13 prepositioning ships which operate in three widely dispersed squadrons. Each squadron is loaded with the equipment for one Marine Amphibious Brigade, thus shortening the time required to support such a formation if it was airlifted to a trouble spot.

Below: The greatest weakness of the US Navy is its shortage of mine countermeasures forces. *Engage*, shown here, is one of the *Aggressive* class of 19 minesweepers, all of them well over 30 years old. A new class is under construction, with a target of 17 ships in service by the early 1990s.

action group and one underway replenishment group could also be assigned to operate in these areas.

The Third Fleet has responsibility for operations off Alaska and in the Bering Sea, the Aleutians, the Eastern Pacific, and the Mid-Pacific region. In wartime there would be much overlapping and trading back and forth between the Seventh and Third fleets. This happened in the Pacific during the Second World War. To cover that vast area we must assign two carrier battle groups and one underway replenishment group.

These requirements compel us to deploy a 600-ship Navy, as outlined in the accompanying table. In peacetime, we deploy in the same way to the same places we must control in war, but at one-third the tempo of operations. This allows a bearable peacetime burden of six-month deployments and 50% time in home ports. We thus require the same size of fleet to meet peacetime commitments as we do to fight a war. This adds up to the following:
- 15 carrier battle groups
- 4 battleship surface action groups
- 100 attack submarines
- An adequate number of ballistic missile submarines
- Lift for the assault echelons of a Marine amphibious force and a Marine amphibious brigade

When escort, mine warfare, auxiliary and replenishment units are considered, a total of about 600 ships emerges. This is a prudent force level, reflecting geographic realities, alliance commitments and dependencies, and the Soviet fleet that threatens them. Unless Congress reduces our commitments or the Soviet threat weakens, there is no way to reduce the size of the US fleet and leave it still able to carry out its missions.

Current US Navy force requirements

	Peacetime	Wartime
Sixth Fleet		
CVBG	1.3	4
BBSAG	0.3	1
URG	1	2
Second Fleet*		
CVBG	6.7	4
BBSAG	1.7	1
URG	4	3
Seventh Fleet**		
CVBG	2	5
BBSAG	0.5	2
URG	1	4
Third Fleet*		
CVBG	5	2
BBSAG	1.5	—
URG	4	1

*Includes forces in overhaul. **Includes Indian Ocean forces. **CVBG** = carrier battle group. **BBSAG** = battleship surface action group. **URG** = underway replenishment group.

Does the Navy have a role in the national strategy?

While the Carter Administration questioned whether the Navy could influence a "short war" in Central Europe, such a proposition is indefensible today. The coalition of free nations bound together in NATO must have maritime superiority as a prerequisite of any defence strategy. Maritime superiority alone might not assure victory but the loss of it would certainly assure defeat – and sooner rather than later. The chronicles of warfare are a consistent testament to the influence of sea power upon history, in which great continental powers do not long prevail against an opponent with mastery of the seas. Today, NATO's continental defence rests on early achievement of maritime superiority. The Soviet Union, as evidenced

by its continuing naval expansion, understands the experience of history far better than our trendier military reformists.

Does the Navy have a strategy? Is it the right one?

Now consider the charge, levelled by some parlour Pershings, that our current naval buildup lacks an underlying strategy. Not since the days of Theodore Roosevelt have the Navy and Marine Corps exhibited such a strong consensus on the comprehensive strategy which now shapes our naval planning. Briefly, our strategic objectives are as follows:
● To prevent the seas from becoming a medium of attack against the United States and its allies.
● To ensure that we have unimpeded use of our ocean lifelines to our allies, forward-deployed forces, energy and mineral resources, and trading partners.
● To be able to project force in support of national security objectives and to support combat ashore, should deterrence fail.

To achieve these objectives we need a global strategy envisaging forces that are forward-deployed and superior to those of our probable opponents. Global because our interests, allies and opponents are global; forward-deployed because we protect those interests and allies, and to deter those opponents, we must be where they are; superior because if deterrence fails it is better to win than lose.

Cape Cod is one of a class of six modern destroyer tenders, each of which can provide services to six guided missile destroyers at one time. They also have facilities for servicing nuclear powerplants.

But do we have the correct strategy? Today's debates would benefit from a more precise understanding of the role of strategy. Strategy is not a formula for fighting each ship and deploying each tank in the battles that might take place around the world. That function belongs not to the military establishment inside the Washington Beltway but to the theatre commander, who is responsible for achieving the defence objectives set by the national command authorities. Strategy's role is to give coherence and direction to the process of allocating money among competing types of ship and aircraft and different accounts for spare parts, missile systems, defence planning, and the training of forces. It provides guidelines to aid us in allocating both resources and tolerating shortages.

Title 10 of the US Code charges the Secretary of the Navy with ensuring the highest level of training appropriate to the responsibilities placed upon the Marine Corps and the Navy. That is what strategy gives us: a framework within which to train. For example, US naval forces recently conducted a major training exercise, Ocean Safari 85, with our NATO allies and the US Coast Guard and Air Force. The force assembled off the East Coast of the United States and fought its way across the Atlantic, moved north of England and east of Iceland, and ended up in the Norwegian Sea. Approximately 155 ships and 280 fixed-wing aircraft and helicopters operated for four weeks in the presence of 19 Soviet ships and submarines and 96 aircraft sorties.

Very effective training like that is being carried out as part of a coherent plan which is linked to the way that the theatre commanders would fight a war. One will search in vain, however, for a Navy manual that tells those commanders when to move aircraft carriers, or how or where to move attack submarines or Aegis cruisers in war. There should never be any such book, and it should certainly never come from Washington.

Those who criticise our strategy for being the wrong manual, or for failing to act as one, do not understand strategy.

Other critics argue that our Navy should be less global, less forward-deployed or less superior, so releasing resources for a stronger continental defence. To be less global means to abandon some area of our vital interests. To believe that in the case of the Northern Flank of NATO, for example, a "passive" defence line thrown across the Greenland-Iceland-United Kingdom Gap would somehow protect our sea lanes or defer an engagement with Soviet forces demonstrates a lack of understanding of the fundamental mechanics of war at sea, the workings of NATO and the Soviets' own operational requirements. No coalition of free nations can survive a strategy which begins by sacrificing its more exposed allies to dubious military expediency. To suggest that naval support of Norway or Turkey is too dangerous because it must be done close to the Soviet Union is defeatist. To suggest that such a strategy is provocative of the Soviets just indicates the lengths to which some critics will go to portray Soviet intentions as solely defensive.

As for strengthening our continental defences, we and our allies are also doing just that. But to discard maritime superiority in an attempt to match the larger Soviet ground forces would give us neither conventional deterrence on land nor secure access by sea unless the Western democracies were prepared to militarise their societies to an unprecedented, and unwise, degree.

Are we buying the right Navy for the strategy?

Because research and development projects span decades, and ships take many years to build, the makeup of our fleet can not change radically with each administration. Instead, the fleet evolves over time in concert with changes in policy and technology. The fleet today reflects the wisdom of the deck plates, the labs, and lessons learned from our exercises. The size and design of our ships and weapons reflect the inputs of sailors in contact with Soviet Victor submarines, *Kiev*-class carriers, and Bear aircraft. Common sense and the highest available technology are among the tremendous advantages brought to the design of today's Navy and Marine Corps.

Of course, there are many kinds of ship not in the fleet today that could do very well in US Navy hands. The British *Invincible*-class vertical/short take-off and landing (VSTOL) carriers are quite capable anti-submarine warfare ships, and it would be nice to have some of them in the US Navy. There are many attractive European frigate designs, and we could make good use of them. There are also diesel submarines in our European alliance navies that perform very effectively.

If the taxpayers of our allies around the world were not buying these vessels, the burden would fall upon us. But happily they are carrying a significant share of the cost of naval defence and American taxpayers do not have to fund a Navy greater than about 600 ships.

The issue most debated on the front pages and in television talk shows is probably whether our aircraft carriers should be large or small. There is no absolute answer to this question, but in my view the evidence still seems overwhelmingly in favour of the 90,000-ton *Nimitz* (CVN-68) class as the best way of taking air capability to sea.

Could we gainfully employ more mid-size carriers like our 64,000-ton *Midway* (CV-41) and *Coral Sea* (CV-43)? Yes indeed. They would be very useful and the Navy would like to have five more of them if it could be afforded. At the very least, we will keep these two smaller carriers steaming in the force for a long time to come.

Similarly, we could buy more nuclear attack submarines if we compromised on their capabilities. But our tremendous edge in technology over the Soviets is built into our culture and economic system. We must exploit this advantage and not trade it away for cheaper, smaller, less capable ships built in greater numbers, which is the forte of a totalitarian, centralised economy.

It would be a great mistake for us to adopt a defence strategy that attempts to match totalitarian regimes in sheer numbers of cheap, mass-produced items. Time and again, the high-tech solution has proved to be the wisest investment, and by far the most advantageous one for the United States and its allies. This is true of our missiles, our aircraft and our ships. We have the world's finest fighting equipment.

So we are getting the right Navy. Although there

are plenty of other kinds of ship we would like to have, and we could certainly use the larger Navy long advocated by the Joint Chiefs, we have stayed consistently with the 600-ship fleet because we are prepared to bet that our allies will continue to maintain modern, effective navies and air forces. In order to have an affordable Navy we are prepared to accept the risk that our nation will make the right decisions to prevent losses of forces early in a conflict.

Can we afford the Navy this nation needs?

Numerous studies and surveys, among them a tome by the Congressional Budget Office, suggest that we cannot afford to sustain, or properly man, a 600-ship Navy. Just the reverse is true. Consider the facts. We now have under construction and fully funded *all* of the ships necessary to attain a 600-ship Navy centred on 15 carrier battle groups, four battleship surface action groups, and 100 nuclear-powered attack submarines.

Our long-term plans now reflect reductions in our shipbuilding and aircraft procurement programmes to the sustaining rate for the 600-ship Navy, or an average of 20 ships a year in new construction. The actual number will be higher or lower in a given year, depending on the block obsolescence of various types of ship.

The 20-ship average is a sound basis for planning, in part because of improved maintenance and the resulting increase in longevity. Instead of the average 26 years of life achieved in the 1960s and the 1970s, we are now getting 30 years' service from our ships

because of better maintenance, the absence of a big backlog of overhauls, and the higher technology that we are putting into new vessels.

This good news should not blind us to the requirements of the future. A steady 20 new ships a year will require 3% budget growth. A succession of zero-growth budgets would mean that we would be unable to sustain a 600-ship Navy – or, for that matter, a capable defence. We know from painful experience in the 1970s that the damage done by no-growth funding is far greater than the mere percentage budget loss would indicate. With zero or negative-growth budgets, the industrial infrastructure vital to fleet construction and support shrinks dramatically. The result is a loss in competitive bidding and a return to sole-source monopolies. Rates of production must then be cut, individual unit costs increase dramatically, productivity falls and, in the final accounting, the American taxpayer gets much less bang for the buck. Even worse is the decline in the quality and morale of the people who man the fleet, as we saw in the late 1970s.

Is 3% real growth beyond our means? Throughout the past two decades many commentators favouring a reduced defence effort have repeatedly predicted that the American people would not support sustained defence growth. That assertion is now put forward by some, including the Congressional Budget Office, as a fact of life. While it may express their hopes, it is not supported by history. That view takes as its basis the flat or even declining figures of the immediate post-Vietnam War period. In fact, except for those years, post-Second World War naval budgets have grown in step with our national economy. The middle and late 1970s, by contrast, are now being seen as an anomaly in US history. It is not apparent, the Congressional Budget Office notwithstanding, that the American people wish to restore that aberrant pattern of declining ship numbers, morale and readiness.

When it comes to procurement, we should not assume that Congress will refuse to make the necessary legislative changes in the way we in the Department of the Navy are permitted to conduct our business. Indeed, I suggest that in the current climate of public concern over budget deficits and government spending there would be few more cost-effective and money-saving moves that Congress could undertake than the removal of the excessive regulation and red tape with which the Navy has to contend. For example,

Left: **While the Royal Navy has turned its back on hovercraft, the US Marine Corps is planning to acquire 90 of these Landing Craft Air-Cushion. The first was delivered in December 1984.**

Above right: **Seattle is one of a class of four fast combat support ships of about 53,000 tons full load. They are designed to provide the fleet with fuel, dry stores, refrigerated stores and munitions.**

there repose in the Library of Congress today no fewer than 1,152 linear feet of statutory and regulatory law governing procurement alone!

Along with over-regulation, we are faced with excessive, layered bureaucracies, and the accretion of authority without concomitant responsibility into a confusing labyrinth of congressional oversight committees and federal agencies without end. The Congressional Budget Office staffers and others who look at the Navy's future costs assume that this bloated, inefficient system will remain in place. I do not accept that. Moreover, we have shown in the Navy a historic reversal of the trend of inevitable cost increases.

For example, the last contract that we signed for a follow-on Aegis cruiser set the price at $900 million. Four years ago these cruisers cost more than $1.2 billion each, and were projected to reach $1.6 billion by the end of 1985. It did not happen, though, because we brought competition into the programme. Both producing yards brought in new efficiencies and instituted strict cost discipline, while we in the Navy learned to contain our gold-plating lusts. All of our shipbuilding programmes show the same pattern. We have gone from only 24% competition in 1981 to 90% competition in 1985, producing an average of $1 billion in cost *under*runs for each of the last four years.

Contrary to what the nay-sayers predicted, the costs of Navy aircraft have been going down, not up. This is a sea change, a break with 30 years of uninterrupted cost escalation in naval aircraft procurement. During 1976–1981 growth in aircraft prices averaged about 10% in constant FY 1980 dollars. In 1981 we implemented vigorous cost management programmes which emphasised competition, no design changes, and firm fixed-price contracts. These efforts have paid off in reduced aircraft prices every year since 1982.

For example, we reached agreement with McDonnell Douglas on FY 1985 fly-away price of $18.7 million for the F/A-18 strike fighter. This represents a real saving of 32% on the price paid in 1982. Purchases in 1985 yielded a saving to the taxpayer of $126 million for that year alone.

So there is nothing inevitable about escalating costs and overruns in defence procurement. During the last four years we have proved that underruns can happen just as consistently. Given even conservative assumptions there is no question that we can maintain the size and the current mix of our force through the rest of this century with a 3%-growth budget.

Just as significant, we can also maintain the tremendous turn-around in readiness that we have achieved with President Ronald Reagan's 7%-growth budgets. Over the past four years the readiness of our ships and aircraft has increased nearly 40%. Even these statistics do not do justice to the palpable difference in the fleet itself, in morale, in readiness and in safety. We know what we have accomplished during the past five years. Furthermore, we know we can maintain this record of success with the size of budget currently envisaged by the President.

The German military philosopher Clausewitz once observed that in the balance of power among nations, battle is to deterrence as cash is to credit in the world of commerce. One can live entirely by paper transactions *only* when there is no doubt about one's ability to settle accounts with hard currency when challenged. Similarly, there must be no doubt in the minds of the Soviet leaders that the United States and its allies can and will settle accounts, on both land and sea, if challenged. The 600-ship Navy is essential to the creation of this belief. We can and must afford the naval power needed for the defence of this country's allies and interests around the world.

Argentina's admirals scuttle the sell-off

Adrian English

THE military government which ruled Argentina from 1976 to 1983 embarked on an ambitious naval re-equipment programme designed to produce a balanced modern fleet which would have been the most formidable in South America by the late 1980s. If the ill considered invasion of the Falkland Islands had been delayed by even 18 months, the balance of forces in the subsequent war would have been so radically different as to make a British victory much more problematic. Since the return of civilian government in Argentina, however, rumours of the pending sale of major naval vessels have been rife. Nevertheless, despite the efforts of the Alfonsín administration, the Argentinian Navy seems to have succeeded in keeping its newest and best equipment, disposing only of the ships that it did not want.

At the beginning of the 20th century Argentina emerged from an arms race with Chile as the premier naval power in South America. This in turn provoked a further naval arms race between Argentina and Brazil, from which the latter emerged as the leading regional naval power between 1910 and the mid-1920s, when Argentina once more gained the upper hand. The Argentinian Navy maintained its regional

supremacy for 40 years. Then, in the early 1960s, massive United States military assistance restored Brazil to the forefront, a position which it progressively consolidated over the next 15 years.

The military junta which seized power in Argentina in March 1976 found itself with a largely decrepit fleet of Second World War relics. The exceptions were two Type 209 submarines, completed in sections in Germany in 1974 and subsequently assembled in Argentina, two modern fast attack craft, also German-built, and two Type 42 missile destroyers under construction, one in Britain and the other locally with British technical assistance.

Although the Commander-in-Chief of the Army, General Videla, assumed the office of President as

Left: **San Luis**. In 1968 Argentina ordered two Type 209 submarines from West Germany. Both were delivered in 1974. Of 1,285 tons dived and with an underwater speed of 22kt, they have eight torpedo tubes and a complement of 32.

Below: **Espora** is the first of the MEKO 140 frigates built at Rio Santiago to a design by West Germany's Blohm und Voss. The first two of these 1,700-ton ships were commissioned in July 1985. All are to be fitted with a telescopic hangar for a helicopter and carry eight Exocet SSMs, one 76mm gun, two twin 40mm mountings and six ASW torpedo tubes. They are powered by two 10,200hp diesels, giving a speed of 27kt.

senior member of the junta following the coup of March 1976, its strongman was the Navy's Admiral Massera. As it transpired, Massera was mainly responsible for the decision, six years later, to repossess the Falkland Islands by force. The unusually strong position of the Navy in the military government was reflected in the undertaking of an extensive building programme. Two enlarged Type 209 submarines were ordered from West Germany in 1977, and four similar vessels were to be built in Argentina with German assistance. The construction of six MEKO Type 360 missile destroyers was also authorised, the order being subsequently modified to four vessels of this type, to be built in Germany, and six Type 140 frigates, to be built in Argentina with German technical assistance.

Hercules, the British-built Type 42 guided missile destroyer, was completed four months after the coup of 1976. Her locally built sister ship *Santisima Trinidad*, which had been damaged on the slip by terrorist bombs, was not to be commissioned until five years later. Two French Type A69 missile frigates, built for South Africa but undelivered following the United Nations arms embargo, were bought in 1978; a third vessel of this type was completed specifically for the Argentinian Navy three years later. Although four Dabur-class patrol craft were supplied by Israel in 1979 and the Argentinian Navy had shown an interest in acquiring HMS *Intrepid* or her sister *Fearless* from the Royal Navy to improve its inadequate amphibious assault capability, no further modern combat craft had been acquired at the time of the Falklands invasion in April 1982. The first five of 14 Super Etendard strike aircraft, for operation from the carrier *Veinticinco de Mayo*, were on hand, however, and were to demonstrate

Top: Santisima Trinidad. In May 1970 the Argentinian Government signed a contract for two British Type 42 destroyers, the first to be built in Britain and the second, *Santisima Trinidad*, in Argentina. They were completed in 1976–81 and were fitted with Exocets and Sea Dart surface-to-air missiles. Their helicopters, sensors, engines and electronics were all of British manufacture.

Above: Veinticinco de Mayo. Built as HMS *Venerable* for the Royal Navy and transferred to the Royal Netherlands Navy as HrMS *Karel Doorman*, she was eventually sold to Argentina in 1968. In 1980–81 this 19,896-ton ship was converted to operate Super Etendard aircraft, although the first trials with the type were not carried out until April 1983.

their deadly effectiveness in the conflict which followed.

The almost universal embargo on the supply of military equipment to Argentina following the Falkland invasion delayed the progress of the new construction programme to a certain extent. Three of the MEKO 360s and one of the 140s were already in the water at the time of the Falklands invasion, and the fourth 360, two of the 140s and the first pair of the enlarged Type 209 submarines were at varying stages of pre-launch construction. The first two MEKO 360s, *Almirante Brown* and *La Argentina*, were finally delivered during 1983, to be followed by their sister ships *Heroina* and *Sarandi* a year later. *Santa Cruz*, the first of the new submarines, was also delivered at the end of 1984, followed by the second boat, *San Juan*, at the end of 1985.

The Type 42 destroyers had acquired a bad reputation during the Falklands War, two of five British vessels of this type employed in the conflict being sunk with relative ease by Argentinian aircraft and one badly damaged. The difficulties of acquiring spares resulting from the post-war chilliness between Britain and Argentina further diminished the potential usefulness of the Type 42s to the Argentinian Navy, and both were laid up at the end of 1982. A decision to dispose of them was taken during the first half of 1983. Its finality was underlined by the sale of the sole remaining embarked Lynx helicopter to Brazil, the other having been lost by accident during the Falklands War.

Having inherited a crippling burden of debt from its military predecessors in 1983, and keen to lessen the ability of the Argentinian military to intervene in politics, the civilian administration of Raul Alfonsin tried to persuade the Navy to sell off some of its new construction, hoping to use the proceeds to reduce the country's liabilities to international bankers. At first it was suggested that two of the four MEKO 360s and up to four of the as yet incomplete 140s might be disposed of, in addition to the two Type 42s already on the sales list. But the Navy successfully resisted all pressures in this respect, its position being strengthened by the fact that the funds for the new construction programme had been voted before the return to civilian government and were already in hand. Far from disposing of any of the projected vessels, the Navy made sure that the keels for the three remaining MEKO 140s were laid during 1983–84 and work on the second pair of modified Type 209 submarines began. It was even suggested that the final pair might be built to a further modified design with nuclear propulsion, although rumours of the purchase of a nuclear attack submarine from France proved to be unfounded.

Using funds appropriated during the military regime, the Navy also acquired additional aircraft, including the remaining nine Super Etendards of the original order, eleven Embraer EMB.326 Xavante light strike aircraft, and six Lockheed L.188E Electras converted for maritime reconnaissance. The Marine Corps also received new equipment, including 12 Panhard ERC-90 Lynx armoured cars and 24 VCR/TT armoured personnel carriers to re-equip its reconnaissance battalion. During 1982–83 the paramilitary coastguard, the Prefectura Naval, took delivery of the five Spanish-built *Halcon*-class economic zone patrol vessels which had been ordered in 1979.

Although *Hercules* and *Santisima Trinidad* remained on the sales list and reputedly attracted the transient interest of Iran, Iraq, Libya, Turkey and Brazil in succession, they failed to attract a purchaser. The only major vessels disposed of were the ancient ex-US destroyers *Comodoro Py*, *Hipolito Bouchard*, *Piedrabuena* and *Segui*, the equally antiquated and unserviceable Second World War-vintage submarine *Santiago del Estero* and, somewhat surprisingly, the fleet oiler *Punta Medanos*. Though over 30 years old, this ship represented the Argentinian Navy's only capacity for replenishment at sea, and her disposal without replacement effectively limits the surface units of the fleet to the coast-defence role.

The only apparent victory of the Alfonsín administration in its efforts to liquidate some of the Navy's new equipment was the announcement during the second half of 1986 that Thyssen Nordseewerke, designer of the new submarines and builder of the only pair so far to enter service, and the West German Government had agreed to the sale by Argentina of two of the four boats still to be completed. No prospective purchasers had emerged at the time of writing, and the agreement now seems to have been nothing more than the first step in the government's efforts to dispose of the vessels. That the agreement referred to submarines rather than surface craft is nevertheless of some significance. The Argentinian Navy has never demonstrated any great interest in submarine warfare, acquiring its first three boats from Italy only in the 1930s and to date never having operated more than four at any given time.

The Navy is understood to be highly satisfied with its MEKO 360s, and is unlikely to be prepared to part with any of them. Although no reports of the performance of the MEKO 140s in service have yet emerged, it is reasonable to suppose that the Navy will also continue to resist all pressures to part with any of the four vessels of this type still incomplete. Even if two of the new submarines are eventually disposed of, a fleet of six boats will remain. While probably amounting to a force twice as big as the Navy can effectively operate, this figure seems unlikely to be further reduced. Ironically, the only two major surface combatants the Navy would genuinely like to be rid of, *Hercules* and *Santisima Trinidad*, are reported to be in extremely poor condition after over three years of decommissioned status with minimal maintenance and must become daily less saleable.

The pride of the Argentinian Navy and its major status symbol remains the 42-year-old carrier *Veinticinco de Mayo*, which seems likely to be retained at least nominally in commission until the turn of the century, although her serviceability must become progressively more problematic. Her replacement in the foreseeable future is rendered unlikely not only by Argentina's poor economic position but also by the decreasing availability of suitable second-hand ships. New construction is out of the question on cost grounds. Should Argentina's economy recover sufficiently within the next decade, the Navy seems likely to be in competition with those of Brazil, Chile, Peru and possibly India for the acquisition of the French carriers *Clemenceau* and *Foch* when these ships come on to the second-hand market in 1995 and 1998 respectively.

Although the Alfonsín administration has been largely frustrated in its efforts to part the Navy from the majority of its new vessels, it has at the same time successfully warded off all threats of a military coup. This is no mean feat and perhaps owes something to the discrediting of the Argentinian armed forces in the war against Britain and the systematic erosion of the already shattered morale of the Army, Navy and Air Force so that they no longer represent a threat to the survival of civilian government.

Despite extensive re-equipment during the last months of the military regime, the armed services must be even less able to undertake external military adventures than they were in 1982. A further diminution in military effectiveness has been brought about by the reduction in the annual conscript intake by 70%, so that the Navy now has little more than 50% of the manpower with which it embarked on the Falklands invasion. This in turn must create progressive manning difficulties as the new construction programme is completed. Further, financial constraints are reported to have reduced the annual sea time of major units to two weeks. This combination must neutralise what is superficially a fine modern fleet even more effectively than if it had been persuaded to part with over 50% of its major combatants, as was the government's original intention.

Indomita is one of a pair of 268-ton fast attack craft delivered from West Germany in 1974. Powered by four diesels, their top speed is 38kt. They each carry one 76mm gun, two 40mm guns and two torpedo tubes.

Above: **Commandante General Irigoyen**, one of two **Cherokee**-class ocean tugs built in 1945 in the USA and transferred to Argentina in 1961 and converted into patrol ships. They will be deleted as the MEKO 140s are completed.

Right: Since this pair of 270-ton tugs were completed at Buenos Aires in 1978 the Argentinian naval building capability has expanded to include frigates and submarines.

Below: **Dorado**, one of the ten large patrol craft and ships of the Prefectura Naval. The Prefectura dates from the 18th century, when the Captainship of the Port of Buenos Aires was first established. It has continued since then under various titles and is today responsible for patrolling over 1,000 miles of rivers and coastal waters and for their associated ports.

The Indian Ocean's naval giant

A. W. Grazebrook

LAST year saw a further substantial build-up in India's naval strength. Already the capability of the Indian Navy, with its naval air arm, has reached the point where it is far in excess of anything that could conceivably be needed for the defence of national interests against any other Indian Ocean maritime force or likely combination of enemies. The build-up has five aspects:

• New ships, increasing total numbers and capability.
• New submarines, again increasing total numbers and capability.
• New aircraft, yet again increasing total numbers and capability.
• New and modernised bases, and new forward operating facilities.
• A greatly improved industrial base.

Two carrier task forces

Undoubtedly the most impressive Indian naval acquisition in 1986 was the purchase, at a bargain-

Above: **Viraat**, until recently HMS *Hermes*, is India's second carrier. She will share with *Vikrant* the 23 Sea Harriers now in Indian Navy service. In addition, Sea King, Alouette, Hormone and Helix helicopters can be handled by these two ships. The Indian Chief of Naval Staff recently declared that carriers would be designed and built in India in the future.

Right: The Indian coastline, including offshore islands, totals 4,350nm in length, though the steaming distances are less daunting. Calcutta is a minor base with a building yard at Garden Reach. Vishakapatnam is the headquarters of the Cs-in-C Eastern Command and Eastern Fleet and houses the main submarine base and school, a major dockyard and barracks, and a naval air station. Arakkonam (outside Madras) is a new naval air station, as is Ramanathaparam (Uchipuli). Cochin is the headquarters for C-in-C Southern Command, and also has a naval air station. Goa is the headquarters of Flag Officer Naval Air, and is close to the new major base and naval air station at Karwar. Bombay is the headquarters of the Cs-in-C Western Command and Western Fleet, and is home to a major dockyard and the Mazagon building yard. The Andamans base of Port Blair is 750 miles south-east of Vishakapatnam.

basement price, of the British aircraft carrier *Hermes*, flagship of the Task Force in the Falklands War. Renamed INS *Viraat*, the ship was refitted at Devonport before delivery. The work included installation of new command, control and communications facilities. This is significant, since *Hermes* was preferred to the newer *Invincible* as flagship of the Falklands force because of her superior command and communications facilities.

In Indian Navy service *Viraat*'s aircraft complement will be very similar to the one she operated so effectively in the Falklands War: Sea King helicopters and Sea Harrier fighter/attack aircraft. The acquisition of *Viraat* will give India two carrier task forces, complete with area defence-equipped escorts and underway replenishment ships. India's second carrier, INS *Vikrant*, is soon to begin the second stage of a modernisation which will include an increase in the angle of her ski-jump to improve the take-off performance of her Sea Harriers. *Viraat* is expected to remain in operational service until after the year 2000. *Vikrant*'s modernisation and refit will keep her in service until 1995. It is planned to replace her, possibly with a new ship designed to operate STOVL aircraft.

The two carriers are likely to be supported by three new Soviet-built Kresta II-class guided missile cruisers. Four new Kashin II-class guided missile destroyers have already joined the Indian Navy. A further two are expected, and there are reports of a total programme of as many as nine.

Two underway replenishment ships are already in service. They each carry a helicopter for vertical replenishment, and modern equipment for replenishment at sea. A third ship for this role has been ordered, details of which are not yet available.

The two carrier task forces will be available for offensive operations, as no other Indian Ocean power has surface forces capable of attacking Indian trade outside the range of shore-based aircraft. For the protection of trade against submarine attack India is developing two major escort forces, the first for "blue water" operations, the second for coastal work. Both will be supported by ship and shore-based helicopters and shore-based aircraft.

Ocean escort forces

At present the oceangoing escort force consists of six British-designed, Indian-built Improved *Leander*-class frigates, three Indian-built 3,600-ton *Godavari*-class frigates and two modernised *Whitby*-class frigates. The *Godavari* class, an Indian-designed development

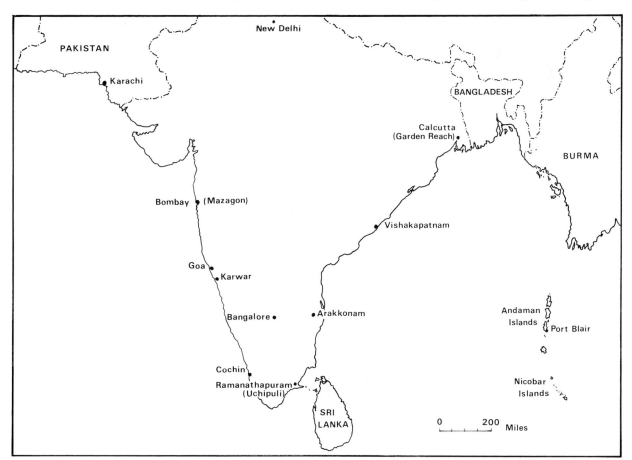

of the *Leander* class, is unusual in being able to carry two Sea King ASW helicopters. A modern Soviet point-defence system and canister-launched surface-to-surface missiles, Italian anti-submarine torpedoes, and a light gun armament complete the ships' weapons fit. At least one ship is fitted with variable-depth sonar.

Three variable-depth sonar arrays have been bought for installation in the *Leander* frigates, as well as two new hull-mounted units. To bring them up to the standard of the two latest ships, the four older *Leander*s are being modernised to accommodate one Sea King helicopter each.

Plans are well advanced for a class of 5,000-ton frigates, with construction of the first expected to start in March 1987 at Bombay's Mazagon Dock. They will be CODOG-powered, with General Electric LM2500 gas turbines and West German MTU diesels, and are expected to be able to accommodate two Sea Kings and carry an Indian-developed variable-depth sonar. Dutch design assistance has been enlisted, although the new vessels will be markedly larger than any escort in service with the Royal Netherlands Navy. While these ships are of great interest, India's plans for new smaller escorts are equally innovative.

Coastal escort force

For some years the Indian Navy has operated two squadrons of Soviet-built Petya II fast frigates. These ships are reported to have been disappointing in service, and two of the class recently paid off. The remainder are obsolescent and lack modern anti-submarine and anti-aircraft weapons and sensors.

To replace them in part, India has ordered the first of a new local design of anti-submarine corvette. The lead ship is expected to commission in July 1987 and the second in March 1988. Two more have been ordered and are now in a second Indian yard. The Indian Navy has not revealed how many ships of this class are to be built.

There are persistent reports that India has ordered five Pauk-class anti-submarine corvettes from the

Above left: **Rajput**, the first of what will eventually be a class of six modified Kashin destroyers purchased from the USSR. Further transfers from the Soviet Navy are reported to include Kresta II-class cruisers.

Above: **Ranvir**, fourth of the Indian Navy's Kashin-class destroyers, was delivered by the Soviet Union in August 1986 and differs from her three earlier sisters in carrying the modern Helix helicopter, 30mm Gatling guns with Bass Tilt radars, and an infra-red attachment to her missile launchers.

Below: The Petya-class light frigates *Amini* and *Andaman* are part of a class of ten transferred by the Soviet Union in 1969–74. They have not been entirely satisfactory and one of the class was deleted in 1986.

Soviet Union. These 580-ton craft achieve a lot on their displacement, boasting a speed of 34kt, a point-defence missile system, dipping sonar and close-range anti-submarine weapons.

On the other hand, it is possible that reports of Indian purchases of Pauk-class ships may have arisen from confusion with the surface attack version of the Pauk, the Tarantul. Having the same hull as the Pauk, the Tarantuls are faster, COGAG-driven vessels equipped with surface-to-surface guided weapons and a point-defence missile system. It can be argued that while the Pauks are coastal escorts, the Tarantuls fall into the category of light surface attack forces.

Light surface attack forces

Apart from any Tarantul-class units that may be acquired, the Indian Navy has in service four Nanuchka-type missile-armed attack corvettes, with four more on order. These ships are listed as having a range of 2,500nm at cruising speed and 900nm at top speed, quite enough for them to operate in the Straits of Malacca from the Indian Navy's new forward operating facility in the Nicobar Islands.

In addition to the Nanuchkas, the Indian Navy has 16 Osa-class missile-armed fast attack craft, some of which are being or have been modernised. Two have been modified – changes include the removal of their missiles – for support of clandestine operations. At least one of a new class of 200-ton patrol craft has been commissioned; more than six are planned. At this stage the role of these craft is not clear, as patrol duties are normally performed by the coastguard.

Ten of India's eleven landing ships are Soviet Polnochnys. *Gundal*, shown here, is the latest acquisition.

Mine countermeasures

Mine countermeasures are important in protecting naval bases and seagoing trade and in "sweeping in" amphibious forces to land on hostile shores. The growth in its mine countermeasures forces indicates that the Indian Navy envisages a need for all three types of capability. It operates eight Soviet-built Natya-class 650-ton ocean minesweepers and has another four on order. Six GRP-hulled inshore minesweepers have been acquired from the Soviet Union, with a further six of the same type on order.

India is now seeking a further ten larger mine countermeasures vessels, with GRP hulls and fitted for both minesweeping and minehunting. The first two such ships are to be built overseas, presumably in Europe as there is a shortlist of two types, both of European design. The remaining eight will be built under licence in Goa.

The need for both minesweeping and minehunting capabilities is clear, and they can generally be shown to be defensive in nature. However, there is no apparent defensive need for such capabilities in a ship of over 650 tons. The selection of the Natya therefore suggests that offensive amphibious operations are envisaged.

Amphibious operations

The Indian Navy's inventory of 780-ton medium landing ships of the Soviet Polnochny class currently stands at eight, with the later units having a notably greater payload and (in most cases) a helicopter landing platform. There is also a programme of utility landing craft construction in India, as well as reports of an order for four further Polnochnys from an Indian yard.

While these acquisitions increase the tonnage capability of India's amphibious lift, they do not add to its range or raise its technological level. These objectives are being attained with a new class of 5,500-ton assault tank landing ship, the first of which (*Magar*) has been commissioned and the second laid down. The necessary assault troops are drawn from a recently formed regiment of marines, the senior officers for which have received overseas training in Western marine forces.

Hydrographic and oceanographic capability

Up-to-date knowledge of the oceans and coastal waters is essential to amphibious operations and every other aspect of modern naval operations. To provide this much needed capability, India has in service five oceangoing hydrographic ships, with a further two on order. Five hydrographic research ships have been ordered from a Singaporean yard. An ice-strengthened research ship has been completed in Denmark, and another research ship has been built in France. A number of smaller hydrographic ships are used for work in coastal waters. Vessels of this type provide much invaluable information for submarine operations.

India's growing submarine force

For over a decade India has operated a squadron of eight Soviet-built Foxtrot-class diesel-electric submarines supported by an oceangoing depot ship. These boats are expected to remain in service until 1995, when the first will reach retirement age. The last Foxtrot will be mechanically sound, though long obsolete, until 2004. To expand her submarine force India has started two new-construction programmes.

Above: **Though a number of Western designs are under consideration, most of India's submarines come from the USSR. *Kanderi*, shown here with a Hormone helicopter, is one of eight Foxtrot-class boats delivered by the Soviet Navy between 1968 and 1975.**

Below left: **In 1981 the Indian Navy concluded an agreement with Howaldtswerke of West Germany covering the building of six submarines, two in Kiel and four in Bombay. The first two, of which *Shankush* (S45) is the second, have been delivered, but some delays have been experienced with the first home-built boat. There are also reports of an Indian interest in Swedish submarines and in a new 2,000-ton class to be built in Bombay.**

Right: **In September 1986 *Sindhugosh* was transferred to India by the USSR, making her one of the first Kilo-class boats to be exported. This class of 3,200-ton submarines entered Soviet service only in 1979, indicating the high priority given to Indian orders. A further five are to be delivered to India, at a rate of one a year.**

The first covers ten German-designed, 1,500-ton diesel-electric boats. The first of these has already commissioned and arrived in India early in 1987, with the second expected to commission later in the year. The remaining eight are being built in India. Although there were some initial problems with the first Indian boat, resulting in a delay of two years, it is claimed that the remainder will be built on schedule.

The second programme covers the purchase of a force of the latest generation of Soviet diesel-electric submarine, the Kilo class. The first of six boats has already arrived in India and the order is due to be complete by 1991.

Possible future developments comprise the domestic development of a class of large oceangoing diesel-electric boats, and the acquisition of nuclear-powered submarines from the Soviet Union. But even if these plans come to nothing, the Indian Navy will still be able to deploy around 20 diesel-electric submarines, a major force capable of interdicting Indian Ocean trade, blockading enemy bases, offensive minelaying and long-range reconnaissance. This force will be three times the size of those of Pakistan or Australia, the next two major maritime powers with littorals on the Indian Ocean, while three-quarters of its submarines will be of the very latest type.

While India's margin of submarine superiority may seem exceptionally generous, it is as nothing compared with the predominance of the Navy's much expanded air arm.

Naval air arm

The Indian Navy's air arm is being modernised by the acquisition of five main types of new aircraft:
● Sea Harriers.
● Enlarged Sea King helicopters.
● Bear-F long-range maritime aircraft.
● Dornier Do228 shorter-range shore-based maritime aircraft.
● Helix anti-submarine helicopters, the latest available from the Soviet naval inventory.

At the time of writing, a total of 19 Sea Harriers, including three two-seat trainers, are in service or on firm order. There are reports of an option on a further eight, making a total of 27.

The number of Sea Harriers needed to equip the two carriers depends on the mix of helicopters and fighter/attack aircraft required for the operations envisaged. However, British peacetime practice suggests that the present total of 19 aircraft would be sufficient to equip the two carriers plus training units.

So far 22 stretched Sea King helicopters equipped with the latest anti-submarine sensors and weapons and air-to-surface missiles have been ordered. They will join some two dozen Sea Kings already in Indian Navy service, and will be more than sufficient to equip the two carriers, the *Godavari* and modified *Leander*-class frigates and the earlier examples of the 5,000-ton frigate.

Several Ka-27 Helix helicopters have been ordered, some presumably to operate from the Kresta II guided missile cruisers. However, the later Kashin II guided missile destroyers will also operate Helix. India already has Hormone helicopters for the earlier Kashins.

Perhaps the most interesting naval air acquisition is that of eight Bear-F shore-based long-range maritime patrol aircraft. These huge machines have an enormous radius of action, giving them the ability to cover a large segment of Australia from mainland Indian bases.

Little has been released about Bear-F, one of the latest versions of what was formerly a strategic bomber, except for the fact that its primary role is anti-submarine. The Indian aircraft, the first of which was delivered late in 1986, are reported to have been newly built, suggesting that they have been significantly modified to meet local requirements. Be that as it may, the full role of these aircraft is unlikely to become apparent until they, the Kresta II-class guided missile cruisers and Kilo-class submarines enter Indian service.

Although the Bear-Fs and Helix helicopters will operate with and for the Indian Navy, they will be Indian Air Force aircraft. The reasons for this are unknown, although the IAF's more extensive maintenance facilities for Soviet-built aircraft may be a factor.

Less dramatic but nonetheless significant is the Indian Navy's purchase of Dornier Do228 maritime patrol aircraft equipped with air-to-surface missiles. The first two aircraft, built in West Germany, entered service in 1986. The remainder, built or assembled in India, will join over the next two or three years. A total of 24 aircraft have been ordered. They will provide coverage of coastal waters, freeing the Bear-Fs and Il-38s (which entered service some years ago) for longer-range operations.

Indian Coast Guard

Present plans for the Coast Guard are reported to envisage a total of 24 ocean patrol vessels, each displacing about 1,000 tons. Three have commissioned so far, and at least two more are at various stages of construction. At present these ships are deployed in the east, with two at Port Blair and one at Madras. Although smaller than the comparable British ships of the "Castle" class, they have about 50% greater complement. This may be justified in part by the permanent attachment of an Alouette III helicopter to each ship, but also suggests that they have additional but unpublicised roles.

The Coast Guard also has a large programme of patrol boat construction and acquisitions. These include Indian, Japanese, South Korean and Singaporean designs. All these craft have a clear coastguard role – and an equally clear usefulness to the Indian Navy. The same can be said of the air arm of the Coast Guard, which has its own aircraft and air stations, both growing in numbers. The extent of Coast Guard's integration into the Navy is emphasised by the fact that the Director-General and his deputy are both retired naval officers.

Naval bases

Probably the most interesting recent Indian naval base development is the construction of a new facility at Karwar, about halfway between those existing at Bombay and Cochin. Karwar will include an alongside berth for aircraft carriers and a new naval air station. The base at Vishakapatnam, built some years ago for the modernisation and maintenance of Soviet-built ships and submarines, is being very substantially extended, with Russian support assistance. Funds have been provided for a new dry dock and other works at the Bombay naval dockyard.

Another new naval air station, in addition to that at Karwar, has been opened at Uchipuli, opposite Sri Lanka (also known as Ramanthapura). A third, being built at Arakkonam, North Arcot, Tamil Nadu, is expected to accommodate the Bear-Fs, and a fourth

has been established at Port Blair in the Andaman Islands. The civilian airfield at Vishakapatnam has been taken over by the Navy for its own use.

A much enlarged naval air technical school is being built at Bangalore, requirements having outgrown the original school at Cochin.

Industrial and development base

Indian industry, both free-enterprise and government-owned, is moving rapidly ahead to provide the industrial and development base needed to support a rapidly growing major navy. Indigenous surface-to-surface missiles are under development. The laboratory at Cochin is developing a hull-mounted panoramic sonar for existing and new-construction escorts, and the NST58 (corresponding to the Whitehead A244) torpedo for use by surface ships and aircraft.

Godavari, the first of a planned class of six to a modified British *Leander* design. Her heterogeneous operational fit comprises four Soviet SS-N-2C missiles, an SA-N-4 SAM launcher, a combination of Soviet and Dutch radars, Soviet guns, Italian torpedo tubes, British helicopters, Canadian and British sonar and Canadian haul-down gear.

Naval shipbuilders at Mazagon Dock (Bombay), Goa and Calcutta are expanding to meet the Navy's needs. At Calcutta, Garden Reach has built patrol craft, survey ships and other non-combat craft for some years. Now this yard has completed its first assault tank landing ship and is building two anti-submarine corvettes, its first major combat craft. The new replenishment tanker has been ordered from Garden Reach.

The yard at Goa has built small naval craft for some time, utility landing craft at first and now patrol boats. The yard's capability will broaden significantly as it tools up to build the eight indigenous GRP-hulled mine countermeasures vessels.

Mazagon Dock is the major builder of warships, as opposed to minor war vessels and support ships and craft. The *Godavari* class were completed on time and within budget, and the new ASW corvettes are proceeding well. Mazagon is confident that the initial problems with the submarine construction programme have been overcome and that the rest of the programme will proceed without further delay.

Locally provided equipment includes the gas turbines for the new 5,000-ton frigates which are to be produced by Hindustan Aeronautics Ltd, the diesels for the same ships by Bharat Dynamics and the diesels for the ASW corvettes by the Kirloskar Corporation, all working under licence. These major programmes reflect India's policy of seeking high local content when building to foreign designs.

Training

Following the recent retirement of the elderly cruiser *Mysore*, the Navy is short of seagoing training vessels. All three Type 41 diesel-driven frigates (similar to the British *Leopard* class) have now been assigned to training duties. It is planned to operate two new purpose-built training ships; the first commissioned recently and funds have been allocated for the second.

A new and much enlarged naval academy is being built at Ezhimada and a large training establishment for ratings has been completed near Vishakapatnam.

Deployments

The Indian Navy is venturing further and further from home. Deployments last year included a squadron off the Cape of Good Hope area (it did not enter a South African port) and another to the Philippines. Countries with communities of Indian descent tend to be high on the list for visits.

Command

The command organisation is growing to match the expansion of the Indian Navy. The Southern Naval Command has been upgraded to the status of command-in-chief; the new Chief of Naval Staff is a former Commander-in-Chief, Southern Naval Command. The Navy provides the tri-service fortress commander for the Andaman Islands.

The reasons for the Indian Naval expansion are obscured by vague or unsupported statements by government ministers or their representatives. However, the fact remains that India has the ability to launch and support an invasion of Sri Lanka, to seize the Maldive Islands or the Seychelles, or to mount naval, air and limited land campaigns against, say, Indonesia and Malaysia. These developments have not passed unnoticed by the neighbouring powers: Indonesia, for one, has officially expressed its concern. India's genuine defensive need for a strong army and air force are accepted by the other nations in the region, but they can see no such justification for the dominating strength of the Indian Navy.

Superpower serpents in the Pacific paradise

Capt John Moore RN

Meuse. Four of this class of 17,800-ton ships have been completed and a fifth is building. As well as being able to supply all forms of fuel, stores, ammunition and water, they can accommodate a maritime zone staff and 45 naval commandos. One acts as the French flagship in the Indian Ocean and could be deployed to the Pacific when needed.

FOR most people the words "South-west Pacific" evoke images of prosperous, games-loving Australians and New Zealanders, and happy-go-lucky islanders living a life of ease on sun-drenched, palm-fringed shores. The true state of affairs in this corner of the world, some 12,000 miles from Europe and 6,000 from California, results from the failure of some Western politicians to appreciate important factors which should have guided their approach to the region.

This is in some ways due to recent history. Some British leaders see the Australians and New Zealanders only as the sons of the men who fought so gallantly in the Second World War, the grandsons of the Anzacs of Gallipoli and the Western Front. In 1950 they rallied to the United Nations banner in Korea, and two decades later some fought in Vietnam. The ANZUS treaty linked the two countries with the USA, and they were all stout fellows and good allies. But that was as far as it went. They were kept at arm's length when it came to economic self-interest, and now the farmers of New Zealand, as they join the dole queue under the shadow of EEC quotas, will never again have quite the same feeling for Great Britain as "home".

Western policies towards this part of the globe have lacked a number of essential qualities, including sensitivity to local ideas and aspirations, an ability to sense what it means to be far from the main centres of the Western world, and an appreciation of the effects of the apparent failure of American leadership. Amongst the greatest offenders are the French, who have aroused anger with their stands on nuclear testing and the future of New Caledonia.

France

Having decided to go it alone on the development of nuclear weapons, France needed a test site. The

Americans had used Bikini for that purpose: why not go to the same general area? With implacable nationalist resolve they have been exploding their devices at Mururoa ever since, despite the protests of the locals. Prime Minister Chirac defends his country's actions on the grounds that France has a position to maintain in the Pacific. It would appear that in the French view this position confers complete freedom, extending to the atmospheric testing of nuclear weapons in spite of the protests of the area's permanent inhabitants.

This same determination to remain a regional power has led M Chirac to take a controversial step in New Caledonia. This group of 25 islands lies 1,000 miles east of Australia. France took control of the area in 1853 and designated it an Overseas Territory 100 years later. It is thus hardly surprising that the major landowners are to be found amongst the 28,000 European descendants of the original French occupancy. Nor is it surprising that the remaining 120,000 people of Melanesian/Polynesian origin, include a fair number who are dedicated to achieving independence. This might seem an unwise course for a country whose entire export earnings depend on nickel mining, which is heavily underwritten by French aid. But the previous, socialist, French Government had floated a plan for "independence in association", which would have satisfied the independence movement while providing for continued economic assistance. M Chirac shelved this scheme on taking power in March 1986, and decided to put the question to a referendum. To be held later this year, this is expected, for reasons not unconnected with the lack of universal suffrage in New Caledonia, to produce a majority against independence.

This might appear to be little more than a local squabble over decolonisation, but there are several wider consequences. The states of the South Pacific Forum were incensed and are taking the matter to the United Nations. A more sinister development is the emergence of FLNKS (the liberation movement of the Kanaks, who form 40% of New Caledonia's population) and its external links. In 1984 a group of Kanaks underwent training in Libya, and a meeting of

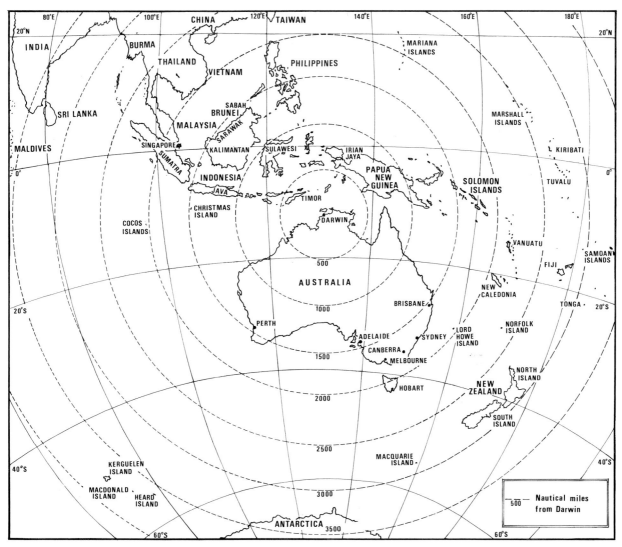

"liberation groups" in Tripoli in 1986 included delegations from the Irianese separatists of West New Guinea, FLNKS, the government of Vanuatu, and FULK (another Kanak organisation). The Libyans expressed support for these groups and, at a time when France and Libya are in conflict in Chad, Colonel Gaddafi might well choose to play the part of a gadfly in New Caledonia.

Although the French Government has declared that "France belongs to the Pacific region as Ayers Rock belongs to central Australia" their footing may be a lot less secure than that of the famous outcrop. Perhaps this is realised in private in Paris: the proportion of security forces to general population in New Caledonia is 1 to 24, compared with, for instance, 1 to 520 in the Soviet Union.

Vanuatu

New Caledonia's neighbour, Vanuatu, is made up of a string of islands stretching some 800 miles and with a most southerly point barely 200 miles from New Caledonia. The history of this group, known as the New Hebrides until independence was achieved in July 1980, has been one of European arrivals and departures. Spain, France and Britain all founded settlements. From 1906 the islands were administered

under an Anglo-French condominium, which instituted various reforms in a vain effort to quell the demand for independence. The present government's foreign policy is the most radical in the South Pacific. In January 1987 the ruling party granted the USSR fishing rights and (yet to be confirmed) gave permission for Aeroflot to fly in relief fishing crews. This Soviet method of acquiring influence, now over 20 years old, has been used before in the Caribbean, West Africa and the Indian Ocean. The next step will take the form of visits by warships and survey vessels of the Red Fleet.

Left: **French A69-type frigate. The normal peacetime deployment of the French fleet includes three frigates in the Pacific. These 1,250-ton ships carry two Exocet missiles and a 100mm gun. Their range of 4,000nm at 15kt is adequate for the huge distances involved.**

Centre left: Revi. **This 1,450-ton French supply vessel was completed with her sister in 1985. Both are based at the Centre d'Experimentation du Pacifique, the nuclear test site at Mururoa. There are also two LCTs and four tugs at this base, which will be the home for the new 4,900-ton landing ship due for completion in October 1987.**

Bottom left: **French survey ship *L'Esperance*. The French naval presence in the Pacific is the largest of any country with no mainland on the ocean's shores. The total, normally about 16, does not include surveying ships, one of which is permanently based at Papeete.**

Below right: **The Australian submarine *Orion*. The huge spaces of the Pacific make ASW exceedingly difficult. Submarines are ideally suited for long-range sonar detection of passing ships but are not practical substitutes for surface ships in a peacetime island-visiting role. Australia has six of these boats and is planning for a new class in the 1990s.**

Kiribati

Some 1,200 miles to the north is Kiribati (previously the Gilbert Islands), which concluded a fisheries agreement with the USSR in October 1985. This was cancelled a year later: some said the Soviets felt they were getting too little for their roubles, others that they had not paid enough. It may however have been simply a matter of geography: Kiribati is a string of small islands lying at the intersection of the equator and the International Date Line, and is thus well north of the main area of interest in the South-west Pacific. There have been no reports of Soviet approaches to neighbouring Tuvalu (previously the Ellice Islands), but other island states have attracted the Kremlin's attentions. Papua New Guinea (PNG), Fiji and Tonga have all been on the visiting list. The first of these is shortly to consider a deal with the USSR. If it is concluded, the Russian fishermen will have access to PNG's exclusive economic zone, within which fully 35% of the South Pacific tuna landings are made.

Treaty of Rarotonga

The Kiribati agreement is a fair pointer to the regional interests and intentions of the Soviet Union, which has thus penetrated the periphery of the South-west

Pacific and is receiving clear signals of local discontent with the activities of other states foreign to the area. France's position in New Caledonia is only one of several irritants, while the refusal of that country to sign the protocols of the Treaty of Rarotonga has resulted in even wider objections. This treaty, formulated by the 13-strong South Pacific Forum, requires members to prohibit the manufacture or stationing of nuclear weapons and the dumping of nuclear waste within their boundaries. The passage of nuclear-powered or nuclear-armed ships through the area is not banned, but permission for port visits by such ships is left to the discretion of individual nations. By March 1987 the Treaty had been signed by Australia, the Cook Islands, Fiji, Kiribati, Nauru, New Zealand, Niue, Papua New Guinea, Tuvalu and Western Samoa; the Solomon Islands, Tonga and Vanuatu have yet to sign.

The external reaction to the treaty is significant. The USSR and China have both backed it, though the former has reservations about its provisions on the passage of nuclear-armed ships. The Second Protocol requires an undertaking from the five major nuclear-

weapon powers – China, France, the USSR, Britain and the USA – to refrain from the threat to use or the use of nuclear weapons against the treaty's signatories while the Third Protocol, applying only to France, Britain and the USA, requires those three countries to refrain from testing nuclear weapons in the area. France refused to sign any protocol, Britain is considering her position, and the USA has also refused to sign despite having previously agreed to similar protocols to the Treaty of Tlateloco in Latin America.

The Forum countries have reacted vigorously. The Australian ambassador in Washington spoke of the US Government being "unresponsive to an important regional concern," and warned that the American attitude would affect local support for "Western security objectives". The Australian Minister for Foreign Affairs, speaking in Canberra on February 6, 1987, was blunter still: "Hostility to and suspicion of the USA has helped the Soviet Union to make interesting progress in a number of instances in the South Pacific."

It cannot have been easy to speak of an ally in such terms, but unfortunately there were good grounds for doing so. The tuna-fishing saga is an example of Washington's insensitivity. The huge numbers of tuna that migrate regularly across the South Pacific represent a significant source of food and income for those states whose 200-mile EEZs lie in their path. For years these areas have been plundered by American fishermen using fast and highly specialised craft. The tiny resources of the governments in the region were unequal to the task of curbing these activities, which yielded no return to the local exchequers. After 30 months and 10 meetings, it was finally agreed at a conference in Tonga in October 1986 that the USA would pay $12 million a year for five years to the Forum states involved. Slightly over half of what had originally been requested, this sum compares badly with the settlements achieved by individual states: Kiribati received $1.7 million from the USSR for its one-year agreement, Japan paid $1.9 million a year to Papua New Guinea until the latter cancelled the agreement because the price was too low, while the Soviet deal with Vanuatu is reported to be worth well over $2 million a year. The Americans, having balked at paying a sum equivalent to the cost of a couple of sonar sets, are now seen as a nation of Shylocks who have belatedly, and only partially, seen the light.

The Soviet Union

The Soviet progress reported by the Australian Foreign Minister has been underway for several years. Aid in kind and money during the war with the USA brought the Russians into Vietnam. This presence was well entrenched by 1975, and over the last 12 years it has expanded markedly. Today the main centre of Soviet influence in this area is the naval base at Cam Ranh Bay. At least seven new piers have been built for the Soviet South China Sea squadron. At the nearby air base, groups of Soviet Flogger fighters and Badger and Bear bombers are ranged to support the surface fleet and to carry out reconnaissance over large areas of the adjoining oceans.

When Mr Gorbachev delivered a major policy speech at Vladivostok on July 28, 1986, he knew that Cam Ranh Bay was a reasonably secure base in the heart of an area which has close ties with the Western democracies, and that his envoys were making inroads in the South Pacific. He offered olive twigs to China, pledged Soviet support for the principles of the Treaty of Rarotonga, and spoke of the "peace zone" in the Indian Ocean and the possibility of a peace conference. He expressed a desire to establish more effective trade relations in South-east Asia. All in all, the Soviet Union would be a helpful friend and would treat everybody better than the Americans had. What he didn't say, but which is evident nonetheless, is that the USSR intends to become an important part of the South Pacific community. He named eight of the smaller partners in the Forum with which he intended to establish closer ties as part of a policy of increased "dynamism" in Soviet relationships in the Pacific. He had little to lose by supporting the nuclear-free zone: Soviet ships and submarines would continue to deploy as in the past, and port visits would be there for the asking as bilateral agreements were concluded. He certainly gave the new Pacific branch of the Soviet Foreign Ministry a lot to do, but time and the failures of the other major powers are on their side.

A major Soviet aim has always been the disruption of Western accords. Some of the Pacific nations could scarcely be expected to make outright affirmations of friendship and collaboration with the USSR. In such cases the Russians seek instead to weaken existing ties with their neighbours or the major powers opposing Soviet policies. In the South Pacific two obvious targets for this activity are Australia and New Zealand.

Australia

Australia's relations with her two nearest neighbours, Papua New Guinea and Indonesia, have not been especially harmonious lately. The government of the former is, and has been for most of the time since independence in 1975, hampered by factionalism. With an election due in June 1987, a whole array of problems face the present five-party coalition, many of them requiring external financial support for even a

partial solution. One source of such help resulted from a five-year aid agreement with Australia in late 1985. In 1986 the sum on offer was abruptly cut by A$10 million, apparently with very little consultation between Canberra and Port Moresby. This embarrassed the PNG exchequer and called into question the integrity of the Australian Government.

While Papua New Guinea and Indonesia have contrived an improvement in relations, which deteriorated following border problems within Irian Jaya, Australia's contacts with Indonesia have become more acrimonious. There have been a number of recent irritations, including an irresponsible article in an Australian newspaper about President Soeharto's family, and a brief ban on overflights of Indonesia by Australian military aircraft which overshadowed Australia's acceptance of Indonesia's occupation of East Timor. Such niggles can only delay moves towards much needed co-operation by the two states and, while the idea of actual conflict between them is absurd, careful handling of relations in the future is essential.

Above: **Australian patrol craft** *Bunbury*, **the last of 15 such vessels commissioned in 1980–84. They are of particular value off the north coast, where their cruising range of 4,800nm is very useful. But in the south, and particularly in the Bass Straits, sea conditions sometimes severely restrict them.**

Below: **Australian survey ship** *Flinders*. **Accurate charts are a necessity when navigating off Australia. At present the Maritime Science Force consists of three large ships backed up by two landing craft and three vessels on charter. Four 120-ton inshore survey craft are due to be ordered.**

of the ANZUS Treaty. However, further detailed questioning produced a vote in favour of accepting ship visits. Seeking to explain these apparent contradictions, the report concluded that the case had been misrepresented by those "occupying positions of high authority." Be that as it may, in June 1986 the US made it clear that New Zealand's membership of ANZUS was at an end, and the following August only

New Zealand

The New Zealand Government has gone one step further than any of her partners in applying the Treaty of Rarotonga. In February 1985 USS *Buchanan* was refused access to New Zealand ports unless it could be shown that she had no nuclear capability. In December of that year a bill was introduced to make New Zealand a nuclear-free zone. In July 1986 the Corner Committee reported on the attitude of the population to these developments. Some 75% of New Zealanders supported a non-nuclear policy and the maintenance

Australian and American representatives met in San Francisco. The New Zealand Prime Minister may describe the country's dismissal as a "farce," but there can be no doubt that his government's actions have done major harm to New Zealand's interests and those of her allies.

Naval forces

Though the South Pacific Forum embraces many countries with naval forces, only Australia and New Zealand possess a navy in the true sense. The development of the Royal Australian Navy in recent years has been less than coherent. In 1986 Mr Paul Dibb reported to the Minister of Defence on Australia's defence capabilities. Analysing the RAN, the report sees a need to maintain eight or nine destroyers, and recommends that at least eight "light patrol frigates" be built to a modified existing design. If the aim is to acquire, at a moderate price, ships capable of tasks which have proved to be beyond the

present *Fremantle* class, the RAN is unlikely to turn to Western shipbuilders. They will want a simple design capable of rapid construction in Australian yards, and South Korea is already firmly established in this field.

A strength of the Dibb Report is the emphasis that

Left: **Australian frigate *Derwent*, one of five built to general British designs, the first three in 1961–64 and the others in 1970–71. *Stuart*, the second ship of the class, was the trials ship for the Ikara ASW system.**

Centre left: **Australian frigate *Torrens*, one of the last two of the five "River"-class ships. The huge distances characteristic of the South-west Pacific and the Indian Ocean mean that she carries every form of detection device.**

Bottom left: **Australian minesweeper *Curlew*, sole survivor of six "Ton"-class ships purchased from the United Kingdom in 1961. It is only recently that the need for a much larger mine countermeasures group has been accepted in Australia.**

it places on mine countermeasures. Every major Australian port is vulnerable to minelaying, and some more than others. Adelaide is worse off than Sydney, Brisbane is better than Melbourne, and Darwin presents many problems. Dibb notes that only two high-priority ports – one on the east coast and one on the west – could be cleared and kept open under present plans. This view, though more realistic than most, may even be a little optimistic. Australia today has two inshore minehunters, but to keep one MCM vessel on task continuously at least four are required. The RAN plans to get round this by commissioning "craft of opportunity" to tow precursor sweeps.

This at least is a positive programme compared with what Dibb describes as the "poor planning and procrastination" of previous years. The first major paper on submarine mining of Australian ports was put to the Naval Board in 1955, and by 1962 six minesweepers had been bought from Britain. But these vessels then paid off over the years, with no replacement until the first of two "Bay" class inshore minehunters commissioned in 1986. The new Australian-developed magnetic and acoustic sweeps and new degaussing methods offer a major advance.

The RAN's submarine and anti-submarine communities have a similar tale to tell, with long-felt deficiencies at last being put right. It has finally been decided to buy eight Sikorsky SH-60 Seahawk to equip the navy's ASW frigates. The purchase of six new submarines is supported by the Dibb Report, which also strongly advocates the use of towed arrays. If these boats are kept as up to date as have been the elderly *Oberon*s currently in service, and if the constructive thinking of the present generation extends into the future, the submarine branch will remain a vital element in Australian defence.

To an outside observer the Dibb Report is an objective and sensible indication of the way ahead.

Australian frigate *Darwin*, the last of four built in the USA to the FFG-7 design. Although the first ship was commissioned in 1980 and *Darwin* in 1984, it was not until 1985 that funds were set aside for the purchase of helicopters for this class, two more of which are currently under construction in Australia.

Above: **New Zealand frigate *Wellington*. In 1982–83 two broad-beamed *Leander*s were transferred from the Royal Navy to New Zealand, HMS *Bacchante* becoming *Wellington* and HMS *Dido* becoming *Southland*.**

But will the Australian Government respond to its logic? Only the next defence review will tell.

The state of New Zealand's naval defences is well exemplified by the astonishing plan to replace the older frigates with submarines. Advanced by the government of a country with over 5,000 miles of coastline, a series of commitments in the South Pacific, a population of a little over three million, and an inadequate defence budget, this scheme was almost beyond belief. Today the idea has disappeared without, it is hoped, any trace. What remains is a navy with a few elderly frigates, nine seaward defence craft which are too small to cope with the heavy seas so frequent in many port approaches, no mine counter-

Left: **Australian fleet support ship *Success*, of the same basic design as the French *Meuse*. Two examples of this invaluable class were to have been built, but the second has now been cancelled. At least three would seem to be needed for a fleet with fuelling stations which are frequently many hundreds, if not thousands, of miles apart.**

Below left: **New Zealand frigate *Southland*, transferred from the Royal Navy in July 1983.**

Below: **New Zealand research ship *Tui*. A hugh amount of research remains to be done in the ocean areas around New Zealand. This work includes not only basic oceanography but also acoustic research to assist ASW. In November 1985 the West German research ship *Meteor* was acquired to assist in this task.**

measures vessels, and a competent survey unit. Currently the only vessel on order is a tanker, needed to increase the range of the four frigates with their embarked helicopters. Well over a third of the navy's personnel are employed in the frigates. Had past programmes included such affordable ships as the Meko 140 frigates and the Spanish *Halcon* patrol ships, with companies of 93 and 34 respectively, a force of seven frigates and ten Halcons would have been possible on the same manpower. Such a fleet might have made the financiers blanch and the numbers would certainly have been cut, but in principle it is far more suitable for New Zealand conditions and requirements than the present force.

The Royal New Zealand Navy as a whole has suffered badly as a result of the ANZUS affair, being deprived of the intelligence, logistic support and exercises traditionally provided by its treaty partners.

Conclusion

The South Pacific has a welter of problems, some self-generated but most caused by the activities of major powers in the area. As far as the Western nations are concerned, these actions are the result of ignorance, inactivity and insensitivity. Consequently, the Soviet Union has been able to make progress in the area where the role and composition of the largest fleet, the RAN, is still under discussion. If the Western powers are not to find themselves faced by a maze of difficulties comparable with those now seen in Africa and the Caribbean, they must quickly adopt a more deeply considered policy towards the countries of the South Pacific Forum.

Submarines: the non-nuclear way forward

Cdr Roy Corlett RN

Peruvian "209"-class *Casma*. Peru ordered two Type 1200s from Howaldtswerke, Kiel, in 1964, two more in 1976 and a final pair in 1977. Of 1,290 tons dived displacement, these boats have an underwater speed of 21.5kt. Each is fitted with eight torpedo tubes and carries 14 torpedoes. The first two have a complement of 35, the remainder 31.

EXCLUDING those of Britain and the United States, 48% of the modern diesel-electric submarines planned or building for or in service with pro-Western navies are based on West German designs. In general, what started out as basic designs have been stretched to meet a wide range of operational requirements. In the process, the potential effectiveness of the diesel-electric submarine has been greatly enhanced. This has led in turn to new operating procedures which increase the time that can be spent dived and on patrol. But what of the future? Is further design stretch possible, or will new developments – such as air-independent power units and integrated tactical/control systems – call for new approaches?

The effect of war experience on design

During the final months of the Second World War Germany was preparing for the mass production of two new classes of submarine, both with revolutionary new design features:

Type XXI, a diesel-electric boat with double the dived speed, endurance and armament of any previous type.

Type XVIIB, an air-independent submarine with a maximum dived speed of 20kt on the power of turbines operated by burning a mixture of fuel and concentrated hydrogen peroxide to generate steam and hot gases.

Fortunately for the Allies, production difficulties with the Type XXI and technical problems with the handling of high-test peroxide delayed the introduction into service of both types. Six Type XXIs finally entered service, but too late to see action. They were surrendered to the victors. Most of the XVIIBs were scuttled, but the Royal Navy did succeed in capturing one vessel intact. She was recommissioned as HMS

Meteorite and operated for four years to evaluate the new propulsion system. In 1956–58 two British variants – *Explorer* and *Excalibur* – entered service, primarily to provide surface anti-submarine forces with experience in attacking fast targets. They did not last long. Known to their long-suffering crews as the *Exploder* class, being afflicted with many fires and explosive incidents at sea, both were soon withdrawn from service. In other countries the Type XXI design influenced all diesel-electric submarine development.

Post-war development

In the decade following the Second World War little money was available to support the armed forces of any country. The reconstitution of civilian life took precedence. The lessons learned about submarine warfare were applied piecemeal by the modernisation of vessels which had survived the war. Deck guns were removed, snorkel masks were fitted and the conning tower became a streamlined fin. New tactics were developed in response to the belief that in future the primary task would be to hunt and attack the enemy's submarines. It was not until the 1950s that France, the USA and the USSR developed new designs based on the surrendered Type XXIs. They were:

France: *Narval* class, mid-1950s.

USA: *Tang* class based on sea experience with the Guppy I–III modernisations of ex-war stock.

USSR: *Whiskey* class (1951–57) followed by a Guppy-type modernisation (1958–61), *Romeo* class.

Britain's first post-war submarine design was the *Porpoise* class, best described as an Anglicised copy of the American *Tang*/Guppy. The first of class commissioned in 1958, only to reveal serious operational and technical deficiencies. Stability and topweight problems limited diving capability, and diesel generators and other major equipment proved unreliable. There followed a continuous programme of modification extending over several years and culminating in a follow-on design, the *Oberon* class. But in spite of all the changes and improvements, the *Oberon*s remained difficult boats to handle, especially when surfacing or diving in bad weather. Between 1961 and 1967, 13 *Oberon*-class submarines were commissioned by the Royal Navy, even though the twin-shaft, double-hulled diesel-electric submarine had been already obsolescent by the end of the 1950s. The streamlined single-screw *Albacore* hull with internal ballast tankage, developed by the US Navy, was becoming the new form for both nuclear and diesel-electric submarines. With the latter, sea experience had shown that the reduction in underwater drag, coupled with a shape which could accommodate larger battery sections without adverse effect on buoyancy or stability, greatly improved dived performance and endurance.

Post-war protocols debarred Germany from building submarines until the mid-1960s, then limited dived displacement to not more than 500 tons. Their task was defined as coastal defence against surface-borne attack across the Baltic. It was not until the beginning of the 1970s that hull size was allowed to increase to 1,000 tons, or that the construction of German submarines for export was permitted. At first sight these appear to be crippling limitations on the development of new technology, but in practice it was not so. Throughout the period of evolution from twin propellors to *Albacore* hull, German specialists observed and analysed submarine developments in other countries. As a result, they avoided an expensive period of technical change and the painful reappraisal of operational procedures. In designing for the future, Germany had the advantage of not being shackled by the conventions of the past.

German submarine design development

In the late 1950s a number of German companies combined to carry out a series of trials and experiments to define a small submarine which – in the first instance – would meet the needs of the Federal German Navy. Operating within NATO, a fleet of these boats would help defend the Baltic against Soviet surface forces. But the long-term plan was to develop a basic hull type and equipment that could be enlarged to meet overseas requirements. Many countries were developing submarine forces for the first time, almost all of them using war-surplus vessels provided at giveaway prices by the United States. For Germany, looking to the future, they represented a major opportunity, for two reasons. First, the submarines acquired by countries such as Argentina, Brazil, Chile and other South American countries with seaboards to defend were obsolete. They were armed with weapons and systems designed primarily to attack surface forces. But, as the war had shown, the new enemy was the submarine itself. Second, by the beginning of the 1970s the obsolescence of the equipment and shortages of spare parts would render these aged vessels increasingly difficult to maintain in operational condition.

To meet this future market requirement, it was decided to develop an integrated package comprising:
1 A basic submarine design, capable of being sized to meet customer requirements without major changes to the general structure.

2   A bow section containing eight torpedo tubes from which the weapons would swim out under their own power instead of being expelled by compressed air. The new arrangement was simple, saved space and was effective at all operating depths.

3   A torpedo optimised to suit the new tubes and able to attack submerged submarine or surface targets, along with new fire-control arrangements. For the first time, weapon and launching platform were designed as a total system.

4   A stern section enclosing diesel-electric generators and a double-armature propulsion motor driving a single slow-revolving, large-diameter propeller. This unit also embodied two new features which would revolutionise operational performance: diesels with sufficient backpressure to permit the use of exhaust gases to clear the line of sea water on starting to snorkel, and remote control of all power and propulsion operations. The latter reduced a complex procedure calling for a high degree of training to a relatively simple start/stop arrangement.

5   New lead-acid battery cells shaped to fit precisely within the new hull, resulting in maximum storage capacity. At the same time, they could be sited low in the hull to provide stability.

6   Finally – but most important – the provision of

Top: **West German Type 206 *U26*. In 1962 the revived West German Navy commissioned *U1* and *U2*, the first submarines to be built in German yards since the Second World War. Neither was satisfactory and both were scrapped. As a result of this experience the Type 205 was developed. The first of this class, the new *U1*, was commissioned in 1967. This was the start of a series of worldwide programmes. The 12 boats built to the 205 design were followed by the larger (498 tons dived) Type 206, 18 of which had been completed by 1975. A follow-on programme of Type 211s is now in hand.**

Above: **Norwegian Type 207 *Kaura*. In 1962 the West German Navy lent the Norwegians the Type 205 *U3*. Two years later she was returned to Germany and scrapped like her sisters *U1* and *U2*. These trials were followed by an order for a large number of Type 207s, developed from the Type 205. Today there are 11 of these 435-ton submarines in Norwegian service, three having been sold to Denmark. They will be replaced in part by six Type 210s (1,300 tons dived) from 1989 onwards.**

facilities to train personnel to operate the new equipment and the encouragement of countries to acquire the new technology and build their own vessels in local shipyards.

Dividing the new design into its major sections, the
rear end's task was to provide electrical power and
propulsion. The bow section contained weapons, the
tubes from which they were launched and stowage for
reloads. In the centre section were the battery
sections, control/tactical systems, accommodation,
and ancillary equipment such as radar/radio,
periscopes, masts and the like. The design could be
stretched by lengthening the mid-section to contain
extra diesel generators and additional equipment to
meet customer specifications. In some instances hull
diameter might also be increased, but in all cases the
overall shape remained the same.

As the past 20 years have shown, this design
philosophy proved highly successful. According to the
latest edition of *Jane's Fighting Ships*, the same basic
German design has given rise to 110 submarines
planned, building or in service with 15 navies, with
dived displacements ranging from 430 to 1,850 tons.
This new breed of diesel-electric submarine has also
permitted radical changes in operating procedures,
the result of improved performance when snorkelling
and patrolling dived on battery power.

Effects on operating procedures

When proceeding on patrol, it had been usual to travel
submerged at best speed, running on diesel-electric
propulsion and ingesting air through the snorkel mast,
until the area of operations was reached. This had
many disadvantages, entailing intensive watchkeeping
and being most uncomfortable in bad weather. This
combination was a physical drain on personnel, and
tired men make mistakes. The major tactical limitations
of snorkelling were the noise that it made and the fact
that it reduced the sensitivity of the submarine's
detection devices. In addition, the exposure above the
surface of periscopes and snorkel masthead and the
turbulence of diesel exhaust gases created an image
which could be detected by radar.

Submarines were thus vulnerable to detection and
destruction when snorkelling to and from operating
areas. Once on patrol, there were further periods of
vulnerability when the submarine returned to
periscope depth to snorkel and replace the energy
drained from the batteries. The advent of the new

diesel generators, permitting easy stop/start
snorkelling, and high-capacity batteries resulted in
new and safer operating procedures which needed
fewer crew and were less physically demanding.

Snorkel/dived transit

Figure 1 shows the transition from the old-fashioned
twin-screw, double-hulled submarine to the modern
Albacore single-screw shape. Figure 2 illustrates the
improvement in dived performance resulting from the
change. Running deep on main motors, a speed of
10kt can be maintained for 18h and 80% battery drain.
On returning to periscope depth and running the

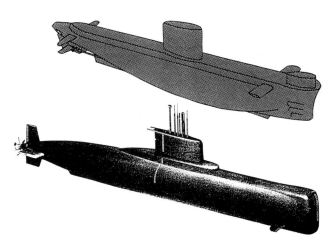

Figure 1   The *Oberon* class *(top)*, with their external ballast
tanks casing and twin shafts, were already obsolete when
they entered service over 20 years ago. The German Type 209
(above) is representative of the designs that were emerging
when the *Oberon*s first went to sea.

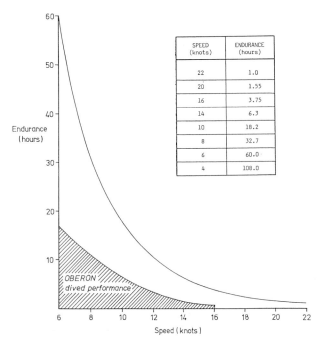

SPEED (knots)	ENDURANCE (hours)
22	1.0
20	1.55
16	3.75
14	6.3
10	18.2
8	32.7
6	60.0
4	108.0

Left: **Figure 2   Based on data obtained during contractor's sea trials, this graph shows that the Type 209's dived performance greatly exceeds that of the *Oberon* class.**

Right: **The double-acting Stirling principle. External heat causes the enclosed working gas, hydrogen, to expand and force down piston P2. The compressed gas beneath passes to P1, the next piston in the cycle, via a cooler which extracts heat and causes the hydrogen to contract, ready for reheating and expansion above P1. Some of the waste heat is recovered by the regenerator and added to the working cycle.**

diesels via the snorkel, the batteries can be recharged in about four hours while maintaining the same speed of advance. At the end of the charging period the submarine returns to running deep for another 18h. This type of snorkel/dived transit to the patrol area is now a standard procedure and has several advantages. A minimum of personnel are needed to keep watch during the deep-run period. The submarine is below the surface duct and the propeller does not cavitate and radiate noise, so detection is relatively unlikely. The return to periscope depth for snorkelling can usually be arranged to coincide with the change of watch, so that extra crew are available for the short changeover period. Stopping the diesels and diving can be carried out by the duty watch. Sea experience has shown that in this way long distances can be covered with minimal crew fatigue and much reduced risk of detection by surface ASW forces.

With a dived endurance of over four days at four knots on patrol, a submarine need only return to periscope depth once a day for 30min to top up the battery. It is unlikely that any enemy forces in the area would be able to detect, classify and track the submarine and develop a firing solution in such a short time.

Today and tomorrow

The German submarine design which has developed over the last quarter of a century has a fine record of safety and reliability, and exceptional operational performance. There may still be a little stretch left for further development, and major systems, such as

diesel generators and batteries, remain well up to current standards. But other manufacturers are competing effectively in areas such as the integration of all sensors, data-gathering, tactical/ship control, and the development of air-independent alternatives to diesel power.

Air-independent power

Nuclear power is now well established in submarines. It provides air-independence, though at a price. Large vessels are needed to house nuclear reactors; they are noisy, complex and thermally inefficient, and highly trained personnel are required to operate them. Because such submarines are large, they can be effective only in deep water, whereas the majority of navies are more concerned with operations over continental shelves, where water is shallow and often crowded with surface traffic. A number of attempts have been made to simplify and miniaturise nuclear reactors, but none has been successful to date. Meanwhile, two low-noise and cost-effective alternatives are being developed: the fuel cell and the Stirling engine.

The fuel cell combines hydrogen and oxygen to release electrical power, with an exhaust effluent of water. This is a well established process which has been used to generate electrical power aboard spacecraft for many years. The process is silent, mechanically efficient and highly suitable for submarine applications. The main problems are cost and the complexities of storing high densities of hydrogen and oxygen aboard a submarine. About six years ago a West German group comprising Ingenieurkontor Lubeck (IKL), Howaldtswerke Deutsche Werft AG (HDW) and Ferrostaal (FS) combined to develop an oxy/hydrogen submarine fuel-cell system, using liquid oxygen in containers external to the submarine's pressure hull and metallic hydride beds (in place of one lead-acid battery section) to store hydrogen. A functional shoreside model was designed, and between 1983 and 1984 a shore plant was built and put on test. Once again, German submarine technology was leading the world.

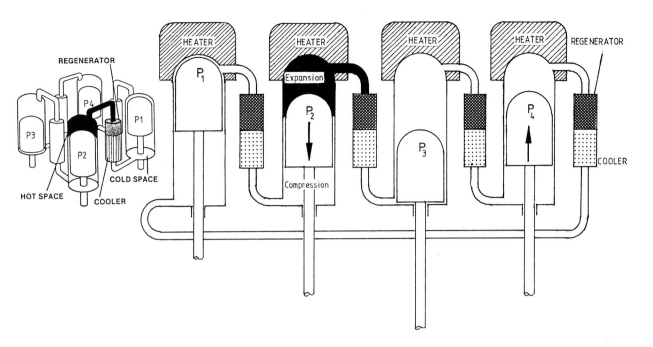

Unfortunately for IKL/HDW/FS, in January 1986 Kockums AB signed a contract with the Royal Swedish Navy for the installation of a 100kW Stirling-engine power system in a *Näcken*-class submarine, and also announced a range of Stirling generator systems for offshore underwater power applications. The Stirling engine is piston-driven by a gas enclosed in a working cycle which obtains its energy via heat from an external source. The working cycle is double-acting, and because there are no periodic detonations of fuel in the cylinders, as with a diesel, and no clattering valve gear, the Stirling engine makes little noise. It is directly coupled to an alternator to generate electricity.

The new heat engine has been under development by a consortium of Swedish companies for several years. The fact that a system is to be installed aboard a submarine gives Sweden a clear lead over Germany in the development of the first production-engineered air-independent power module to go to sea. Air-independence apart, the Stirling engine offers other potential advantages:

1 Because diesel fuel is the energy source, no special provision need be made. This contrasts with the fuel cell, which requires that part of the main battery be replaced with hydride beds to contain the hydrogen.

2 Storage of liquid oxygen demands a very high level of thermal insulation. Externally stowed aboard the German fuel-cell submarine, the containers will be in contact with the sea. Salt water has relatively high heat conductivity, making even more insulation necessary. The Swedish Stirling system stows oxygen inboard, where, it is claimed, it can be retained for months at a time.

3 The Stirling engine can be driven by any type of heat source. This means that fuel and snorkel-ingested air would be just as effective as the pure oxygen cycle. In turn, this may mean that the Stirling could replace the diesel in the first instance. The fuel cell will also run on air, but there are problems: all impurities and other gases (such as carbon dioxide) must be removed, otherwise the fuel-cell electrodes and electrolyte become contaminated. Hydrogen must still be used as fuel, but hydride storage space aboard the submarine is limited.

The first application of air-independent power systems aboard submarines will be hybrids, with conventional diesel-electric propulsion used for snort/dived transit, and fuel cells or Stirling generators providing the reduced power needed for low-speed patrolling. In both cases the electrical output floats in parallel with the main battery, so that maximum power is always available if needed.

The first non-nuclear, non-diesel air-independent submarines should be at sea before the end of the century. They will be small, silent, cost-effective and highly efficient ASW weapon systems. Whether they will have fuel cells or Stirling engines remains to be seen, but Sweden is in the lead at present and the Stirling cycle appears to offer greater power output and more flexibility for future development.

Personnel and ship control

Until fairly recently a major limitation of diesel-electric submarines was the fact that they were labour-intensive. A large, highly trained crew was needed to operate complex equipment, and sophisticated drill procedures were evolved to link the various personnel units into an integrated combat system. The German designs brought a degree of automation of the control of power and propulsion, and autopilots for rudder and hydroplanes. The effect of these changes is obvious in the crew reductions it brought about: compare the British *Oberon*'s complement of 69 to the 32 of a Chilean T.209. However, this still left a need for drills to link the tactical, navigation and weapon control systems and sensors into a fighting unit. One limit on full integration has always been lack of communication – and often business rivalry – between the suppliers of equipment fitted in submarines. In an important side-effect, the full power of microprocessors to control and link the major systems of a submarine and its weapons has yet to be fully exploited.

The first country to appreciate the importance of combining company interests to form an integrated design team was Italy. In 1984 a powerful new consortium was formed around leading companies of the FIAT group, together with Elettronica San Giorgio Spa (ELSAG), to compete in the field of underwater systems:

Whitehead Torpedoes, weapon discharge systems and associated equipment.

SEPA Weapon control, automated platform control and related systems.

The WELSE Submarine Integrated Control System. The use of interactive microprocessors to replace complex drills significantly reduces stress on the crew and cuts the manpower requirement.

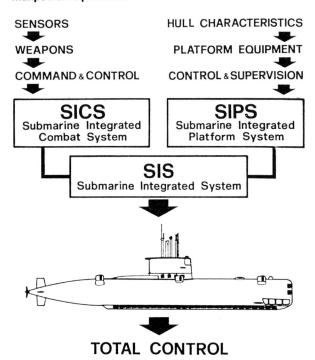

SENSORS → WEAPONS → COMMAND & CONTROL →

HULL CHARACTERISTICS → PLATFORM EQUIPMENT → CONTROL & SUPERVISION →

SICS Submarine Integrated Combat System

SIPS Submarine Integrated Platform System

SIS Submarine Integrated System

TOTAL CONTROL

ELSAG Underwater acoustic systems, signal processing, command and control systems.

The consortium's name, WELSE, is derived from the initials of the companies. As the German companies did a quarter of a century earlier, the Italian consortium has developed a scheme for full integration of submarine and command/tactical/weapons control. It consists of two major systems:

Submarine Integrated Combat Suite (SICS)
This is designed to detect, evaluate, classify and indicate potential targets, and navigate the submarine in a hostile environment. It handles the control and presentation of all acoustic, optical and electronic data, and the selection, preparation, discharge and control of weapons. The Combat Suite is completely automated, but there is operator override at all tactical decision levels.

Submarine Integrated Platform Suite (SIPS)
This handles submarine steering, operating depth, trim, propulsion, auxiliary machinery, the surveillance and presentation of all operating data, and the evaluation of tactical options such as the best profile for a selected snorkel/dived speed of advance, and speed/endurance relative to battery state. As with SICS, all controls are automated but are subject to operator override.

SICS and SIPS combine to form the Submarine Integrated System (SIS). All data are shared between consoles, which have a high degree of display commonality as regards data display. Because there is a high level of computer/data-storage redundancy and system interactivity, losses due to action damage can be made good by using the extra capacity available at other units.

Interlinked subsystems and the Combat and Platform suites' data processing replace the complex drills still used aboard most submarines. The result is a significant reduction in the number of personnel needed to operate the submarine and a potential increase in the time that can be spent on patrol, since the crew is less subject to stress and combat fatigue.

Tomorrow's submarine

Because a nuclear submarine generates a great deal of noise, sophisticated techniques are used to improve sound insulation and reduce machinery vibration and resonance. These measures increase the bulk and weight of equipment, requiring extra buoyancy and space and therefore a larger pressure hull. But because the hull is larger, it also has a greater surface area to resonate and radiate noise. This upward spiral is obvious in the size increase of American and British nuclear submarines:

Class	Year	Dived displacement (tons)	Size increase
USA			
Skipjack	1960s	3,513	
Los Angeles	1980s	6,927	+ 197%
UK			
Valiant	1960s	4,800	
Trafalgar	1980s	5,208	+ 10.85%

The British size increase is more modest, but in both cases unit cost has grown by more than 300%. Attack capability – in terms of number of torpedo tubes and weapon reloads – has actually decreased. Complement has remained the same aboard American submarines but increased by 11% in British boats. What should be worrying the West is the fact that comparable Soviet submarines are moving in the opposite direction:

Class	Year	Dived displacement (tons)	Size decrease
Victor I	1960s	5,300	
Alfa	1970s	3,700	– 143%

A comparison of Western and Soviet crew requirements is also significant:

Class	Complement	Change over 20 years
USA		
Skipjack	143	
Los Angeles	143	None
UK		
Valiant	116	
Trafalgar	130	11% increase
USSR		
Victor I	90	
Alfa	40	225% decrease

To sum up: while Western nuclear submarines grow larger, cost more and still appear to use personnel instead of microprocessors for skilled tasks, over the past 20 years Soviet underwater technology has moved in the opposite direction, towards smaller vessels and fewer crew. In addition, the Alfa can dive twice as deep and travel 40% faster than its Western contemporaries; reliable evidence also suggests that Soviet submarines are now radiating much less noise than they did 20 years ago. It would therefore seem to be time for the West to accept that it has lost its claimed underwater superiority over the Soviet Navy, and that some alternative to the nuclear hunter-killer submarine should be developed now that more efficient air-independent power sources are becoming available.

In the years ahead, two air-independent power sources for submarines will emerge, the fuel cell and the Stirling engine. Of these, the heat engine is likely to be front runner because it has a number of advantages:

1 Since the Royal Swedish Navy is installing a 100kW Stirling generator in a *Näcken*-class submarine, it is a system that has already reached production status.

2 In the Stirling engine heat is generated by the combustion of diesel fuel with oxygen. The engine would perform equally well burning fuel with air ingested via a snorkel. Thus the time could come when the Stirling engine replaces the diesel, with just a small battery section to provide emergency power; the empty battery compartments would provide extra stowage space for liquid oxygen.

3 Given bigger engines and more oxidant storage space, the diesel-electric/air-independent hybrid could be transformed into a submarine able to operate for long periods without atmospheric oxygen; a snorkel would be fitted for emergencies and long-range transits.

Apart from having been beaten by Sweden in getting the first viable system to sea, the Germans have to contend with two other major disadvantages of their fuel-cell power source: its dependence upon hydrogen, which is difficult to store safely aboard a submarine; and the fact that it cannot use air as an alternative to pure oxygen for electrical conversion. These difficulties may be overcome but the Stirling generator is likely to remain in the lead for some time to come.

Another important design consideration must be the use of microprocessors, combined with multiple redundancy for safety, in place of highly trained men. Why should it take so many personnel to drive a *Los Angeles*-class submarine but so few to fly a large commercial aircraft? The latter is every bit as complex to operate as a submarine. A radical reduction in complement would lead to smaller submarines, with less space and buoyancy needed to support personnel. But above all, cost must be reduced. A form of Parkinson's Law seems to apply in Western naval procurement: cost increases first, then the operational requirement expands to justify the extra price. If it is to be effective in war, any weapon system should be both expendable and affordable. At present, British and American submarines are neither.

Soviet submarine technology forges ahead

Capt John Moore RN

AMONG the many problems which faced the British in 1939 was the fact that too few people in the Royal Navy had studied the capabilities of submarines, while the Navy as a whole was unprepared for the war which was then beginning. Today, though the strategic situation is very different, one thing remains the same: keeping the countermeasures abreast of the technical advances in submarine construction is very difficult. And when the potential adversary is forcing the technological pace, as is happening at present, the problem becomes even more formidable.

The main attributes of the submarine are its invisibility and its ability to detect other submarines and ships by passive sonar at long ranges. Its success in these areas currently depends on the development of quiet and high-power propulsors, the ability to operate at great depths, and the effective silencing of the submarine for long periods. Thus the designer has to provide for the integration of speed, silence, endurance, habitability, hull strength, adequate power for all on-board equipment, and hull form. To ensure that the submarine can operate effectively on

Alfa is the most revolutionary of modern submarines, with an excellent streamlined form. The propulsion machinery includes two small nuclear reactors with lead bismuth coolant, two steam alternators and an electric motor. It is likely that superconductivity principles have been applied, allowing much increased power from a much smaller motor and resulting in a maximum submerged speed of 42kt.

patrol and execute its wide range of tasks, the sensors, weapons and communications equipment must be the most modern available. At the same time, the ship's company must be the smallest possible, in order to minimise crewing expenses and the training commitment.

As the Soviet Navy is the only likely naval opponent of the NATO nations during the remainder of the century, we review here the capabilities of its submarines and assess the severity of the problem they pose for Western ASW forces.

Speed and propulsors

The original Soviet SSNs were as fast as their USN counterparts, the normal propulsor being pressurised-water reactors and steam turbines. In the early 1960s work began on a radically new design, the Alfa class. When eventually completed, this class possessed high speed (about 42kt), a deep diving capability (about 900m) and a well streamlined hull form. After initial disaster, the use of a lead-bismuth-cooled reactor and, probably, a superconducting motor provided high power in a small space.

Other methods of propulsion – fuel cells, magneto-hydrodynamic thrust (MHD) and various types of nuclear reactor – have been widely discussed and must be expected to be in development or production. If such methods are introduced, the result will be quieter submarines. The fuel cell has no moving parts, and MHD requires no propeller.

Quieting

In the early days of nuclear propulsion Soviet boats were extremely noisy. But, starting in the early 1960s, a great deal of research has been carried out in the USSR in an effort to overcome this problem. This work ranged from studies of dolphin shapes, compliant coatings, anechoic tiles and the reduction of turbulence and wakes to the development of anti-vibration mountings for machinery and investigations of active silencing. The first class to benefit from this effort were the Victor IIIs. This design's sound signature was nearly 20% less than the 170 decibels of its predecessors, making it comparable with the more modern US submarines at their noisiest. Subsequent

Below: **Victor II, an improvement on the 1967 Victor I, shows the continuing evolution which is typical of the Soviet building programmes for both submarines and surface ships.**

Bottom: **Victor III is somewhat larger than Victor II but much quieter. Like all modern Soviet submarines, this class carries both 21in and 25.6in torpedoes as well as SS-N-15 ASW missiles, SS-N-16s with nuclear depth bombs, and the SS-N-21 1,600-mile-range cruise missile.**

classes such as the Oscar and Akula boats are even quieter. While it is impossible to make a submarine absolutely quiet under all conditions, this sudden and signficant improvement makes passive detection by any sensor far more difficult.

Depth and hull strength

There is a limit beyond which there is little to be gained from increased diving depth, while the effort becomes prohibitively costly. However, the greater a submarine's diving limit, the larger the volume in which it can manoeuvre. This complicates the enemy's choice of ASW weapons and, combined with high speed, makes the task of the hunting torpedo far more difficult.

Submarine hulls are normally built of high-yield steel, which becomes more difficult to work as the specification is increased. Titanium is expensive and can only be welded in a clean atmosphere of inert gas. Many forms of laminate have been tried in both West and East; this technique may have been developed further in the USSR than in the West.

Diving depths of around 450m are frequently achieved with steel hulls, while the Alfa class, with a titanium alloy hull, has a limit of around 900m. Some new Soviet classes also use titanium alloy, the USSR having large deposits of the necessary raw material and fewer financial constraints on defence procurement.

Modern Soviet submarines are normally double-hulled. The greater the stand-off distance between the outer and inner hulls, the smaller the effect of a warhead detonation on the outer hull. Soviet submariners place great stress on such aids to survivability.

Endurance, habitability and auxiliary power

Nuclear power confers almost limitless range on modern submarines and provides sufficient power for all forms of auxiliaries and sensors. As a result, the internal atmosphere is maintained at a steady state. This means that the crews are cleaner and more alert,

Below: **The Yankee class, the first ballistic missile submarines in the Soviet Navy to carry their weapons within the hull, began entering service in 1967. The variations on this design ran from Delta I to the most modern Delta IV, each change being dictated by the need to get the maximum number of new missiles to sea.**

Bottom: **The first Sierra was commissioned in 1984, the class probably being intended as the successor to Victor III. The pod on the stern fin, similar to that first seen on the Victor IIIs, is the cause of some debate in Western circles. One theory holds that it is a form of silent auxiliary propulsion.**

while the only two limits on the length of a patrol are the quantity of victuals carried and the crew's tolerance of confinement. The Soviet scale of victualling is less generous than that of many Western navies and the standards of discipline harsher, with the result that patrol periods may be longer.

Sensors and fire control

It is significant that much of Soviet naval espionage is concentrated in this area. Basic radar and sonar as well as advanced computers and all aspects of signal processing are high on the target list, and have been for many years. As a result of these efforts the Soviets have made major advances, though it is difficult to estimate their current standing. It is however known that there are certain gaps in their capability. Despite some theories about the nature of the pod on the stern of some new submarines, the Soviets do not appear to deploy towed-array sonar, although they do have several varieties of variable-depth sonar.

In view of the recent extraordinary advances in so many areas of Soviet submarine technology, it would be unwise to underrate the USSR's current capabilities in the use of sensors and the conversion of the resultant information into a firing solution.

Weapons

The main difference between Soviet weapons development and that of the West is that the Russians have moved ahead in all aspects of submarine capability while Western navies have concentrated on only a selection. The Soviets have worked on five areas: ballistic missiles, cruise missiles, torpedoes, anti-submarine weapons and mines. This means that Western countermeasures against Soviet submarines must be applied at varying ranges from the assumed target, accounting for ballistic missiles at 4,500 miles, cruise missiles at 25–2,000 miles, torpedoes at 2–50 miles, and mines to within a few miles of the target, be it port, channel or strait.

Ballistic missiles are primarily aimed at land targets but may be used against naval forces, and can be

The Echo II class were the first Soviet nuclear-propelled cruise missile submarines. A total of 29 were completed in 1961–67, all of which are still in service. The eight missile tubes have been converted in ten of the class to carry the 295nm-range SS-N-12 in place of the original SS-N-3.

launched from boats lying in any suitable ocean area between the Arctic ice and the Equator. Cruise missiles can also be used against land or sea targets. Torpedoes may be of several types, the most dangerous being the 650mm weapon fitted with a wake-homing head. Soviet mines can embody the full range of means of activation, but would require the submarine laying them to be at or near the target. Delayed-action mines could be laid before the onset of hostilities, and mobile mines could be launched from 20 miles range to move into harbour entrances.

Communications

The time when a submarine had to come up from deep, either to periscope depth or the surface, to carry out wireless routines is now past. Communications buoys and buoyant aerials have been introduced in concert with the development of very-low-frequency (VLF) and extremely-low-frequency (ELF) transmitters. The former permits normal transmission to dived submarines at long ranges. The latter, so far used only by the US and Soviet navies, permits transmissions at very slow data rates to deep submarines at great ranges. Because its main use is to alert deep submarines of the imminent transmission of longer messages by VLF, the US Navy nicknames its ELF system the "Bellringer". These developments have significantly increased the invulnerability of submarines to ASW operations.

Training

The most important element in a submarine's capability is its crew. The submariner has to be trained to react instantly at all times; he must be carefully screened for any tendency to claustrophobia or aggravating habits and attitudes; he must be

The small Bravo class demonstrates the breadth of capability of the Soviet submarine design teams. Though work was in hand on a wide range of nuclear and non-nuclear boats in the late 1960s, space and time were found to produce four of these 3,000-ton submarines to act as padded targets for weapon firings.

impervious to boredom, fit and devoted to his calling. All ratings below chief petty officer in the Soviet Navy are conscripts serving a three-year period; the best are transferred to submarines. Training in many aspects of naval affairs may have taken place before a conscript is called up, but indoctrination into submarine operations can only be carried out after his initial six months in the navy. None of the Soviet Navy's officers or ratings has ever experienced war, when the initial encounters with the enemy are the most frightening. The main aim under such conditions is for the ASW forces to strike early and hard. To achieve this, targets must be quickly detected and localised.

The strengths and weaknesses described above have the following implications for Western anti-submarine warfare planners:

Speed and propulsors
The maximum dived speed to be expected is now 35–42 kt. This may increase greatly with the development of more effective propulsors.

Quieting
The last ten years have seen a notable decrease in Soviet sound signatures. With the development of active silencing, the possible replacement of propellers with other ways of generating thrust, and the introduction of a number of other techniques, the passive detection of Soviet submarines may become problematic by 2000.

Depth and hull strength
As submarines go deeper and faster, the ASW torpedo must have a significantly higher speed, greater range and a minimum depth capability of 950m. The warhead must be of the shaped-charge type to defeat the stand-off distance between the outer and inner hulls.

Endurance
The ability of modern submarines to operate for two or three months without replenishment requires close observation of their movements at all times. This may become impossible as their sound signatures are reduced, making the surveillance of replenishment ships imperative.

Sensors
In view of the efficiency of Soviet overt and covert intelligence, the worst possible case must be assumed: that the capability of Soviet Navy sensors is equal to that of Western systems. This implies long-range detection of surface ships and early warning of any Western submarines that are not adequately silenced. Radar is of little importance except in close encounters or for navigation.

Weapons
Soviet strategic ballistic missiles have ranges from 1,600 miles to about 5,000. Cruise missiles now have a range of 1,500 miles, which may be extended to 2,000 + miles and run down to 300 miles and then 25 miles. Torpedoes range from a few miles to 50 +, the latter with wake-homing heads. ASW weapons have a range of some 20 miles. Mines can be laid from harbour entrances to the edge of the continental shelf (about 185m depth), and some may be similar in design to the US mobile mine.

Communications
Modern methods would require a Soviet submarine to come to a shallower depth only if warned by ELF that a longer message by VLF was imminent.

ASW methods
Passive detection may well become increasingly ineffective during the next ten years. Alternatives may be:

Ensonification The use of high-power active sonars by large numbers of ships and submarines working in concert.

Very-low-frequency passive sonar This might detect certain accidental emissions from transmitting submarines.

Non-acoustic detection During the last 30 years much research has gone into such things as "thermal scars," internal waves and magnetic signatures. So far this work has yielded few results.

Soviet naval developments hold their course

Capt John Moore RN

Kiev, the first Soviet-designed aircraft carrier with an offset island and angled deck. Of 37,100 tons, she has a complement of about 32 aircraft, both V/STOL and helicopters. In addition, she has eight launchers for the 295nm-range SS-N-12 missile, four twin surface-to-air missile launchers, an ASW missile launcher and two ASW rocket launchers, two twin 76mm gun mounts, eight Gatling guns and ten 533mm torpedo tubes. This formidable armament is directed by means of 20 radar sets and hull-mounted and variable-depth sonars.

THE signal "No change" is frequently the most informative source of intelligence. But it can also be the most worrying. Why is there no change? Does this suggest a planned retreat or, possibly, an advance? Does it point to a change of plan? "No change" can mean a hundred things, so the fact that the Soviet naval building programme has sprung no major surprises in the past year certainly does not give Western analysts leave to sit back and take a rest.

Over the last 30 years Soviet naval building has consistently wrongfooted NATO observers, and in many cases has achieved significant advances on current capabilities. In September 1955 a Zulu-class boat was the platform for the first launch of a ballistic missile from a submarine. The Kashin class of 1963 onwards were the world's first all-gas-turbine destroyers. The underwater launch of cruise missiles from a Charlie-class submarine in 1967 was another first, and three years later the lead boat of the Alfa class became the fastest (42kt) and deepest-diving (700m) submarine in the world. 1967 also saw the emergence of the first true helicopter carrier, *Moskva*. In fact that year represented a watershed in Soviet naval planning. The subsequent two decades saw a series of evolutions of various designs, culminating in revolutionary changes in the 1980s.

Amongst major surface ships, these changes were indicated by the marked differences between the third and fourth *Kiev*-class aircraft carriers, and, in 1983, the laying down of the first true carrier – in this case

Left: **Kashin class.** This class of destroyers, the first all-gas turbine design in the world, was introduced in 1963. They were originally planned as ASW ships, but from 1972 six of the total of 20 were lengthened by 3m and fitted with four surface-to-surface missile launchers. Apart from one lost following an internal explosion in 1974, all remain in service. The Indian Navy has recently taken delivery of the fourth of six ordered from the USSR.

Below: **Delta III class.** Of the same length as the preceding Delta IIs, these boats carry 16 SS-N-18 missiles, which have less range than the Delta II's SS-N-8s but carry multiple independently targeted re-entry vehicles (MIRVs). This class was overtaken in 1984 by the Delta IVs, 5m longer and carrying 16 examples of the SS-N-23, a longer-range weapon with greater accuracy and throw weight. Three of this class had been completed by 1987 and others are following at a rate of one a year.

Above right: **Sierra class.** The first of this class was launched at Gorky in July 1983. Of 1,600 tons dived displacement, she carries both 533mm and 650mm torpedo tubes. These can be used for launching torpedoes (the 650mm weapons have a low-speed range of 50 miles), mines of all types, SS-N-15 ASW missiles, SS-N-16 missiles carrying a nuclear depth bomb, and SS-N-21 nuclear-tipped cruise missiles with a range of 1,600nm. By 1987 two of this class had been completed, with others following at a rate of one a year.

nuclear-propelled – for a Russian navy. The first of the *Kirov*-class battlecruisers was commissioned and the first *Udaloy* and *Sovremenny* destroyers were completed in 1980.

The submarine story was even more dramatic. In spring 1980 the first Oscar-class SSBN was launched, followed a few months later by the first of the huge Typhoon-class SSBNs. The new Mike and Sierra-class SSNs emerged in 1983, followed in 1984 by the first of the Akula class. At this time the initial Victor III SSNs were still under construction, as was the conventionally propelled Kilo class. This flood of new designs began to condition Western analysts to expect something new almost every year. In fact what has been happening recently is a continuation of past programmes matched by an improvement in a number of weapon systems.

The Soviet submarine-building programme has now slowed down, averaging 5–6 nuclear and 1–3 non-nuclear boats per year. The SSBN programme is concentrated on the Typhoon and Delta IV classes, with one of each being commissioned every year. But despite the reduction in numbers, little time is wasted in getting these boats into service. The first of the Delta IVs was commissioned less than a year after launch, which is a few months less than is required for the US Navy's *Ohio* class and about half the time needed for a British SSN. There has also been a steady advance in the missile armament of these submarines over the last six years. The testing of SS-N-20 for the Typhoons took place in 1980, and the SS-N-23 for the Delta IV was on the range by 1983.

Both missiles carry multiple independently targeted re-entry vehicles (MIRVs) to greater ranges than were

possible with the Mod 1 and Mod 3 versions of the SS-N-18, first tested some five years before SS-N-20. SS-N-20 and 23 are both propelled by solid fuel, a great improvement emphasised by the explosion of a liquid-fuelled SS-N-6 aboard a Yankee-class boat in 1986.

Since the original Whiskey Single Cylinder in the mid-1950s, Soviet cruise missile boats have carried special launch tubes for missiles of very varied performance. It was in 1967 that the first SS-N-7 missiles appeared in the Charlie class. These weapons represented a major step forward, being capable of launch from a dived boat. Then came the Papa and Charlie II classes, carrying SS-N-9s with a range of 60nm, almost twice that of SS-N-7. Finally, in 1980, the first Oscar appeared. With a displacement treble that of the original Charlies, the Oscars have three times as many missile tubes, capable of accommodating 24 SS-N-19 missiles. These supersonic weapons have a range of 295nm and are intended primarily for ship attack. Since 1980 four Oscars have been completed, the last pair at annual intervals.

Paralleling the development of the SS-N-7, 9 and 19 was that of a much longer-ranged cruise missile, the SS-N-21. This is a tube-launched land-attack weapon with a range of 1,600 miles, which confers a new status on many of the Soviet Navy's attack submarines. Just as the introduction of Tomahawk cruise missiles into the US Navy inventory has given American SSNs a strategic as well as an attack role, the Soviet submarines carrying this new weapon will have similar dual capabilities. At a time when attention is focused on defence against ballistic missiles, this equally deadly threat will soon be made more acute by what is currently known as SS-NX-24. With a larger body and a longer range (possibly over 2,000nm), this missile is currently under test in a converted Yankee. The size of the SS-NX-24 weapon will probably dictate a new class of submarine, and this should make its appearance in the near future.

Thus by 1990 the Soviet Navy will deploy a wide variety of cruise missiles:

Missile	Range (nm)	Launch platforms
Ship attack		
SS-N-19	295	7 Oscar (24 missiles)
SS-N-12	295	10 Echo II (8 missiles)
SS-N-9	60	6 Charlie II (8 missiles)
		1 Papa (10 missiles)
SS-N-7	35	?11 Charlie I (8 missiles)
SS-N-3	250	?16 Juliet (4 missiles)
		?19 Echo II (8 missiles)
Land attack		
SS-N-24	2,000	New class
SS-N-21	1,600	Approx 30 SSNs (up to 18 missiles each)

Note: The SS-N-3, 12 and 19 could also be used in the land attack role.

This adds up to a formidable capability which would stretch the ASW resources of an enemy to a very great degree. In the event of hostilities the deployment of these submarines could cover the path of any fleet or task force at varying ranges, while other boats could be placed at intervals beyond the enemy's coast, threatening command and communications centres. These weapons can carry either nuclear or conventional warheads and, if launched at a time when satellite surveillance was least effective, would be difficult to detect and hard to stop. A surprise attack on a port could have devastating results.

But missiles are not the only weapons available. All the submarines in the Soviet fleet, with the exception of a small number of research craft, can carry torpedoes and mines. These constitute the main armament of all attack submarines when they are employed on normal tasks.

Enormous advances have been achieved since the first Soviet nuclear-powered boat, of the November class, entered service in 1960. The first Victor-class boat appeared in 1967; 11 years later the Victor III was in service. At 6,300 tons dived, these boats are 1,000 tons larger than the first Victors. But the most distinctive feature of the Victor III design is not its size, nor the pod on its tail fin. What makes Victor III special is its extreme quietness, the most valued element in a submarine's make-up and the most difficult to achieve. The Alfa boats can go faster and dive deeper but are notably noisy. Since 1978 new classes entering service have been progressively quieter, further exacerbating the Western ASW problem.

The year 1984 represented another turning point in Soviet submarine design. In less than twelve months the first of the Sierra and Mike classes entered service and the lead boat of the Akula class was launched. Sierra and Akula are much bigger than Victor III, while Mike, though of a similar length to the other two, is of the same dived displacement as Victor III. The three classes differ markedly from one another in appearance: the fins are different and Mike lacks the prominent stern pod carried by the other two. Why were all three built simultaneously at different yards? It could be that Mike is – as Papa was for the SSGNs – a trial boat embodying new design and propulsion features which may be incorporated in a future class. This could be either an attack submarine or of a specialised type. The other two classes differ in hull form – Sierra has a greater beam on almost the same length as Akula – and mast arrangement. The implications of these variations are not immediately clear.

Great headway has also been made by Soviet naval weapon system designers. The first requirement of an attacking submarine – or indeed one seeking to evade – is the ability to locate, classify and track the target by means of sonar. After a shaky start in the 1940s and 1950s the Soviet Navy has made significant advances in this area. The early active and passive sets have given way to systems with a wider frequency range, and modern Soviet submarines are now equipped with active, passive, active/passive, fire-control and under-ice sets. The one omission appears to be a towed array, there being little foundation for the theories suggesting that the Akula/Sierra-style stern pod is used for this purpose. "Good but could be better" probably sums up the present standing of Soviet sonar.

The main armament of an attack submarine, whether torpedoes, mines or missiles, has to be discharged through the torpedo tubes. The original scheme for two sizes of tube, 400mm and 533mm, was applied to very few boats. Production ultimately centred on 533mm (21in) tubes and a variety of torpedoes propelled by steam and oxygen or silver-zinc batteries. None of these weapons was particularly remarkable, the main methods of guidance being a form of pattern running (developed from the German Lut) or fairly simple passive sonar. Nuclear heads have been available for these torpedoes from the time of the early November class, and currently form part of a normal outfit.

The late 1960s saw the introduction of a new guidance method: the wake-homing head, designed to attack a ship or force from astern. Ten years later, as the early Victor IIIs were commissioning, a new and very potent weapon was introduced. This was the 650mm torpedo, longer as well as fatter than its predecessors, and therefore able to carry more fuel, yielding in turn a longer range and a larger warhead. From then on attacks could be carried out from, by torpedo standards, very long ranges: 25 miles at 50kt or twice that at about half the speed. At the climax of the engagement the wake-homing head gave a further advantage.

The Russians have been keenly interested in mines for well over a century. They built the first submarine minelayer and today have over 200,000 influence and 100,000 moored contact mines, the world's largest stockpile. Of these, possibly a third are available for submarines. They include antenna contact mines, and rather elderly moored acoustic mines. The more modern designs incorporate all three influence methods: magnetic, acoustic and pressure. The majority are moored, although an adequate number are available as bottom mines, as in the case of those laid by the Libyan ship *Ghat* in the Red Sea in 1985. There are also rising mines, which lie at depth until a target is detected overhead, and mobile mines, which can be discharged up to 15–20 miles from a target area and set to track into a harbour entrance or other constricted waterway. Warheads range from 100 to 500lb, and the depth of water in which the mines are laid can vary from 1,000 fathoms for a rising mine, to the 20-fathom line for other varieties. The present inventory is being steadily updated and represents a major threat which is far from being matched by the MCM efforts of the NATO navies.

The increasing silence of modern Soviet submarines is being achieved by rafting of machinery, providing maximum stand-off between the outer and inner hulls; streamlining of the outer hull to lessen turbulence; attention to boundary-layer control; and the use of polymers. The methods of propulsion now foreshadowed by many articles in Soviet naval and scientific journals could well result in the elimination of the greatest noise-maker of all, the propeller. Whether this is achieved by hydrodynamic thrust (electrically operated water jets) or by other means, there seems little doubt that Soviet research into such methods is further advanced than the comparable Western effort.

Until the late 1960s it seemed that the Soviet Navy was specialising in ships designed for surface action. Only the *Moskva* class of helicopter carriers, which appeared in 1967, was clearly intended for anti-submarine operations. But then came the Kresta II cruisers, the first of which commissioned in 1969, and the Krivak frigates, which joined the fleet in 1970. Both carried a new missile, the SS-N-14, which was initially seen in the West as a sea-skimming surface-to-surface weapon. As a result, the application of the designation *protivolodochny korabl* (anti-submarine ship) to the Krivaks and Kresta IIs was regarded as

Above: **Moskva**, the world's first helicopter carrier, is capable of carrying a large complement of rotary-wing aircraft (14 Hormone A and B). She is also equipped with an ASW missile launcher (SUW-N-1), two 6,000m-range rocket launchers and a variable-depth sonar. She was commissioned in 1967 and her sister, *Leningrad*, in 1968. It is possible that further ships of this class were cancelled in favour of the much larger *Kiev* class, capable of carrying VTOL aircraft.

Below: In the Krivak II class the two twin 76mm mountings carried aft by the Krivak Is have been replaced by two single 100mm guns. A total of 11 of this variant are in service. Designed as ASW escorts, these ships carry four SS-N-14 ASW missiles, two rocket launchers and eight 533mm torpedo tubes which can be used for ASW weapons. A large assortment of radars is complemented by hull-mounted and variable-depth sonars. A second variant of this class, the Krivak III, is now in production for the KGB. The SS-N-14 mounting has been replaced by a single 100mm gun forward and the after guns have been removed to make way for a helicopter platform and hangar.

nothing more than disinformation. But SS-N-14 subsequently turned out to be primarily an anti-submarine missile carrying a homing torpedo to a range of 30nm. Thus, in the early 1960s, the Soviet Navy had appreciated the threat from nuclear submarines and had begun planning a surface ship counter-force.

In 1971-79 the Kara-class cruisers continued to add to this capability, while more Krivaks and smaller ASW vessels joined the fleet. Although the total of ASW ships was rising, it was some time before Soviet sonar equipment proved equal to coping with modern submarines. It was not until the early 1980s that new active equipment was introduced, and even now several of the later classes of ship carry sonars which must soon be outdated. A form of variable-depth sonar went to sea in *Moskva* in 1967, and was subsequently fitted to the Kara and Krivak classes. In the early 1980s a new version was seen in the *Kirov*, *Udaloy* and later *Kiev* ships.

Soviet ASW weapons have advanced very little during the last 15 years. The SUW-N-1 of 1967 and the SS-N-14 of about the same era are still the standard surface ship ASW missile systems. The multi-barrelled *Raketnaya Bombometnaya Ustanooka* (rocket-propelled depth charge) systems remain in service in many surface ships. With ranges varying from 600 to 6,000m and warheads comprising between 21kg and 55kg of explosive, these weapons are very much a last-ditch defence against a modern submarine, although the RBU's ability to fire anything from 6 to 16 depth charges in rapid succession might disrupt a close-in attack or deflect incoming torpedoes.

Helicopters did not get to sea as an integral part of the Soviet Navy's ASW capability until 1967. Apart from the specialised carriers, no ship carried more than one until the *Udaloy* class of 1980. The first of these aircraft was the Ka-25 Hormone, which comes in three versions: ASW, missile targetting with a video data-link, and reconnaissance. In 1980 came the Ka-27 Helix, at 12.5 tonnes some five tonnes heavier than the Ka-25, and with a greater range and speed. It is now embarked in the later Soviet ship classes.

The use of ship-based aircraft had long been a source of debate in the Soviet Navy. Although Stalin had shown interest in aircraft carriers, the only ship of this type to wear the Soviet ensign before the present

Top: **Kara class. This class, successor to the Kashin IIs, was first seen in 1973. The seven ships have a helicopter deck and hangar aft above the variable-depth sonar. The two twin 76mm gun mountings are just abaft the bridge, while the main armament, two quadruple SS-N-14 ASW missile launchers, is placed either side of the bridge. Four twin surface-to-air missile launchers and four Gatling guns make up the AA armament. The ASW battery is completed by four rocket launchers and ten 533mm torpedo tubes. Six gas turbines give a speed of 34kt and ranges of 3,000 miles at 32kt and 12,000 at 15kt.**

Above: **Since the first of the *Udaloy* class commissioned in November 1980 a further seven have been built. Construction is expected to continue at a rate of one a year from 1987. These 8,000-ton ASW ships carry two helicopters and are capable of 32kt. Like the Karas they carry two quadruple SS-N-14 ASW missile launchers. Their four gas turbines give a speed of 32kt and ranges of 2,000nm at maximum speed and 6,000nm at 20kt.**

Right: **Frunze, second of the modern Soviet battlecruisers. The first, *Kirov*, brought a new dimension to modern surface warship design. Displacing 28,000 tons, this class has a hybrid propulsion plant using both nuclear reactors and steam boilers. On a fairly conventional hull *Kirov* carries 20 SS-N-19 missiles, 14 surface-to-air launchers and a reloadable twin SS-N-14 launcher. In *Frunze* this ASW outfit has been replaced by a new vertical-launched SAM system. By early 1987 two ships of the class had been completed, one was fitting out and one was on the building slip.**

day was the captured German *Graf Zeppelin*, which, grossly overloaded with booty such as railway engines, capsized en route to the USSR in 1947. *Moskva* was therefore a major advance when she appeared with her 14 Hormone helicopters in 1967. Only two of this class were completed; one reason for this unusually brief production run may have been the successful performance of the first Soviet VTOL aircraft, the Yakovlev Freehand, which first flew in public in the same year as *Moskva* commissioned.

The first modern Soviet carrier, *Kiev*, was laid down in September 1970 and commissioned in May 1975. She carries about a dozen Yak-38 VTOL Forgers and up to 19 Helix or Hormone helicopters. This looks like a small complement for a ship of some 40,000 tons, but the whole forward section is taken up by eight launchers for 295nm-range SS-N-12 missiles and their reloads. Other armament comprises two types of surface-to-air missile, two twin 76mm gun turrets, eight 30mm Gatlings and ten 21in torpedo tubes. Radars include 3D air search, air and surface search, fire-control, aircraft control and navigation sets. Underwater search is handled by active hull-mounted and variable-depth sonars, the latter having a large towed body and probably being capable of active and passive operations at medium frequencies. An SUW-N-1 is mounted forward for long-range ASW work, with two RBU-6000s coming into play at ranges below 6,000m.

This multi-purpose design philosophy was followed in the *Kirov*-class battlecruisers, the first of which was laid down three years after *Kiev*. So far two of these 28,000-ton (full load) ships have been completed, with another due in 1988 and a fourth still on the building slip at the Baltic Yard, Leningrad, with a possible completion date of 1992. These large ships incorporate a number of capabilities, including surface-to-surface and surface-to-air missiles, 100 or 130mm gun armament, Gatlings, ten 21in torpedo tubes, and ASW armament. Three helicopters are carried in both

completed ships, though there is a major difference in their ASW/AA armament. In the first, *Kirov*, an SS-N-14 mounting with reload facilities is sited in the bow. In the second, *Frunze*, this has been replaced by twin silos for the new SA-N-9 short-range (10 miles, 60,000ft) missile. Similar silos are placed either side of the quarterdeck, making necessary a resiting of Gatlings and the use of the new twin 130mm turret in place of *Kirov*'s two single 100mm guns. Further aft and set into the transom is a large door masking the very big VDS towed body.

The propulsion system of this class is unique. Two nuclear reactors, which make this the first class of nuclear-propelled major surface warship in the Soviet Navy, are complemented by oil-fired boilers. It is not known whether the boilers are used to superheat the steam from the reactors or whether they have their own turbines on the same shafts as those of the reactor, but the result is a speed of 33kt.

This class demonstrates the readiness of the Russians to make radical changes to an accepted design as lessons are learned and new equipment becomes available. This is an expensive way of doing business but is clearly considered cost-effective. Indeed, the approach may have been taken even further in the latest major surface warship class. In 1983 an aircraft carrier was laid down in two sections at Nikolayev. At about the same time a flight deck mock-up – with ski-ramps, an angled section, two catapults (possibly for development purposes) and arrester wires – was laid out at the nearby Saki naval air station. No catapults were included in the ship's design, suggesting that the plan is for conventional fixed-wing aircraft – for which the ship seems to be intended – to take off from a ski-ramp.

If catapults are not fitted and the ski-ramp scheme does not work, a possible rearrangement would comprise the removal of the ski-ramp, fitting of surface-to-surface missiles up forward, removal of the arrester wires, and substitution of a new V/STOL

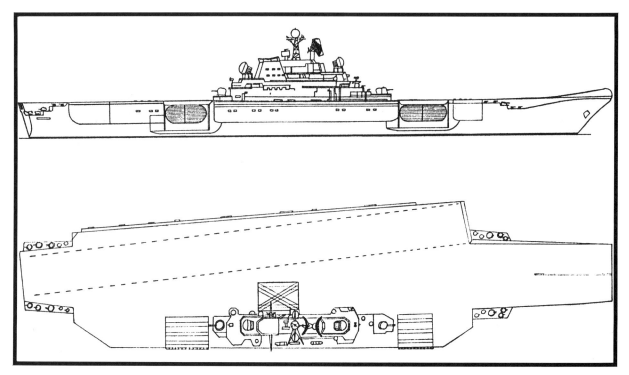

aircraft for the fixed-wing carrier aircraft that is rumoured but has yet to emerge. The currently estimated in-service date of 1992 must be revised if this ship's air group, apart from helicopters, is to be all-V/STOL. In that case, the first of class could be operational by 1989 and the second in 1991.

The development of the escort fleet took a marked step forward in 1980–82. In 1980 the first of the *Sovremenny* class was closely followed by the first *Udaloy*. Of about 8,000 tons full load each, these ships are classified in the West as destroyers, though in the Soviet terminology the *Udaloy*s are "large anti-submarine ships". Once again the Soviets have opted for specialised ships. The eight *Sovremenny*s (with

three building) each carry eight SS-N-22, an improved supersonic version of SS-N-9 with a range of 70nm. The *Udaloy*s carry the same number of SS-N-14s for anti-submarine operations and two helicopters in place of the single targetting aircraft in the *Sovremenny*s.

1982 saw the introduction of *Slava*, bridging the gap between *Kirov* and the *Sovremenny*s. Built at Nikolayev, this cruiser has a displacement of 12,500 tons full load and carries 16 SS-N-12 surface-to-surface missiles, a twin 130mm turret, surface-to-air missiles, a helicopter, eight 21in torpedo tubes, and short-range anti-submarine weapons. With four gas turbines she can equal the speed of *Kirov*, but, unlike *Udaloy*, she has no variable-depth sonar.

Left: This drawing shows the main features of the nuclear-propelled aircraft carrier currently fitting out at Nikolayev, with a second under construction. While the first apparently has no catapults, the second could well be fitted with two if the present trials at Saki are successful.

Below left: The first of the *Sovremenny* class commissioned in August 1980. A further seven have been built since then, with three more building. About the same size as *Udaloy*, these ships have steam turbines, a cheaper solution than gas turbines. Armament comprises eight SS-N-22 missiles with a range of 70nm, two twin 130mm turrets, four torpedo tubes, two short-range rocket launchers (ASW) and a single helicopter. Role of the *Sovremenny* is anti-surface ship operations.

Right: Slava class. The first pair of these 12,500-ton cruisers had been completed by the end of 1986, with a third due in 1987. They come midway between the *Kirov* battlecruisers and the new destroyers, carrying a powerful armament of 16 SS-N-12 surface-to-surface missiles, a twin 130mm gun mounting, six Gatlings, eight torpedo tubes and two ASW rocket launchers. A single helicopter is tasked primarily with missile guidance. Four gas turbines give a speed of 34kt and a range of 10,000 miles at 18kt.

Below: Ivan Rogov, the first of two 13,000-ton assault ships, appeared in 1978. Capable of carrying two large hovercraft and an LCM in the docking bay, and with room for a Naval Infantry battalion of 522 men, 20 tanks and other supporting vehicles, they represent a marked improvement in the Soviets' amphibious capacity.

Above: **The thirty-five 790-ton Natya-class ships are the largest vessels in the Soviet mine countermeasures force, which currently numbers almost 400 hulls, more than the whole NATO MCM fleet.**

Below: Berezina. **Although the Soviet Navy relies very largely on merchant fleet support, there are many specially designed replenishment ships. *Berezina*, at 40,000 tons, is the largest.**

Conclusion

The Soviet submarine force is showing continuing improvements in silencing, weapons, speed and deep-diving capabilities. Weaknesses continue to be the lack of towed sonar arrays and, despite the fact that the submarine arm is allocated the cream of the fleet, the poor standard of conscript crews.

Advance in the surface fleet has relied on variations in armaments and sensors rather than on new designs. But one thing is certain: Soviet naval equipment is rugged and, necessarily, sailor-proof. Its effectiveness in action depends upon crew quality, and with a third of a fairly low-grade ship's company being changed every 9–10 months the overall standard must be lower than that of an all-volunteer navy. The complete lack of war experience within the Soviet Navy must also count against its ability to do well in the opening stages of a conflict.

S90: only trial will tell

Nigel Ling

Introduction

Argument about the "short, fat" hull form for naval vessels as opposed to the conventional "long, thin" shape is not new. A meeting of the Institute of Naval Architects in 1869 devoted the entire proceedings to the matter. The differences of opinion on the subject were as marked as they are today, but there the similarity ended. The main protagonist of the short, fat design was the Chief Naval Constructor, and his advocacy was backed by naval officers who had commanded such ships. The fact that these vessels were actually operating in the fleet suggests a broad-minded approach which is lacking today. Admittedly ships were cheaper and funds more readily available then than they are now. But, as the extraordinary virulence of the attacks on the S90 design shows, the attitude of today's official examiners in both Britain and the USA is very much at variance with that of their Victorian predecessors.

During comparative 1/10th-scale model trials carried out in the Solent the S90 model *(right)* showed her seakeeping capabilities to be superior to those of the *Leander* model *(left)*. This method of model trials, approved by the Royal Corps of Naval Constructors, is invaluable when employed under strict scientific conditions, as the S90 trials were.

The issue has been examined by an unofficial panel under the chairmanship of Admiral of the Fleet Lord Hill-Norton, which concluded that the S90 case warrants examination by Government committee. After many delays this is now in hand. The author of this summary of the background acted as an adviser to the minister at the meetings of the Defence Scientific Advisory Committee (Hull Committee) which originally discarded the S90. As a naval architect he is in a unique position to provide a balanced view.

J. E. Moore

THE publication of the Hill-Norton Committee report on the case for the S90 hull design has refuelled a controversy which has raged over the past few years in the technical press and in letters pages of the quality newspapers. It has also led directly to the setting up of an official inquiry into the selection procedure for the procurement of the Royal Navy's Type 23 frigate, for which the S90 hull was proposed.

The S90 was a private-venture design by a small group of naval architects based on the Isle of Wight, Thornycroft Giles and Associates. That such a small organisation should be able to put forward a radical new design for a major class of warship was in itself remarkable. But more remarkable still was the subsequent controversy, with vitriolic letters in the press, widespread media cover and professional reputations being staked in a series of arguments which have tended to generate more heat than enlightenment. Cause of the strife was the largest of a series of designs for a warship with a much larger beam than that normally found in vessels of frigate and destroyer size. Smaller versions included the Mexican Azteca patrol boats and the Danish Osprey 50m patrol craft.

All these craft owed their origins to design work by Sir John I. Thornycroft, who pioneered the development of the torpedo boat towards the end of the last century. He had then settled on the "long, thin" hull, dictated by the poor power-to-weight ratios of steam machinery at that time. Sir John was however always aware of the inadequate seakeeping and structural integrity of such designs, as well as their high cost, and spent the last 20 years of his life experimenting with a variety of wide, fast hulls which appeared to be directly contradictory to his original designs. After his death the advent of lightweight diesel machinery, providing an adequate power-to-weight ratio, enabled his grandson, Cdr Peter Thornycroft, to develop the Nelson family of fast launches, based directly on the work of Sir John. The satisfactory performance and seakeeping of these craft is now legendary, and they set the standard by which all other similar-sized craft are judged.

The basic design was then enlarged into the 130-ton Azteca patrol craft for Mexico. With 36 built or on order over a ten-year period, these craft can be considered highly successful. Further enlargement led to the Osprey design, examples of which were built by Frederikshavn Vaerft A/S (FHV) for Denmark, Burma, Kuwait, Morocco and Senegal. A number of variants are currently being built in other parts of the world.

Osprey is a 50m patrol craft with a displacement of 500 tons and a speed of 20kt on about 4,500hp. The first of the type, the Danish Havørnen, was built in Denmark in 1979 at a cost of £1.4 million. Thornycroft Giles' claim that their designs could be built more cheaply than conventional arrangements appeared to

have been borne out by the fact that HMS Sandpiper, built two years previously and with around one third Havørnen's displacement, also cost £1.4 million.

Derivatives based on the standard Osprey hull were also projected, including a full armed version costed at £3.5 million and an interesting design study for Kuwait. The latter was to have a speed of 36kt on the power of four MTU diesels and a length of 55m, and to be armed with a 76mm Oto Melara gun, 50mm Bredas, four Exocets and other systems giving the combat performance of a small frigate. The complete package, with performance guarantees, was estimated at £11.5 million.

As a result of this work, Thornycroft Giles and Associates (TGA) was invited by the British Ministry of Defence to submit a private proposal for the Type 23 frigate. TGA submitted its scheme to the Controller of the Navy on May 21, 1982, and it was formally considered at a meeting at the Ministry of Defence on July 14, 1982. It was agreed that the validation programme for the design, now designated "S90," would be funded jointly by the Department of Trade and Industry, British Aerospace, Frederikshavn Vaerft and TGA (later joined by other companies), with no MoD assistance. It would address only the questions of basic design, resistance, propulsion and seakeeping, using the results of tank tests at the British Hovercraft Corporation (BHC) and National Maritime Institute (NMI). It was never intended to submit a fully detailed design, as this would form part of a later project-definition contract if the validation programme supported the original estimates.

Evident in this picture is the height of the S90 mast, which can carry a search radar far higher than that of any current destroyer/frigate of the same tonnage. The result would be a markedly greater radar horizon.

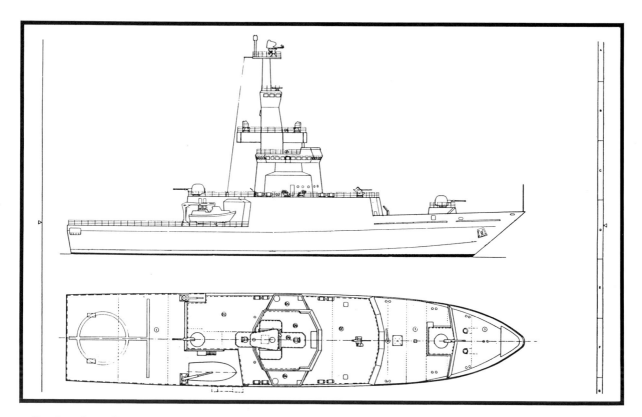

During the validation programme TGA was invited to present a paper to the DSAC Hull Committee. Submitted on March 10, 1983, *The S90 and the Action of Water* confined itself to philosophical design issues because the major part of the trials work remained incomplete.

On May 20, 1983, with the major tank tests completed, a 250-page summary was delivered to MoD, with copies to the MoD's Ship Department, YARD Ltd (the research and development arm of Yarrow Shipbuilders) and the DSAC Hull Committee. The two-volume summary covered, among other topics, speed (resistance and propulsion), seakeeping, resistance and seakeeping test illustrations, an S90 *Leander* seakeeping comparison, stability, structure and running costs. Frederikshavn Vaerft contributed an outline specification, Dowty Fuel Systems Ltd details of the fuel transfer system, NEI-APE Ltd a propulsion summary and schematic drawing, and BHC subjective motion magnitude calculations. Test data covered S90 resistance and self-propulsion tests by BHC, and resistance, propulsion, Osprey 1/10th-scale correlation, and controlled seakeeping tests by NMI. FHV contributed figures on dimensions, weights, stability, hydrostatics, loading and trim. All drawings were to a small scale and of a preliminary nature. This information was considered by the Hull Committee, and YARD and the Ship Department performed their own calculations on resistance and powering.

The verdict was generally unfavourable, resulting

Following the DSAC's rejection of the S90 design, a smaller version was entered for consideration as an offshore patrol vessel. Evident in this drawing are this variant's heavy armament and exceptionally high search radar mounting.

in the S90 being rejected in favour of the conventional Type 23. Though this decision was announced on October 18, 1983, it was not until July 1986 that the DSAC Hull Committee's critique of the proposal was made public, in *Jane's Defence Weekly*.

Fundamental to the S90 design was the fact that the vessel was intended to derive dynamic lift from her movement through the water and would therefore not operate in a pure displacement mode. The YARD/Ship Department calculations assumed traditional theory and totally discounted any possible benefit from dynamic lift. It is thus not surprising that their calculated results were different from those provided by NMI and BHC.

As often happens when arguments become heated, fundamental basic points were either missed or became clouded. Analyses comparing a "Ton" class mine-sweeper with an Osprey hull form with the same basic parameters have been carried out. The "Ton" class is a pure displacement hull, while the Osprey is not. Basic comparative calculations show that it would be totally impracticable to power a "Ton" class for 20kt, let alone the 40–50kt that tank tests have shown could

be reached by an Osprey hull if installed power were simply increased.

It is generally not disputed that a hull form increased in beam to give greater displacement and volume could be built much more cheaply than a hull lengthened for the same purpose. The first approach allows the use of heavier, simpler scantlings in the structure, and while the materials cost is slightly higher because of the increased weight of structure, many fewer constructional man-hours are needed. It is this reduction in building time that produces the greatest cost saving.

The DSAC committee's assertion in *Jane's Defence Weekly* that TGA "underquoted for structural weight of a conventional hull by 12%" came as something of a surprise to the S90 team, as the figures had been taken from the paper *The Design of Cheap Warships* by the MoD's own distinguished designer D. K. Brown. The committee claimed in the same article that TGA had underestimated the structural weight of the S90 by 45%. However, they reached this conclusion after dismissing the possibility of dynamic lift and adding to the proposed weight to allow for the extra power and fuel they insisted would be required.

Top: **The "Ton" class minesweepers were designed for one purpose: the removal of mines from coastal waters. Comparison with ships designed for ocean work is therefore misleading.**

Above: **The modern "Hunt" class minehunters have a length-to-beam ratio of 6:1, compared with 5.2:1 for the "Ton" class. Though they can thus be described as "short and fat", there the resemblance to the S90 design stops. While the Ministry of Defence complained about the rolling behaviour of the original "Osprey" design, it had nothing to say about the "Hunt" class.**

The reduction in price claimed by TGA does not relate to the weapons (although the cost of their installation is likely to be lower) but to platform cost, which can be shown to be about half that of a conventional destroyer/frigate form. "Double the weapons for less than half the price" is a nonsensical claim invented by the press and never advanced by TGA. The saving actually claimed for S90 against a conventional hull form with the same weapons capability was in the order of 25%.

Short hulls display greater structural integrity

under bending loads. Though it has been implied that conventional warships suffer no difficulty with bending stresses, the addition of doubler plates to the Type 21 frigates to cure their alarming tendency to structural failure would suggest otherwise. Indeed, it is understood that the Royal Navy considered disposing of the whole class as a result of these failures.

Virtually every destroyer-sized class of warship built in Britain since the Second World War has suffered some degree of structural failure, often in moderate weather. This includes extensive setting-up of bottom plates in "Tribal" class frigates, transverse cracking of *Darings*, Type 16s and *Leanders*, and reports of similar defects in ships currently serving. This is not to claim that merchant ships and similar structures are immune from such failures, but it does indicate that the problem cannot be summarily dismissed.

The *Jane's Defence Weekly* article continues: "The DSAC Committee members tried to deal with TGA's most controversial claim that, for a given speed, a 40 per cent increase in beam is possible without increase in power." This is not quite what was claimed by TGA, which instead specified "a given length, displacement and speed" and expressed its results in terms of power per ton of displacement. All this is made quite clear in the Hill-Norton Report.

The advantage in this area is due partly to the increased propulsion coefficient claimed for the S90 form. While the designers admit that this effect is not fully understood, they believe it may be influenced by the same pressure distribution under the hull that gives rise to dynamic lift. They base their claims on the full-scale results produced by trials with an Osprey hull.

The major source of disagreement over the performance of the S90/Osprey form is TGA's claim that it produces dynamic lift. The DSAC committee simply discounted dynamic lift and based their findings on computer predictions which took no account of this phenomenon. Applying similar predictions to Osprey, for which full-scale results are available, it can be demonstrated that the performance actually achieved is theoretically impossible. The Osprey trials results must therefore owe something to dynamic lift and increased propulsion coefficient, and it is these same benefits that are claimed for the larger S90.

The Hill-Norton Report considers the question of

Below: Gurkha, one of the "Tribal" class of frigates built in the early 1960s. These ships have a length-to-beam ratio of 8.5 : 1, more generous than some other classes of British destroyers and frigates. Despite this the first of class cracked her keelson while on passage under normal conditions. The remainder of the class had this section in the engine room reinforced.

Bottom: Dundas was one of the Type 14 frigates classified as "Second Rates" and designed to carry out the menial tasks of the fleet. Unfortunately, this involved encounters with heavy weather in the North Atlantic, which caused distortion of the quarterdeck area. Additional pillars and strengthening were required.

dynamic lift so important that a full appendix is devoted to it. The appendix finds that a senior MoD official made a simple error in stating that no benefit could result from dynamic lift, as "displacement varies as the cube of the dimensions and dynamic lift as the square". This appears to be the theory upon which the DSAC Committee rejected the TGA propulsion figures, and which the Hill-Norton Report dismisses as "wrong in fact," pointing out that lift "varies not only as the square of the length but also as the square of the speed". Although the whole DSAC report relating to resistance and powering is flawed by that one error, it has not generally been spotted by the detractors of the S90. For its part, TGA accepts that it does not fully understand the whole effect of dynamic lift – although its tests continue to reveal additional information – and would welcome a further, more detailed, series of tests to provide extra data. The question of dynamic lift is so fundamental to the concept of the Osprey hull form that to dismiss it summarily on erroneous grounds must raise doubts as to the validity of the other counterarguments.

It is generally accepted that a hull form designed for maximum efficiency at high speed is often inefficient at lower speeds as a result of transom immersion. In terms of power/ton, the S90 is more resistant at speeds in the 15–18kt range than the equivalent conventional form. To offset this effect TGA proposed a fuel transfer system allowing the vessel to be trimmed by the bow to raise the transom out of the water during extended passages. The transfer time of 15min for 140 tonnes, quoted in *Jane's Defence Weekly*, assumes

Below: **York** is one of four Batch 3 Type 42 destroyers now in service with the Royal Navy. Compared with the previous eight ships of this type, the Batch 3s have 50ft more length, improving their speed and seakeeping.

Bottom: Type 21 frigate *Amazon*. This comparatively inexpensive design was developed to boost escort numbers in the fleet in the mid-1970s. They have had their problems, the main evidence of which is the large strengthening piece welded amidships to prevent hull and upper-deck cracking. Not so evident but equally significant is the 130 tons of ballast needed to improve their stability.

the use of Bunker C residual fuel; Navy diesel could be transferred in less than 5min by the proposed system.

Once again, the fundamental point was missed. The bows-down attitude would be adopted for extended passages at economical speed in peacetime or for passage to an operational area. In "sprint and drift" operations with a towed sonar array, the bows-up "sprint" trim would be adopted, as the towing speed is below the range in which the S90 form is less efficient. As the US Navy has found out, long-stay towed arrays are in any event more efficiently handled by vessels derived from offshore supply ships. These were in turn based on stern trawlers, which trim bows-down for economical passage to the fishing grounds, and then immerse their transoms to begin fishing. S90 proposes the same procedure using fuel rather than water as ballast. A further advantage of the TGA system is its usefulness as a damage control facility.

The allegedly excessive stability of the S90 has been widely misrepresented. MoD figures for warship stability are classified, so direct comparisons cannot be made. However, whatever the criteria, some British warships currently in service must have very marginal stability reserves. It is understood that the stretched Type 42s incorporate 138 tonnes of lead ballast and that the additional guns fitted to the Type 42s after the Falklands War required the removal of boats and the addition of permanent ballast. The Type 21s are reported in *Jane's Fighting Ships* to be permanently ballasted, and the addition of a towed-array winch to the *Leander*s has required drastic and expensive surgery to reduce topweight. With such a background, high reserve stability has to be viewed as something of a blessing, especially as it can be demonstrated that the majority of warship losses are caused by loss of stability rather than loss of buoyancy, i.e. they usually capsize before they sink.

The metacentric height of 5.0m attributed to the S90 in some publications would indeed result in an unacceptably quick roll. However, this figure applied only in the early stages. During the more detailed design process special attention was given to the roll period and, by careful weight distribution, the metacentric height was reduced to 3.9m, corresponding to a roll period of 8.04sec. This compares with the

Top: **This 10-year-old picture of a *Leander*-class frigate shows the original configuration. Since then a series of conversions has taken place, all requiring the surrender of vital equipment to allow for modernisation. In Batch 1 the guns were removed to accommodate the Ikara ASW system. In Batch 2 the guns gave way to Exocet missiles. In Batch 2TA, to compensate for the 70 tons of towed-array equipment the forward Seacat mounting was removed, the 40mm guns replaced by 20mm, the boats supplanted by an inflatable craft, the torpedo tubes lowered a deck, and the Type 965 air surveillance radar removed. The fourth conversion includes the fitting of quadruple Exocets and a Sea Wolf SAM mounting, and removal of the twin 4.5in gun mounting and Type 965 radar.**

Above: **Type 22 frigate *Broadsword*. The bias towards missile armament in this design meant that only small-calibre guns could be fitted. The last ten of the 14 ships of this class have been lengthened by 55ft, and the last four have had a single 4.5in gun added.**

*Leander*s' 9.3sec at a metacentric height of 0.84m. During the Second World War the American "Captain" class destroyer escorts were regarded as highly successful. Their reserve stability allowed them to carry a good weapons load and spared them the "waves down the funnel" traumas suffered by some other classes. Their period of roll was about 8sec. TGA has never fitted bilge keels or stabilising fins on any of its designs, and has never had any reason to do so.

The design was criticised as being only a two-compartment ship, i.e. capable of remaining afloat if no more than one bulkhead was breached. The

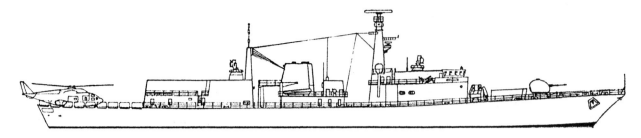

The Type 23 has been preferred to the S90 design as the "cheap" frigate for the future. Although their beam is within a few inches of that of the Type 22, they are over 50ft shorter than the later ships of that class. The logic of this design is difficult to follow: it is now almost twice as expensive as originally planned, and it is slower than its predecessors.

provision of two or three-compartment integrity is a matter of subdivision and not hull form. In general, a large reserve of stability is of great advantage in damage control.

The arguments relating to seakeeping ability are long and complicated. One-tenth-scale model tests have been supported by MoD designers, and if it is accepted that comparative tests of such models are fair and valid, anyone seeing the *Leander* and S90 models in action under the same conditions will require no further convincing of the latter's superiority. Extracts have been shown on television, and mere figures cannot adequately show the obvious differences.

TGA has been criticised for not paying attention to noise reduction, shock and NBC protection, and the provision of clean conditions for the electronics. There is the simplest of reasons: those factors were outside the terms of reference laid down by MoD/DTI for the S90, and would have been covered in the later project definition.

Examination of the early S90 presentations reveals that some of the initial information provided by TGA was not clearly expressed. Moreover, the various papers were written as the research programme was continuing, and figures such as the metacentric height and machinery weights changed from time to time. Understandably, this gave rise to a certain amount of confusion, compounded by what appears to have been a lack of willingness by the MoD to liaise closely during the appraisal phase. Many of the simple misinterpretations could have been readily resolved. For example, when the dispute over the metacentric height and damage stability became known, the writer, as an impartial observer, obtained a full printout of stability and weight distribution data within 48h as the result of a single telephone call to Frederikshavn. The DSAC committee appears not to have taken such simple steps to resolve confusion, and to have restricted itself to the papers as presented, although in fairness that may have been the brief.

Regrettably, opinions have now become firmly entrenched and it is difficult to predict a settlement. The situation has not been helped by sensational reporting in the media. Many of the reported claims for the S90 are as outrageous as those describing the Type 23 as "invisible" because of the features incorporated to reduce her radar signature. The letters pages have contained correspondence in which "fact" has proved to be only opinion, informed or otherwise.

There can be no doubt that conventional theory, if applied to the existing Ospreys, shows that they should not be able to reach their actual trials speeds. Some effect that is not fully understood is therefore likely to be present. There is also no doubt that TGA is attempting to make serious proposals for a cost-effective warship, which should surely be the object of all warship designers.

TGA has continued to investigate its hull forms and believes that the speeds they can attain are higher than were first thought and are purely a function of installed horsepower. The company's research shows that speeds in the region of 40–50kt are possible. Coupled with what TGA claims to be improved seakeeping performance by comparison with a conventional hull, this would, for the first time since the introduction of the nuclear submarine, give an ASW ship a speed advantage over her quarry. Current ASW ships are some 12kt slower than the fastest Soviet submarines. Reversing that speed advantage would produce such a large gain in capability as to alone justify further work on the project.

It is quite natural that conservatism should prevail in the military environment. However, if an aircraft promised such an advantage a prototype would surely have been built for testing. The £15 million or so that an S90 prototype (with concrete in place of weapons) would cost pales into insignificance when compared with the £1 billion poured into the AEW Nimrod, the enormous sums wasted on the development of unsuccessful torpedoes and the £200 million recently thrown away on seven other cancelled projects.

Professional reputations should now be put to one side and the matter resolved, with whatever funding may be required, so that the Royal Navy can enter the next century with the best capability that can be afforded.

Guns still good for the close-in battle

Brian Spilman and Mike Round*

Last hope of the warship under close-in missile attack: Contraves Seaguard CIWS spits 25mm cannon shells from its quartet of Type KBB cannon.

THE ADVENT of the anti-ship missile has revolutionised naval warfare. The first awareness of being attacked that a victim ship might have is when an object apparently the size of a football and travelling near the speed of sound appears over the horizon. This is followed a few seconds later by the impact and detonation of several hundred kilograms of high-explosive warhead. In practice a task force of ships would rely on a layered defence comprising combat air patrols, electronic jamming, anti-missile missiles and guns to counter such an attack. This article considers only the last stage of the defence, using fast-firing guns, otherwise known as close-in weapon systems (CIWS).

Anti-ship missiles can be programmed to follow any one of several different trajectories, including sea-skimming and diving from high angles of elevation, and several can arrive from different directions simultaneously, using multiple-waypoint manoeuvres (see Fig 1). To be effective against such attacks, the defensive system must have a very short reaction time, almost hemispherical coverage, and a high kill probability against multiple attacks.

* Respectively manager, Weapon Systems Engineering Group, and ship designer, Vosper Thornycroft (UK) Ltd.

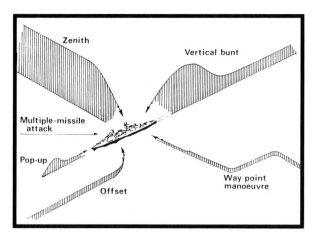

Left: **Figure 1**   Anti-ship missiles can be programmed to follow a variety of trajectories.

Below: **Seaguard search** (left) **and tracking radars.**

Right: **Figure 2**   Effect of dispersion/bias on single-shot hit probability.

Radar considerations

Of all the problems involved in defending a ship, those of detecting and tracking small targets close to the sea surface, at a sufficiently long range against a background of clutter and jamming, must be among the most difficult. The following examination of some of the major problems and possible solutions shows some of the decisions and compromises that the system designer must make.

Detection in clutter and jamming

● High power tends to burn through jamming but is comparatively difficult to control at high frequencies.

● Low frequencies are less susceptible to weather interference and have better atmospheric penetration; as a result, they give longer-range detection. Within reason, the choice of frequency has to fit into the frequency plan of the ship in order to avoid mutual interference.

● Increase in antenna height extends the radar horizon.

● There is now available a range of signal-processing techniques for tracking and detection to reduce the effects of clutter and jamming. They include frequency agility and pulse-to-pulse coherency, which decorrelate the clutter and force the jamming power to be spread over a wide frequency range: sidelobe suppression; fast Fourier transform (FFT) processing; moving-target indication (MTI); and coded waveform transmission.

Low-angle effects

● When the target is at a very low angle, lobes can be created in the radar beam, resulting in missed returns and nodding of trackers. In general, higher frequencies give a smaller resolution cell for a given size of antenna, permitting accurate tracking at the expense of long-range performance. Some systems use dual frequencies to overcome this effect.

● Increase in antenna height helps to increase the

range at which lobing occurs, and frequency agility tends to destroy the pattern.

● A common solution is to use integrated optronics sensors in conjunction with the radar tracker, ie TV/ infra-red tracking and laser rangefinders. Image-free tracking can then be obtained by whichever sensor is appropriate.

Minimum reaction time

● Minimum reaction time from detection to actual tracking is crucial. To detect and establish a track on a target can take between five and ten rotations of the search antenna, so the rotation rate must be high. To obtain enough pulses for processing, the pulse-repetition frequency (PRF) must be very high; the resulting "blind speed" problems can be overcome by staggering PRF.

● The tracker also needs time to acquire the target. This necessitates matching the detection radar window (target indication, TI) to the tracker radar window in terms of range and bearing resolution. If the TI window is large, time is lost by the tracker radar in scanning it. A small TI window depends on antenna dimensions and power output.

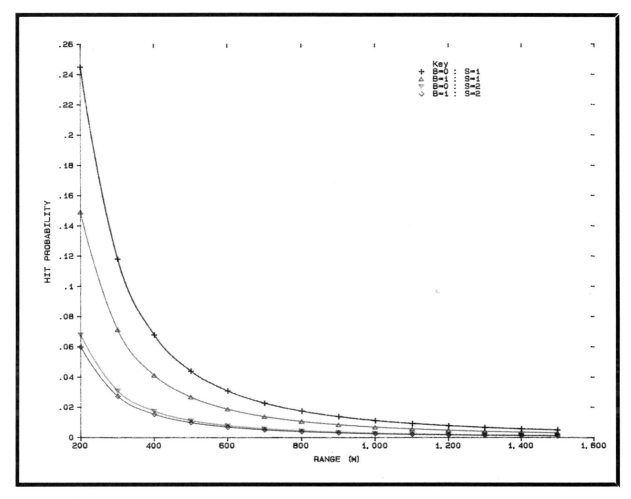

Coverage

● The sensor coverage volume required must be carefully considered. High-gain antennae give long-range detection but low angular coverage, so search rates are still low. The solution is to produce a multi-beam antenna using electronic-array processing with each PRF.

Gun requirements

Open-fire range

Maximum engagement range is defined as that point beyond which the system's random dispersion (**S**) and bias (**B**) make the hit probability unacceptably low. Bias errors can arise out of misalignment, incorrect setting of muzzle velocity, poor atmospheric data, and any uncompensated ship velocity or motion. Random errors are essentially those which are uncorrelated from round to round: ballistic dispersion (which is a function of burst length), general fire-control errors (due to target glint and scintillation), and the effects of support flexibility, which gives rise to structural deformation under recoil forces.

Assuming that the random errors in both the vertical and horizontal planes follow a Gaussian distribution, the probability **P** of a round falling within a circle radius **r** is given by:

$$P = (1 - e^{-r^2/2S^2}) . e^{-B^2/2S^2} \text{ for } S^2 < rB$$

(**r**, **S** and **B** all in millirads)

The effect of these factors on single-shot hit probabilities over a typical range bracket is shown in Fig 2.

Fortunately for the defender, the overall hit probability depends not only on the single-shot probability but also on the total number of shells fired at the missile over the engagement range. This in turn depends upon the rate of fire and missile speed. Fig 3 shows the overall hit probabilities for various combinations of rate of fire and missile speed for the single-shot probabilities shown in the lowest curve of Fig 2.

In practice there is a trade-off between rate of fire and accuracy. Larger guns are more accurate but their rate of fire is lower. It should be noted that accuracies are quoted in terms of angular rather than linear measure: ie, to hit a given size of target at 2nm requires twice the accuracy compared with that needed for the same target at 1nm.

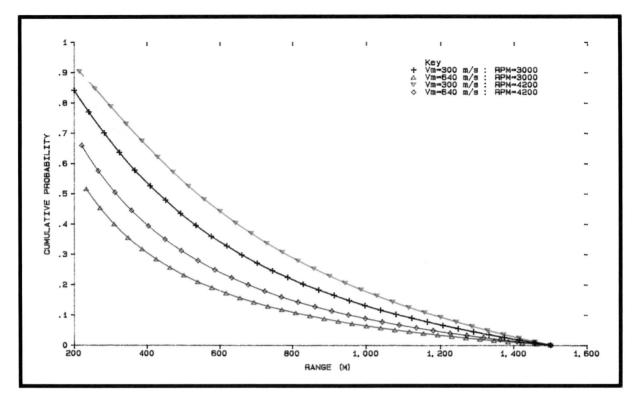

Key
+ Vm=300 m/s : RPM=3000
△ Vm=640 m/s : RPM=3000
▽ Vm=300 m/s : RPM=4200
◇ Vm=640 m/s : RPM=4200

Minimum range

It is not necessary for the missile to hit the ship in order to perform its destructive task: extensive damage can be caused by blast and fragmentation effects. In particular, antennae can suffer permanent damage at overpressures of $>5\text{lb/in}^2$, general structural distortion begins to occur at $>13\text{lb/in}^2$, and permanent structural damage occurs at $>30\text{lb/in}^2$. As a result, a missile warhead comprising, say, 200kg of RDX, must be destroyed at a range greater than 150m. The non-aerodynamic shape of blast fragments means that their energy is soon expended. Even so, depending on fragment mass, >150m is the minimum safety distance for damage by fragments.

Proximity-fuzed or direct-impact ammunition?

Not only must the gun system place the shells accurately, but each shell must have a high kill probability, through either a direct hit or a close fragmentation blast. A direct hit on a missile is necessary to detonate the warhead. If a proximity-fuzed shell does not obtain a direct hit, it will explode as it passes the missile. Shell fragments, together with the payload of high-density balls, will pierce the missile body and rupture the final guidance and control system, possibly causing the missile to ditch.

At ranges less than 600/700m it is necessary to explode the warhead. Below this range there is a high probability of the missile hitting the ship on a ballistic trajectory even if it is extensively damaged; this minimum ditching range increases with missile speed.

If proximity-fuzed ammunition is used at longer range, the time available for missile ditching is extended.

Proximity fuzes have to be smart enough to see the target and not be triggered by clutter or susceptible to ECM.

Muzzle velocity

A high muzzle velocity has several benefits: it gives a shorter time of flight (hence better prediction performance and flatter trajectories) and provides higher initial kinetic energy. To maximise muzzle velocity the shell in the barrel should present to the propelling gas a large area with low mass. In flight, to maintain velocity a low aerodynamic area and high mass are needed. The classic means of achieving high

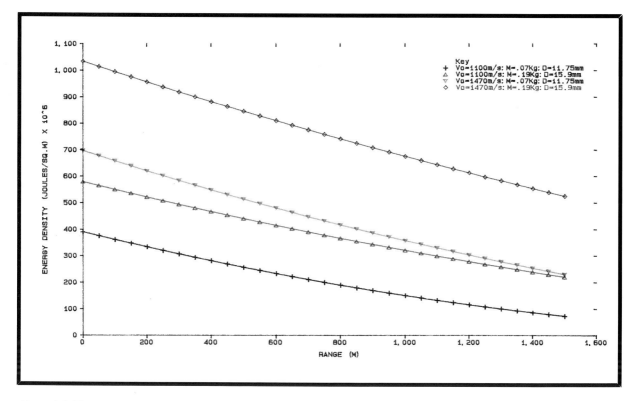

Key
+ Vo=1100m/s: M=.07Kg: D=11.75mm
△ Vo=1100m/s: M=.19Kg: D=15.9mm
▽ Vo=1470m/s: M=.07Kg: D=11.75mm
◇ Vo=1470m/s: M=.19Kg: D=15.9mm

Above left: **Figure 3   Effects of rate of fire and missile velocity on hit probability. B = 1, S = 2.**

Left: **Short burst of fire from Contraves Seaguard scores a direct hit on a small target at a range of 600m.**

Above: **Figure 4   Effect of shell mass and MV on energy density.**

Below right: **Figure 5   Errors in target plane. MA = missile actual position, MP = missile predicted position, BA = bullet actual position, BP = bullet predicted position.**

area/mass ratio in the barrel and low area/mass ratio in flight is the combination of discarding sabots and high-density bullets.

Warhead destruction

In order to explode the warhead the shell must be slender and stable enough to penetrate the frame and any surrounding armour and still have sufficient energy to detonate the explosive. Long, slender projectiles tend to be unstable in flight, so a compromise between in-flight stability and penetrating capability must be reached.

Modern explosives are extremely difficult to detonate. Even striking them with a hammer is not sufficient to cause detonation, a high energy density also being required. The latter is a function of muzzle-velocity decay and cross-sectional area, combined with missile velocity. The effects of muzzle velocity and shell size on energy density over a possible engage-

ment range are shown in Fig 4. A figure of about 10^9 joules/m^2 is often quoted as the threshold at which detonation is initiated.

Closed-loop fire control

This is a process whereby the system corrects the gun's aim by assessing the distance by which the round(s) have missed the target. Fig 5 shows the effect of errors in the target plane; ideally, both bullet and missile should pass through the point MP. There are two different types of error: those which are constant over a firing burst, known as systematic or fixed errors, and those which vary, known as random errors. The missile might not pass through the predicted position as a result of random errors caused by sensor glint or manoeuvre, or systematic errors due

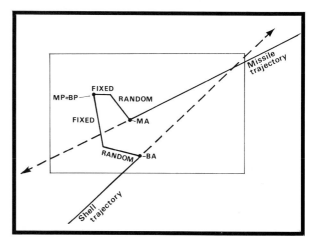

perhaps to poor velocity estimation; such errors are magnified by longer flight times. The shell might not pass through MP for similar reasons.

In practice the centre of gravity of a number of rounds would be measured, since trying to correct the trajectory on the basis of the random dispersion of a single round could be unreliable. It might take 0.5sec to measure the bias caused by the systematic errors and apply it to the next shell. Thus these corrections do not come into effect until (0.5 + time of flight) seconds after the engagement starts, ie, towards the end of the engagement.

In measuring the miss distances the objective is to obtain an unbiased estimate of the average miss distance; this will not be achieved if part of the burst pattern is missed by the measuring radar.

Despite the problems of measurement and application, closed-loop fire control must increase system effectiveness, particularly in longer-range engagements. It is not however an alternative to good system design, which must have as its objective the minimising of random and systematic errors.

Multi-barrel operation

In order to achieve a high firing rate, either separate asynchronous cannon or rotating gatling-type barrels are used. The use of the Gatling principle eliminates parallax problems but introduces potential inaccuracies associated with the dynamics of moving barrels. At the expense of a decrease in accuracy, the Gatling's barrel wear and mean time between failures must be lower for a given firing rate.

System aspects

A major consideration in the choice of a CIWS is the degree of integration of the various components. At one extreme there are highly integrated modular systems in which surveillance radar, tracker, vertical reference and gun are mounted very close together and operate as a single autonomous system. At the other are systems comprising physically separate units functionally linked together.

A high degree of physical integration is beneficial, eliminating parallax problems and the effects of the ship's bending and twisting. Of the latter, one of the most troublesome is apparent target velocity error as a result of relative movement between the tracker and vertical reference. Integration problems are reduced or eliminated, and to a degree such a system can give better performance and a faster reaction time.

However, the dedication of expensive equipment to one function is not economical, while in a less modularised system it might be possible to mount the

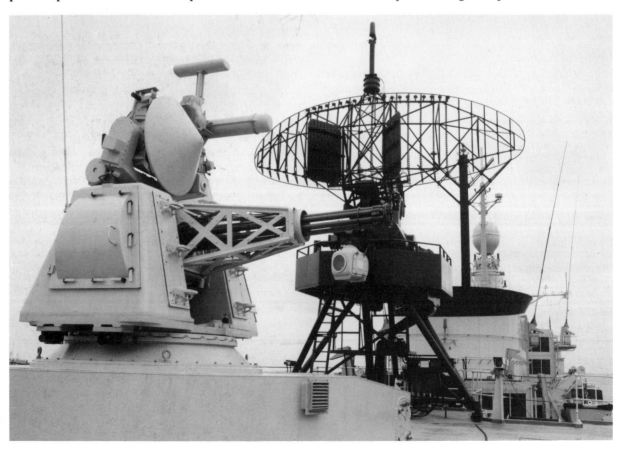

component so as to improve their individual coverage. A centralised detection system can exploit information from sources in addition to the surveillance radar, such as data links and electronic support measures (ESM). Finally, in a totally modular system the failure of a major component could be disastrous, since there are fewer reversionary modes than in a more loosely federated system.

Whatever configuration is chosen, both tracker and gun mount need very high slew and elevation rates to counteract sea motion and deal with sequential attack over a wide area. While CIWS are largely intended for point defence, they have to be able to cope with the very high crossing rates generated by missiles aimed at distant parts of a large ship.

The location of the CIWS in the vessel is generally a compromise. To avoid stability problems it is best to keep a system low down on the ship. However, this very often conflicts with the need to establish good operating arcs. In an integrated system, the effect of radar sidelobes on surrounding structure might give rise to a higher false-alarm rate.

When the sensors are separated from the gun mounting, misalignment or flexure of structure between devices can cause confusion. Stabilisation systems can be fitted at each position, but they must be good enough to give the increased pointing accuracy required by a hard-kill CIWS.

Fire-control channels should offer balanced cover around the ship, with each positioned to optimise the firing arcs. In particular, firing arcs should overlap as far as possible, to minimise dead zones lacking defensive cover. Fig 6 indicates a position providing good CIWS firing arcs.

Left: **Hollandse Signaalapparaten Goalkeeper mounted on the helicopter hangar of the Dutch *Kortenaer*-class frigate *Callenburgh*.**

Below: **Figure 6   Vosper Thornycroft Vita missile corvette fitted with Contraves Seaguard CIWS. The location of the system in this application gives good aft firing arcs, unrestricted by structure and equipment.**

A mounting high in the ship structure can create problems of ammunition supply from magazines below the waterline. Too large a ready-use magazine increases stability problems and makes the vessel more vulnerable to action damage. However, enough ready-use ammunition must be available to cope with the predicted weight of attack.

Some CIWS interface directly with other sensors such as ESM, while others operate independently or interface through the action information organisation (AIO). In the last case, the command team must be able to relate the situation presented by the AIO to target data from the CIWS. The weapon system engineer must therefore consider how CIWS information can be handled so that target identifications are correlated with those of the overall weapon system. Even when control of CIWS relies simply on a veto from the AIO, it still makes sense for vetoed data to be available to the command team.

CIWS: the choice

Some of the systems currently available are outlined below. No information on Phalanx was releasable for publication.

HSA Goalkeeper

This system, completely integrated on a single mounting, comprises a surveillance radar, dual-frequency tracking radar, fire-control unit, and GAU-8/A seven-barrel 30mm Gatling gun. Operation is automatic from target detection to kill assessment, termination of firing and selection of next target.

The I-band surveillance radar has good electronic counter-countermeasures (ECCM) features and a high antenna speed. Advanced processing techniques, including digital pulse compression and fast Fourier transform techniques, give good detection of very small targets in dense clutter environments. The threat evaluation and target designation module automatically determines threat priority and initiates the engagement. The train and elevation drives of the mounting are controlled by digital servos. High-bandwidth servo loops eliminate pointing errors due to ship's motion. High-speed servo motors and a high control data rate make possible a very responsive and fast-slewing mount, necessary for engagement of multiple fast-moving targets with the 30mm Gatling gun.

Bofors Trinity

This is a fully integrated, stand-alone system. It differs from the other systems in having a single manned 40mm gun. Day and night sighting is included, with or without laser rangefinding. A fire-control radar and associated fire control can be fitted. Trinity

need not be autonomous, receiving instructions instead from a central fire-control system.

The servo system is sufficiently precise and fast-acting to handle both the fire-control radar and the gun mounting. It has the damping ability and power to slew the mounting with the necessary accuracies. This is achieved by a precision hydraulic drive using microprocessor-implemented servo control. The built-in heading attitude reference compensates for ship hull flexure.

Above: **Bofors Trinity is unique among the systems described here in having a manned turret.**

Right: **Breda-Bofors L70 40mm gun mounting.**

Below: **Selenia-Elsag NA30 with Breda-Bofors L70 40mm guns.** *(Selenia)*

The acquisition and fire-control radars are designed to provide maximum resistance to jamming by use of frequency agility, binary pulse compression, and MTI. In extreme jamming conditions the IR tracker and laser rangefinder take over.

Selenia-Elsag NA30

This system's sensors and weapons are mounted separately. It can control both surface-to-air missiles, normally the Selenia Albatros, and medium/short-range guns, handling three guns at once and being capable of ballistic calculations for two different calibres. The guns normally associated with NA30 are the Oto Melara 76/62 and the Breda-Bofors 40/70 twin. The system can also supply target information to surface-to-surface missiles. Automatic reaction to high-speed aerial targets includes threat evaluation and assignment of the most appropriate weapon.

The basic NA30 comprises the Orion 30X tracking radar fitted with an infra-red thermal camera and a closed-circuit daylight TV; transmitter and receiver units for the tracking radar; supervision console; data-processing unit; and servo unit. The system has all the interfaces needed for full integration with the ship's main surveillance radar, weapons and data network.

Contraves Seaguard

Similar to NA30 in having sensors and weapons on different pedestals, Seaguard includes:
● A dual-beam C-band radar for surveillance, detection and indication of missile targets as well as general air and surface targets in severe ECM conditions.
● A three-axis, multi-sensor (Ku-band radar, forward-looking infra-red laser) tracking mount.
● A canted two-axis gun mount with four Type KBB 25mm independent cannon.

Seaguard is modular in design, with distributed processors linked by data bus permitting the system to be readily reconfigured and giving the capacity to control other weapons such as medium-calibre guns and SAMs. The radars are ECM-resistant, with high data rates.

The "Zenith" capability avoids limits in performance against high-speed diving targets above 55°, where missiles can be countered irrespective of their terminal trajectories. The high tracker/gun mount dynamics allow high-speed crossing targets to be countered throughout the hemisphere.

Marconi-Breda Sea Cobra

Sea Cobra comprises a Breda Compact 30mm naval mounting with the director of a Marconi 400-series tracking radar mounted on top. The system is fully automatic from detection of the threat by the radar in its surveillance mode, through lock-on and tracking, to the point where the target is in range and the operator fires the gun.

The radar units (transmitter, signal processor, synthesiser, data extractor) are carried in the gun cupola. A separate control console carries all radar and gun controls, together with radar and TV displays. It also houses the predictor, which gives linear and goal-orientated options for four types of ammunition.

The radar has an all-weather capability, operating in I and J-band. The surveillance radar provides a high data rate, scanning at 60rpm. It is frequency-agile, yielding powerful ECCM features and minimising multi-path effects, and coherent, increasing sub-clutter visibility. The system is gyro-stabilised for precision tracking.

The ideal CIWS

The ideal close-in weapon system offers the following:
● Reliable, long-range target detection over a wide coverage arc, with sophisticated ECCM, anti-clutter and all-weather capability.
● Fast reaction time, with completely automatic functioning from threat evaluation and designation to destruction.
● Image-free tracking from dual-frequency radars together with whatever sensor(s) are appropriate for the conditions.
● Accurate fire control incorporating automatic spotting corrections, particularly for longer-range engagements, and curved-course prediction for use against missiles with pre-programmed course-change capabilities.
● High-response mount with "stiff" servos for rapid reaction and engagement of close-in targets, and wide arcs of fire.

Above: **Seaguard demonstrates its maximum-elevation capability.**

Below: **The Marconi-Breda Sea Cobra combines a Breda Compact 30mm gun mounting with the British company's 400-series tracking radar, mounted on top of the turret.** *(Marconi)*

- Cannon with high muzzle velocity and rate of fire.
- Ammunition with low ballistic dispersion and high energy content, plus proximity-fuzed rounds for use at longer ranges.

Most of these attributes could be embodied in a modular fire-control system consisting of a single very accurate medium-range gun (40mm or 57mm) with close associated radar and optronics trackers and vertical reference. Target detection, selection and designation would be carried out by a separate centralised facility. Separately mounted but driven from the same fire-control system would be a high-rate-of-fire 30mm Gatling gun. Being more accurate, the medium-range gun would fire proximity-fuzed ammunition, opening fire at a range in excess of 2m. The 30mm multi-barrel mount would open fire at a range of about 1,200m. This would maximise the kill probability over the total range bracket. Such a composite system might be expected to give the kill probabilities shown in Fig 7.

Conclusion

Despite developments in close-in weapon systems, the initiative still lies with the attacking missile. It will do so for the foreseeable future, due particularly to the development of the supersonic missile, which will reduce engagement times to seconds. Advances in armour technology will make the missile warhead even harder to detonate. It is conceivable that the continuing trend in robust micro-electronics will lead to "smart" small-calibre bullets, allowing trajectory corrections to be made in flight. All things considered, the gun will remain a worthwhile means of producing an affordable kill well into the next century.

Figure 7   Cumulative kill probability for combination gun. Missile velocity = 640m/sec.

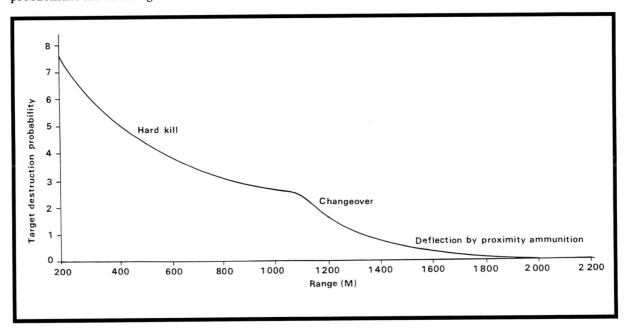

Anti-ship missiles: no let-up for defences

Roy Braybrook

An MBB Kormoran anti-ship missile spears into the flank of a target ship. *(MBB)*

IF WIRE-GUIDED torpedoes are disregarded, then anti-ship missiles began with Germany's aircraft-launched Fritz-X (FX-1400) of the Second World War. A radio-controlled glide bomb weighing 3,500lb (1,590kg), it was first used operationally by the Dornier Do217K-2s of KG100 on September 9, 1943, in an attempt to prevent Italian warships falling into Allied hands. Two direct hits on the battleship *Roma* caused a fire which led to a catastrophic explosion in the main magazine, but a single hit on her sister ship the *Italia* did not prevent this vessel from reaching Malta.

The Fritz-X was also employed against Allied warships supporting the landings near Salerno, along with the Henschel Hs293, which was also radio-controlled but had a liquid-fuel rocket motor for increased range. The Hs293 weighed 2,175lb (975kg) at launch and cruised at 450mph (720km/hr). Six ships were sunk and damage was done to a further 10, including the RN battleship *Warspite* and cruiser *Uganda* and the USN cruiser *Savannah*.

The Japanese lacked the electronic sophistication needed to produce such command-guided missiles, so they developed a manned missile, the Yokosuka MXY-7 *Ohka* (Cherry Blossom). This was dropped from Mitsubishi G4M2e Betty bombers at a launch weight of 4,720lb (2,140kg), of which the warhead amounted to 2,650lb (1,200kg). A solid-fuel rocket motor gave a stand-off range of up to 55 miles (88km), although a longer-range turbojet-powered version was also studied. The *Ohka* was first used operationally on March 21, 1945, but on this occasion all the launch aircraft were shot down before they could release their missiles. It is probably fair to say that the threat of the *Ohka* system and suicide attacks with conventional aircraft was restricted to manageable proportions by standing patrols of carrier-based fighters and proximity-fuzed AAA fire.

In the early post-war years there was little effort in the West to develop anti-ship missiles, probably because the German guided weapons were regarded as desperate last-ditch efforts that gave results only against docile, undefended targets. The only major success had been the *Roma*, which had mistaken the Dorniers for friendly aircraft. In any event, there was no threat of war, and no funds for unnecessary R&D efforts.

The Korean War of 1950–53 provided little opportunity for anti-shipping strikes, but the US Navy experienced substantial losses from AAA when attacking land targets such as bridges. This led to the development of the command-guided Martin ASM-N-7 Bullpup, which weighed 540lb (245kg) at launch, carried a standard 250lb (113kg) warhead from a Mk 82 bomb, and achieved a range of 3.0 miles (4.8km) on the power of a solid-fuel rocket motor. Its light weight enabled the FJ-4B Fury (the USN derivative of the F-86 Sabre) to carry five rounds, and its small size and Mach 2 cruise made it a very difficult target. On the other hand, its stand-off range proved too short once targets were defended by surface-to-air missiles (SAMs), as happened subsequently in Vietnam, and command guidance has severe limitations. Although cheap, simple and resistant to jamming, this system required the launch aircraft to continue towards the target until the missile impacted. In addition, the pilot (who was watching flares on the missile and flying it by means of a miniature stick) could control only one round at once, and could be distracted by tracer fire. Bullpup was first deployed on the FJ-4Bs of attack squadron VA-212 which sailed in USS *Lexington* in April 1959 to join the 7th Fleet in the Western Pacific.

The Vietnam War (1965–75) again produced few naval targets, but Bullpup was used by both the USN and USAF against bridges. It worked reasonably well against all but the Thanh Hoa bridge, and this led to the development of a "Big Bullpup" with a 1,000lb (454kg) warhead. In 1967 this was supplemented by the Walleye TV-guided glide bomb, which has a limited stand-off capability and the same size of warhead. Walleye gave a much smaller miss distance, but it was still limited to daylight clear-weather operation, and did not provide adequate stand-off range in the presence of SAMs. The first SA-2 kill (an F-4C) occurred on July 24, 1965, and within two years around 200 SAM sites, including mobile batteries, were in operation in North Vietnam.

Various other anti-ship missiles were developed in the West during the early 1960s, but this aspect of armament received comparatively little attention until the Yom Kippur War of October 1967, when the Israeli destroyer *Eilat* was sunk by three SS-N-2 Styx surface-to-surface missiles (SSMs) fired by two Egyptian Komar-class fast patrol boats (FPBs). In spite of the fact that missiles such as Styx represented a threat primarily in coastal waters, the West initiated several urgent development programmes to defend its warships against stand-off attacks by sinking the vessels from which such attacks might be carried out.

By the early 1980s several Western anti-ship missiles had been deployed, and two of the new types were used in the Falklands War of 1982. Most of the publicity went to the Aérospatiale AM.39 Exocet, which was launched from Argentinian Navy Super Etendards, immobilising the Type 42 destroyer *Sheffield* on May 4 and destroying the container ship

Aérospatiale AM.39 Exocet seen just after launch from a Mirage F.1. *(Cazaux Flight Test Centre)*

Atlantic Conveyor on May 25. In the case of the *Sheffield*, the official British account states that "the missile hit fuel tanks amidships and serious fires started, which filled the central section of the ship with acrid smoke. After nearly four hours, with the fires increasing in intensity, the captain gave orders to abandon ship." *Altantic Conveyor* was hit by two Exocets (according to the British Ministry of Defence). The ship was set on fire and abandoned with the loss of 12 lives. But a third attack on the Task Force (on May 30) was countered successfully by means of helicopter decoys and chaff rockets. In addition, on the night of June 11/12 two Exocets were fired from a shore base against the destroyer *Glamorgan*. One of them hit, but the resulting fire was extinguished and the ship remained available for action. In total, seven Exocets were fired in all, of which four hit their targets, according to the Ministry of Defence. An independent study claims that *Atlantic Conveyor* received only one hit, reducing the successes to three.

Apart from providing a first indication of the hit probability likely to be obtained with Exocet, the Falklands War illustrated various aspects of anti-ship missile attacks. For example, all the air-launched attacks were based on preliminary target data from external sources. On May 4 the target was shadowed by an SP-2H Neptune, and later attacks used target data provided by the radar controllers at Port Stanley (by tracking the carriers' aircraft). Second, although the Super Etendard pilots could designate individual radar targets for attack, they had no means of identifying them. In the case of the May 25 attack, the pilots saw three radar returns and both fired at the largest, imagining it to be one of the carriers. In reality

it was *Atlantic Conveyor* with containers stacked three-high along either deck-edge to minimise salt-water damage to the aircraft parked on deck. At the time of the strike the carriers *Hermes* and *Invincible* were respectively only 2nm (3.7km) and 10nm (18.5km) away from the target.

The air-launched Exocets were fired at 24–31nm (44–57km), giving a flight time of 2.5–3.0min, the missile switching on its active-homing radar at 30sec from impact. Reports at the time indicated that at least one of the missiles that hit did not actually explode, and that Exocet impacted well above the waterline. In theory the Super Etendards should have been detected by the targets' radars at the launch point, and the aircraft and Exocet radars by electronic support measures (ESM) systems. However, it has been reported that at the time of the attack *Sheffield*'s main radar was switched off because she was using satellite communications, and that (although MoD states that "countermeasures to deal with Exocet were available to the task force") the ship was ill-prepared to deal with a missile strike, unlike *Glasgow*.

In principle a single Exocet launched under daylight clear-weather conditions may be vulnerable to the British Seawolf SAM, although it is not clear whether this is true for an Exocet at minimum sea-skimming height. It is known that in the attack of May 25 the Seawolf-equipped Type 22 frigate *Brilliant* picked up

---

An MM.40 Exocet is test-fired from the French Navy frigate *Premier Maître l'Her*. This version of Exocet can take target data from external sources, including helicopters. This permits over-the-horizon targetting. *(Aérospatiale)*

Above: **British Aerospace Sea Skua mounted on a Sea King helicopter of the West German Navy.** *(BAe)*

Right: **Main components of Sea Skua.** *(BAe)*

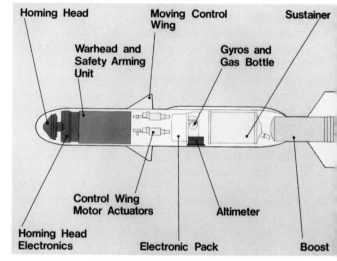

Homing Head — Moving Control Wing — Sustainer

Warhead and Safety Arming Unit — Gyros and Gas Bottle

Control Wing Motor Actuators — Altimeter

Homing Head Electronics — Electronic Pack — Boost

the two Exocets on its radar but did not open fire because they were out of range.

Exocets are reported to have been used in large numbers by Iraq in attacks on ships in the Arabian Gulf in the course of the war with Iran. Although the hit probability appears to be high, the most likely result seems to be damage that is uneconomical to repair (rather than the ship sinking), and there have been some cases of the missile failing to explode. Iraq is also believed to have fired large anti-ship missiles, probably Soviet AS-5 Kelts, from Tu-16 maritime strike aircraft. Iran has used the TV-guided Hughes AGM-65 Maverick.

Returning to the Falklands War, another missile used operationally for the first time was the British Aerospace Sea Skua, which was fired against various Argentinian patrol boats by Royal Navy Lynx helicopters. According to the Ministry of Defence, it scored eight hits with eight firings, destroying one patrol craft and seriously damaging two other ships.

Apart from the Exocet and Sea Skua, which are both modern, sea-skimming missiles, the conflict saw operational use of the older AS.12 wire-guided missile. In the retaking of South Georgia a total of eight were fired by two RN Wasps against the Argentinian submarine *Santa Fé*, which had been depth-charged by a Wessex and was running on the surface. Four missiles hit the conning tower, and the submarine limped back to Grytviken and sank beside the jetty.

Basic requirements

The history of anti-ship guided missiles can be said to fall into two generations, the first consisting mainly of small command-guidance weapons and some larger Soviet missiles with homing systems, and the second being represented by sea-skimming homing weapons, many of which were developed in direct response to the Styx threat.

In discussing today's missiles, it is convenient to start with a broad outline of the requirements that they may be designed to meet. For any nation that develops its own armaments, there is a strong argument in favour of a single weapon type that can be launched from land, sea and air, and possibly also by submarines. If a single type is to be used, it should be capable of day/night all-weather operation, which suggests radar guidance. On the other hand, if two or more types can be used, there are strong attractions in imaging infra-red (IIR), which in principle can provide target identification and a hit on the ship's most vulnerable area, given suitable atmospheric conditions. Likewise, it would be foolish to rely completely on an anti-radar missile (since the target may cease transmissions), though such a weapon would be very useful in conjunction with one using active radar homing.

Missile range should be sufficient to keep the launch vehicle beyond the reach of the target's defences. If the target is an FPB, then a missile range of about 8nm (15km) is enough. Conversely an attack on a carrier battle group must take into account wide-ranging defences. In order to exploit firing opportunities at extreme radar range, a weapon range of perhaps 200nm (370km) is needed, clearly demanding an air-breathing engine. However, even longer ranges can be achieved when mid-course guidance updates are available, the Soviet AS-3 Kangaroo having a reported range of 350nm (650km) and the AS-X-15 1,600nm (3,000km). On the other hand, range (like warload and cruise speed) has a direct effect on launch weight and production cost. The AS-3 weighs around 17,600lb (8,000kg), while at the opposite end of the scale the Aérospatiale AS.15TT anti-FPB missile weighs a mere 212lb (96kg) at launch. The low weight and moderate cost of

the AS.15TT also reflects the fact that it employs automatic command guidance, the Thomson-CSF Agrion 15 radar of the SA.365 helicopter tracking both missile and target, and generating corrective signals. Agrion also enables the helicopter to supply its parent vessel with the co-ordinates of over-the-horizon targets for engagement by surface-to-surface missiles.

One of the limitations of the simpler forms of command guidance is the fact that only one missile can be guided at once. As a result, the launch vehicle has no chance to swamp the target's defences with a ripple firing. It is also desirable that the weapon system should be able to engage ships lying close to the shoreline. Various reports have suggested that Exocet (with active radar homing) was unable to attack ships of the British landing force when they were at anchor in San Carlos Water. Norway's Kongsberg Penguin was developed specifically as an anti-invasion weapon capable of attacking a specific ship in a formation, even among small islands. To meet this requirement it has an infra-red (IR) target seeker and can be programmed in altitude to clear intervening

---

This Aérospatiale SA.365F Dauphin 2 carries four AS.15TT missiles and the Thomson-CSF Agrion 15 nose-mounted radar. *(Aérospatiale)*

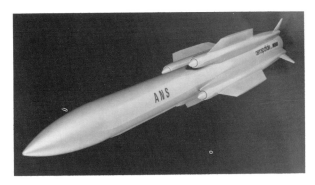

Above: **Mock-up of the Aérospatiale/MBB ANS *(Anti-Navire Supersonique)* anti-ship missile, which is powered by rocket boosters and ramjets.** *(MBB)*

Below: **For submarine launch the Harpoon is enclosed in a buoyant capsule that is fired from a torpedo tube. At the surface the capsule ends are jettisoned and the booster ignites.** *(MDC)*

Below right: **This Harpoon has just cleared its shipboard launch canister. The wings have unfolded and the tail surfaces are partially extended.** *(MDC)*

(3m). The BAe Sea Eagle measures wave height and adjusts its cruise height accordingly.

Penetration capability also depends on missile speed. Most existing ASMs cruise at around Mach 0.9, but the ANS *(Anti-Navire Supersonique)* being developed by Aérospatiale and MBB will fly at more than Mach 2.0. China's rocket-powered ship-to-ship FL-7 has a maximum speed of Mach 1.4. The Soviet Union's AS-4 Kitchen is credited with Mach 2+, and the AS-6 Kingfish with Mach 3. High speed reduces warning time and firing and jamming opportunities for the defences, increases the defences' miss distance, and, since the target has less time to change position, delays the point at which the missile's homing system must be switched on.

The chances of a successful penetration are also improved if the missile guidance permits a dogleg course, so that the attack can come from an unexpected quarter or from behind terrain. Such a capability was demanded from the outset in the case of Penguin, and it is one of the improvements introduced with the Block 1C model of the McDonnell Douglas Harpoon, which has three programmable waypoints.

The missile's effectiveness is likewise increased if it has small visual, radar and IR signatures, and if it presents the defences with a very small target. The more sophisticated missiles may be able to identify a chaff cloud by its movement relative to the main body of the target. Susceptibility to jamming is reduced if the homing system is activated very late in flight. Harpoon has a home-on-jam facility. The Block 1B model introduced a sea-skimming terminal phase at the request of the RN, but it retains the original pop-up and dive attack capability, developed to spoil the

terrain. The BAe Sea Skua was also designed to attack ships among islands, using semi-active radar homing.

The ability of an ASM to penetrate defences may be enhanced in various ways. For example, sea-skimming height should be the minimum consistent with the existing sea state. After a Seawolf successfully engaged an Exocet during RN trials in 1983, Aérospatiale pointed out that the MM.38 had been set to fly at its highest level, some 26ft (8m), whereas sea conditions would have allowed a true sea-skimming height of 10ft

fire-control solution of radar-directed close-in weapon systems (CIWS).

Most anti-ship missiles have a blast warhead with a time delay on the contact fuze to optimise damage effects. However, missiles employing a terminal dive could be fitted with directional warheads (eg, shaped charges and self-forging slugs) to combine blast effects with holes below the waterline.

Typical examples

The basic operational demands outlined above can be illustrated by examples from the various ASM categories. The AS.15TT, mentioned earlier, is a lightweight anti-FPB weapon that delivers a 66lb (30kg) warhead over a range of 8nm (15km), using automatic command guidance. One direct competitor is the BAe Sea Skua, which is rather heavier at 324lb (147kg) and employs semi-active radar guidance. This permits ripple firing and gives the launch helicopter more freedom of manoeuvre. Sea Skua also features a multi-step flightpath with a very low terminal sea-skim height which is matched to the target's CIWS range.

The Hughes AGM-65 Maverick is rather larger, weighing around 465lb (210kg) at launch; the difference is the result of a heavier warhead rather than longer range. Two versions may be used for anti-ship strikes: the TV-guided AGM-65B with a 125lb (57kg) shaped charge, and the IIR-guided AGM-65F with a 300lb (136kg) combined blast/penetration warhead. In firings against ground targets both types of guidance are very restricted in range, but this is far less of a problem in anti-ship operations. For naval use the IIR guidance has been modified to give a central strike just above the waterline.

Italy's Sistel Marte 2 helicopter-launched missile is

Above: **Test firing of a Harpoon from the US Navy hydrofoil *High Point*. Following surface/subsurface launches a rocket booster accelerates the missile to flying speed.** *(MDC)*

Below: **Project test pilot Lt-Cdr Terry Callaghan inspects an AGM-65F infra-red Maverick air-to-surface missile before flight. Callaghan piloted the A-7 Corsair II launch aircraft for three successful firings of infra-red Maverick against target vessels off the Californian coast.** *(Hughes Aircraft)*

an active radar-homing derivative of the company's ship-launched, command-guidance Sea Killer 2, which serves with the Iranian Navy. Marte 2 weighs 705lb (320kg) and has a range in excess of 11nm (20km). Norway's Penguin is in the same weight category. The Mk 1 is now operational on 76 frigates and fast attack craft in four navies. The aircraft-launched Mk 2 is planned for use on the F-16 and has a maximum range of 14.5nm (27km). The helicopter version, the Mk 2 Mod 7, has folding wings. The Mk 3 for the USN's LAMPS III advanced shipborne helicopter has a new two-stage motor and a range of 21.5nm (40km). Range is not restricted by the IR sensor, which can search for the target autonomously. The missiles of Israel Aircraft Industries' Gabriel series weigh up to 1,325lb (600kg), and the air-launched Mk III has a range of over 32nm (60km). Gabriel employs active radar homing, cruises at 65ft (20m), and can go down to 5ft (1.5m) in the terminal phase. Provision is made for a mid-course update from the launch aircraft. The 108nm (200km) Gabriel IV is under development.

Exocet is the best known example of the larger rocket-powered, sea-skimming category. The MBB Kormoran is in broadly the same class, with a 1,390lb (630kg) launch weight, but was designed to accept a

more sophisticated warhead incorporating 16 directional charges. Reports suggest that rocket-powered missiles in this weight class can achieve ranges of around 40nm (70km), but such figures may assume high-altitude firings.

Greater ranges demand air-breathing engines, as in the case of the McDonnell Douglas AGM-84 Harpoon, which can be fired from aircraft, surface ships, submarines and helicopters. Typical of missiles in this class, Harpoon is normally fed with target range and bearing information by the launch vehicle, although it can be fired with only bearing data. In practice the USN would use Harpoon in combination with Standard anti-radar missiles, noise jamming, tactical air strikes and Tomahawk cruise missiles. It is estimated that a destroyer would be put out of action by two Harpoon hits, a cruiser by four, and a *Kiev* or *Moskva*-class ship by five.

The BAe Sea Eagle has a launch weight of around 1,325lb (600kg) and is officially stated to have a longer range and better target discrimination than Exocet. It is also claimed to have a larger warhead than any existing Western anti-ship missile. It is operational on RAF Buccaneers and RN Sea Harriers, and will also be used on Indian Navy Sea Kings. The Saab-Bofors RBS15 is in the same weight and range category. It was designed initially for use on torpedo boats, although an air-launched version is also under development. It will supersede the old Saab 04E active-radar homing missiles and the 05A command-guided weapon. One of the largest missiles in this class is the Oto Melara/Matra Otomat, with a launch weight

of 1,700lb (770kg), maximum range of 100nm (180km) and 465lb (210kg) warhead. However, even this pales in comparison with the General Dynamics/McDonnell Douglas Tomahawk BGM-109 cruise missile, which has a launch weight of around 2,650lb (1,200kg) and delivers a 1,000lb (450kg) Bullpup warhead over a distance of 240nm (450km).

Below: **The BAe Sea Eagle, first developed for use on fixed-wing aircraft, is now being adapted for operation from Indian Navy Sea Kings.** *(BAe)*

Bottom: **Main components of the BAe Sea Eagle turbojet-powered anti-ship missile.** *(BAe)*

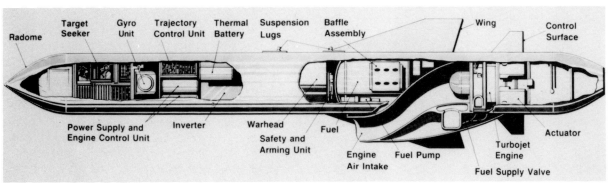

Above: The Saab RBS15 anti-ship missile has been selected for service with the Swedish Navy and Air Force. Seen here is project manager Hans Ahlinder with a full-scale mock-up of the weapon. *(Saab-Scania)*

Left: A Matra/Oto Melara Otomat coastal defence missile leaves its container at the start of a 54nm (100km) test flight. *(Matra)*

Below: The General Dynamics/McDonnell Douglas Tomahawk is the largest Western anti-ship missile, weighing 2,650lb (1,200kg). *(MDC)*

Mix-and-match MEKOs mean export success

Geoffrey Wood

MEKO 360 frigate *Almirante Brown* of the Argentinian Navy.

FOR some time now the manufacturers of equipment for merchant vessels, particularly in the ancillary machinery sector, have been providing shipbuilders with "packaged" systems. Comprising a principal system such as air-conditioning mounted with all its pumps, control gear and other necessary equipment on a common base, such packages are fully operational as soon as the service connections have been made. With the added advantage of having been factory-tested before delivery, packages minimise installation problems, thereby reducing fitting-out time and cost.

About 15 years ago the West German shipbuilder Blohm und Voss, all too aware of the need at least to put a brake on warship cost escalation, saw that packaging, developed to the ultimate, would yield

Operating Theatre

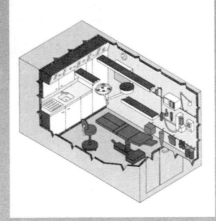

Medical Treatment

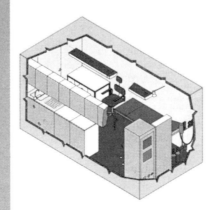

Accommodation

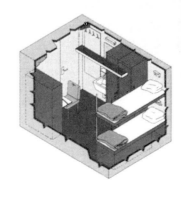

Sanitary Unit

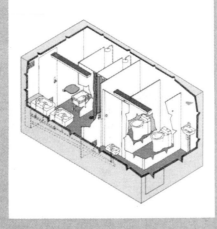

NBC-Decontamination

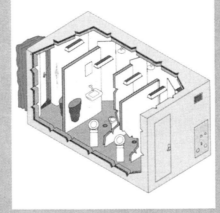

Ventilation

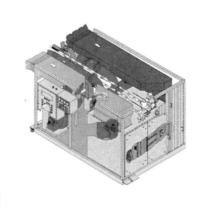

Damage Control Unit (Diver)

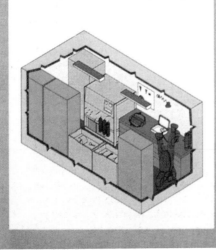

Opening and Passage System

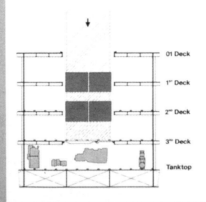

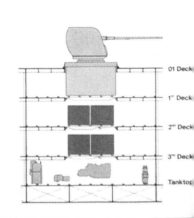

major economies in naval construction. The result was the Multi-role Combination Construction Principle (MEKO), whereby a range of standard hulls – in effect weapon platforms – could be fitted with a variety of containerised weapon and electronic systems, and main and auxiliary machinery. These Functional Units (FES) would be standard-sized and interchangeable, and would have standard interfaces with the basic ship platform. Where containers were inappropriate – as in the case of consoles within a combat information centre, for example – standard pallets would be used.

The MEKO/FES concept not only enabled a standard hull to be used with a wide variety of weapon fits, but was also expected to have advantages during building, maintenance, refit and modernisation. These were seen to be:

• Time and cost savings as a result of parallel construction and outfitting of hull and Functional Units.
• Non-disturbance of units after factory completion and testing.
• Time and cost savings by eliminating duplication of factory setting-up aboard ship.
• Clear division of responsibility between equipment manufacturer and shipbuilder.
• Rapid removal and replacement of Functional Units without disturbing other onboard systems.
• Refit and repair of Functional Units in clean conditions ashore.
• Replacement of obsolete weapon and electronic systems without the need for major structural alterations.

It was argued that under the MEKO/FES concept a comparatively light weapon fit would have an unnecessarily large platform. However, it has been calculated that in the worst case the over-displacement could not exceed 2% and that this was far outweighed by the advantages of the system.

Design studies were so promising that it was decided in 1969 to develop the concept thoroughly. As the Functional Units would be the most important components, construction of a typical example – an Oto Melara 76mm gun on a prototype container – began in 1971. The unit was installed in the Federal German Navy destroyer Z4, and successful sea trials were completed the following year. An electronic container was outfitted with a Krupp Atlas 80 sonar in 1975 and successfully trialled in 1976.

The Nigerian Government was among the first to be persuaded of the concept's merits, ordering a MEKO 360 (3,600 tonnes) frigate in November 1977. Construction of this first vessel proved beyond doubt the worth of the system in terms of time and therefore money. First steel was cut in December 1978, the first section laid on the slip in May 1979, the vessel was launched in January 1980 and she commissioned in February 1982. A total of only 38 months from start to completion is exceptionally fast by contemporary standards.

About a year later Argentina ordered four MEKO 360.H2s, capable of operating two helicopters. The first of these took only 30 months from laying down to commissioning, reduced to 14 months for the last of the series.

The differing outfits of the Nigerian and Argentinian 360s, on a common hull measuring 125.6m length overall × 15.0m beam × 4.30m draught and 3,600 tonnes full-load displacement, are tabled below to illustrate the flexibility of the system:

	Nigerian MEKO 360	Argentinian MEKO 360.H2
Propulsion	CODOG 2 × RR Olympus TM3B 2 × MTU 20V.956 TB92	COGAG 2 × RR Olympus TM3B 2 × RR Tyne RM.1C
Armament	8 × Otomat Mk1 SSM 1 × Albatros SAM system 1 × 127mm Oto-Melara gun 4 × Breda twin 40mm AA 6 × 324mm ASW torpedo tubes	8 × Exocet MM.40 SSM 1 × Albatros SAM system 1 × 127mm Oto-Melara gun 4 × Breda twin 40mm AA 6 × ILAS-33 324mm torpedo tubes
Radar	Decca 1226, Plessey ASW.5D, Signaal WM.25 and STIR	Signaal ZW.06, DA.08A, WM.25, STIR and 2 × LIROD
Sonar	Signaal PHS.32	Krupp Atlas 80
Electronic warfare equipment	2 × Breda SLAR Decca system	2 × Breda SLAR AEG system
Helicopters	1 × Lynx	Two

Left: **Modularity is the heart of the MEKO concept. The first modules to be developed accommodated weapon and electronic systems and major machinery. Second-generation units provide for crew needs and response to emergencies. Also shown here is the method of installing weapon system and other modules.**

The initial Argentinian order was followed in 1979 by one for six MEKO 140 corvettes to be built indigenously. Four MEKO 200 light frigates were ordered by the Turkish Navy in 1982 and three similar vessels by Portugal in 1986.

The MEKO hull

The use of Functional Units requires that the ship's hull be designed to offer standard seatings at as many locations as possible. This led to a system of paired longitudinals arranged symmetrically about and parallel to the ship's centreline; these are supported by transverse bulkheads and deep web frames. Characteristic of the resultant girder system are the large openings of the foundation units, which also provide generously sized access routes for internal Functional Units.

A notable feature of the MEKO hull form is the flared section with its distinctive knuckle, which extends almost the full hull length. The flared section not only provides an advantageous righting moment when the ship is heeled but also increases the available internal space.

MEKO/FES Mod 2

As word of the effectiveness of MEKO/FES spread, more and more weapon and electronic units were adapted, with manufacturers falling over themselves to get in on the act. Mod 2 of the system, introduced in 1984, was centred on the use of Intelligent Functional Units (IFE) equipped with Multi-Interface Computer Units (MICE) and linked by the Data Information Link (DAIL) system. Apart from the operational advantages, the change to a digital system simplified the transfer of data, reducing the number and weight of cables by some 80% and so easing installation work.

Another Mod 2 change, following a study of the Royal Navy's experience in the Falklands War, was the abandonment of horizontally positioned firefighting pipelines in favour of a vertical loop-line system in the midship section. This yielded improved operational availability.

MEKO/FES Mod 3

The Mod 3 development is designed to create a multi-purpose capability, allowing the ship both to counter underwater, surface and air threats and to perform the special tasks which fall to the modern deep-water warships. It is hardly surprising that the resulting design could readily meet NATO's NFR.90 requirement for a common frigate for the 1990s. The MEKO system could easily accommodate the many different national aspirations that will have to be reconciled within this project. The new ship will have to far exceed the performance of most current frigates in meeting the following requirements:

• Effective self-protection against current and anticipated air threats.

Left: **MEKO 360 under construction. Note the generously sized weapon system openings in front of the bridge.**

Below: **The proposed MEKO Mod 3 features vertical-launch surface-to-air missiles fore and aft, surface-to-surface missiles amidships, a general-purpose gun, four close-in weapon systems, and a helicopter in the Seahawk/EH101 class.**

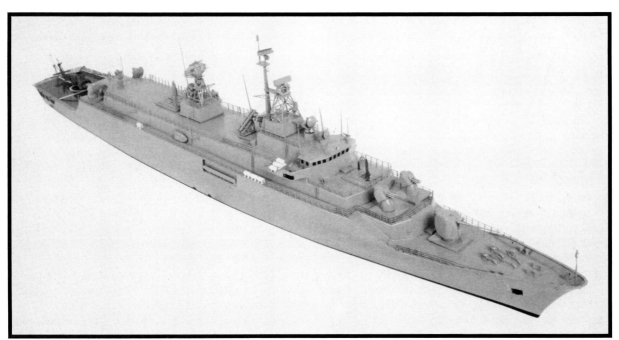

- Effective passive self-protection against damage by fragments of a missile destroyed at up to 500m range by the ship's own close-in weapon system (CIWS).
- Minimal passive and active above-water signatures.
- Economic protection against nuclear electromagnetic pulse (NEMP) effects.
- Effective and economic measures to increase survivability.

MEKO Mod 3 is characterised by the integration of the latest weapon and electronic systems, including vertical-launch missiles (VLMS), into the standard ship platform, which itself has been the subject of developments. The resulting Integrated Missile Defence System (IDMS) looks likely to be particularly powerful, comprising fore and aft VLMS launcher groups, each with its own 360°-coverage fire-control/illuminating radar.

Also included would be up to four CIWS, two forward and two aft, and each with a 360° arc of fire; a combined active/passive fire-control system; trackers forward and aft; and a 360° missile-detection radar mounted on the forward mast. The main sensor would comprise a 3D radar and/or 2D long-range radar, or another combination of surveillance and tracking/illuminating radars. The rest of the operational equipment fit would comprise guns for use against air and surface targets and shore bombardment, deck-mounted SSM launchers, tubes for ASW torpedoes, and medium/short-range decoys.

All systems and subsystems will be designed as Intelligent Functional Units, and the standards for the weapon modules adopted would be those agreed between Blohm und Voss and the US Navy in 1984.

Defence through concealment

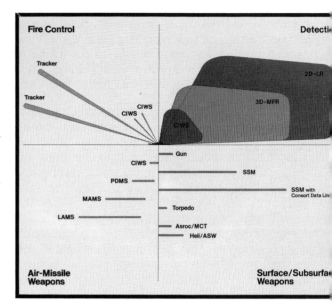

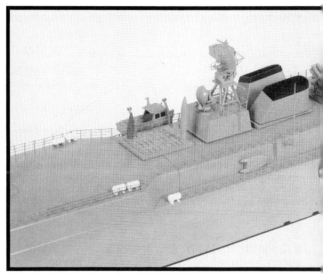

The most effective defensive measure for a modern warship is to minimise its visibility to enemy sensors. This has been made all the more urgent by rapid progress with infra-red (IR)/TV/laser techniques for missile terminal guidance, passive air and shipborne detection, and fire-control systems.

Visibility to infra-red and optical sensors depends on the size of the target ship's above-water hull and superstructure, and in the case of radar, on its geometric configuration. Blohm und Voss has carried out model experiments aimed at reducing a ship's signature since 1970. In 1983 the company was able to prove its model measurements with an extensive series of trials with a MEKO 360.H2 over the Federal German Navy range in Eckernforder Bight.

The results indicated that the trials ship had a radar signature very much lower than that of similarly sized warships and, in some instances, as low as that of a fast patrol craft. Viewed by a powerful radar, this low signature could cause an enemy commander to select the wrong weapons and tactics in an engagement. In the case of lower-powered airborne radars, the reduction in detection range could be significant. Good as these results are, they could be improved still further without a significant increase in cost. The necessary measures include the inclining of superstructure external faces and the rounding of angles between faces.

The exhaust plume of a conventionally stacked gas turbine-powered frigate can be detected at a range of 35nm by infra-red sensors. The changes needed to reduce these depend on the propulsion system, whether gas turbine, diesel or a combination of the two. In the case of diesel-powered vessels (and diesel engines powerful enough for a frigate-sized CODAD plant are now available), the IR signature can be greatly reduced by pre-cooling the exhaust and discharging it just below the waterline. At very low speeds and in harbour, an above-water bypass has to be provided to avoid unwanted backpressures. When under way at some speed a properly shaped discharge orifice will yield an extraction effect, dragging the gases into the aerated water in that area and dispersing it into the wake.

When gas turbines are included in the installation a funnel remains essential. But even then the problem can be eased by pre-cooling the exhaust gases and shrouding the exhaust itself in an air-cooling jacket.

Reduction in the optical signature can be achieved only by presenting the sensor with as small, flat and homogenous a silhouette as possible.

Noise-reduction arrangements to minimise the underwater detectability of a warship have been common practice for some time.

Passive self-protection

It should not have taken the Falklands War to draw attention to the need for splinter protection aboard modern warships. The skimpiness of the average

Above left: **Air, surface and subsurface coverage of the MEKO Mod 3's weapon systems and sensors.**

Left: **Detail of the aft vertical-launch SAM system, missile tracking and surveillance radars, and transversely mounted containerised anti-ship missiles on the MEKO Mod 3. The funnels visible here can be suppressed, and the infra-red signature reduced by underwater venting of exhaust gases.**

Below: **Distribution of compound-armour splinter protection on the MEKO Mod 3. Use of this 20–30mm-thick lightweight armour for the protection of vital spaces such as missile magazines and the bridge adds just 50–60 tonnes to total weight, less than a third of the figure for conventional steel armour.**

structure is such that, for example, it would not protect a computer suite from rounds fired from the types of weapon available to terrorists today.

Equally important is protection from fragments of an incoming missile destroyed by the ship's CIWS within a distance of 500m. To meet this requirement Blohm und Voss has developed a three-component compound armour. Measuring 20-20mm thick, it weighs only 30% of conventional armour for the same level of protection or better. The weight penalty for the MEKO 360 is estimated at only 50–60 tonnes.

In the event of nuclear conflict, it is likely that such weapons would be directed mainly at land targets and at such a distance from warships in open water that the resulting pressure wave and thermal and nuclear radiation would not be a major problem. But nuclear electromagnetic pulse (NEMP), which has the effect of coupling electrical energy in electric and electronic components, is a serious threat to communications and sensor systems. MEKO's containerisation of NEMP-sensitive electric and electronic components largely meets the Stage 1 protection requirement, which calls for shielding factors in excess of 60dB.

Survivability

Fire is a major threat to warships, more than 90% of Western naval casualties over the past 15 years having been caused by this hazard. Ventilation is of prime importance. Hot gases and smoke, which inhibit firefighting efforts, can spread through ventilating ducts. At the same time, lack of ventilation can effect the cooling of vital electronic equipment.

MEKO Mod 3 takes a novel approach to the problem, providing compartment-by-compartment ventilation. Working in collaboration with Noske-Kaeser, Blohm und Voss found that all MEKO types from the 200 up

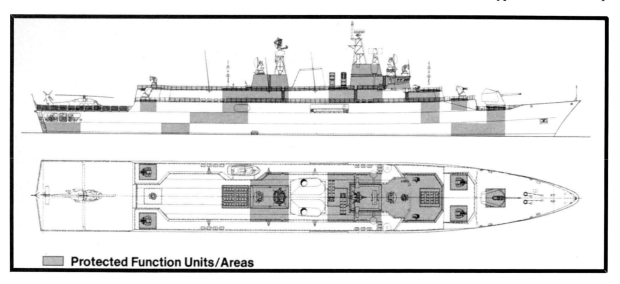

Protected Function Units/Areas

could be fitted with an independent compartment ventilating system handling all kinds of air within a standard 3,600 × 2,400 × 2,150mm container. Such a system would cost only 75% as much as a conventional arrangement and could be installed by way of existing routes.

Firefighting systems in current warships have generally evolved from earlier installations and usually feature a ring main below the main deck. As anti-ship missiles tend to strike about 4m above the waterline, exploding inside and causing the greatest damage above the point of impact, such ring mains are in a high-risk area. The MEKO Mod 3 solution is again a compartment system, with each space between two watertight bulkheads having its own fire pump and sea chest. This simplifies pipework, requiring less co-ordination, giving savings in design, construction and material costs, and resulting in fewer deck and bulkhead penetrations.

Conclusion

The MEKO/FES system has come a long way since its inception, with each new development aimed at producing a better end product and slowing cost escalation. This evolution continues in the form of modular outfitting, with operating theatres, accommodation, sanitary units, damage control units and the like all provided as ready-to-use units.

Another MEKO takes to the water. This is MEKO 200 *Yavuz* for the Turkish Navy.

Naval helicopters: costly but capable

Paul Beaver

In the light helicopter category the SA.365F Dauphin has not sold as well as expected.

THERE IS no doubt that the helicopter is firmly established as a vital weapon system in all but the smallest of navies. Its naval future is assured, particularly in the anti-submarine and anti-ship warfare roles. This has been achieved in spite of the high cost of naval helicopters: a recent survey indicates that while only 12% of the total world rotary-wing fleet is dedicated to maritime tasks, these aircraft account for about 25% of expenditure on helicopters. Both figures look as if they will continue to rise.

So why do naval staffs continue to spend scarce funds on expensive helicopters? The short answer is that their effectiveness outweighs their cost, offering distinct advantages over other weapon systems, particularly in the areas of flexibility and reliability.

Although naval helicopters were originally envisaged as search and rescue (SAR), commando assault and anti-submarine warfare (ASW) vehicles, in the 40 or so years since they entered military service their roles have multiplied to include over-the-horizon targeting (OTHT), anti-surface vessel warfare (ASVW) and, more recently, airborne early warning (AEW). ASW is still the predominant role and looks like remaining so for the foreseeable future, especially among the NATO nations as the Soviet nuclear-powered submarine fleet increases in size, performance and potency. It is widely believed that, next to another nuclear-powered submarine, the ASW helicopter is the best weapon the defending force commander could have in the event of submarine attack.

Within NATO, the ASW helicopter comes in two major types and two basic sizes. The Royal Navy, the primary anti-submarine force amongst the European members of the Alliance, operates the Sea King as an autonomous outer-zone hunter-killer in the medium-weight category of around 21,000lb (9.5 tonnes). The smaller Lynx, weighing in at some 11,000lb (5 tonnes), has a secondary role as an anti-submarine weapons carrier, being primarily an anti-ship/surface strike helicopter.

Other NATO navies follow a similar doctrine but do not have the same two-type system. For example, Canada flies the Sea King while the Netherlands and the Federal German Republic operate an uprated version of the Lynx equipped with a Bendix lightweight dipping sonar for its primary ASW role. The exception is Italy, with its shore-based SH-3 fleet (some to be embarked in a light carrier) and the escort-based Agusta-Bell AB.212ASW. Both are primarily ASW

types but have also been used for anti-ship missile trials.

The United States Navy has deployed the helicopter at sea as a fundamental part of its surface ships' anti-submarine warfare capability for over 20 years. In contrast with RN practice, the aircraft are commanded directly from the mother ship under the Light Airborne Multi-Purpose System (LAMPS) arrangement. The LAMPS I air vehicle is the Kaman SH-2F Seasprite, with the Sikorsky SH-60B Seahawk performing a similar role within LAMPS III on the more modern ASW escorts. The USN has equipped its air wings with the Sikorsky SH-3G/H Sea King for the inner-zone defence of carrier task forces. This type is also used for planeguard and logistical tasks.

The future of Western helicopter ASW appears to lie in two areas: the development of a tilt-rotor convertiplane to replace the Lockheed S-3 Viking fixed-wing anti-submarine aircraft of the USN (with the possibility of export sales to larger NATO and friendly nations), and the continued development of the medium (20,000–25,000lb, 9–11.5 tonnes) and light (7,000–12,000lb, 3–5.5 tonnes) helicopter categories. During 1986 Bell-Boeing announced that development of the SV-22A Osprey tilt-rotor for the US Navy was to begin. This type of aircraft combines the best qualities of a fixed-wing design with some of

Italy continues to produce the AB.212ASW for its own navy and a reported South American customer. The type has been in service for several years and a number of update programmes are under way. *(Agusta)*

136

Left: Artist's impression of the SH-60F Oceanhawk using its Bendix sonar for inner-zone protection of a US naval task group.

Below: **By the mid-1990s the US Navy and Marines will be equipped with several hundred V-22A Ospreys. This impression shows the MV-22A replacement for the CH-46E Sea Knight commando assault helicopter. The Osprey combines the helicopter's hover capability with the ability to reach the landing zone rapidly, so allowing the amphibious assault group to lie further offshore, well clear of the defences.**

Bottom: **Shipboard tests of the Bell XV-15 proved that tilt-rotor aircraft would be useful for naval operations, in either vertical or short take-off configuration.** *(Bell Helicopter Textron)*

the unique characteristics of the helicopter. For example, the Osprey will have both a maximum forward speed of 340kt (630km/hr) and the ability to hover to deploy an advanced lightweight sonar. The tilt-rotor's maximum take-off weight can be increased from 47,000lb (21.5 tonnes) to 55,000lb (25 tonnes) by means of a short take-off run of less than 500ft (152m) with the engine nacelles tilted 20° up from the horizontal.

Although weighing twice as much as the SH-3 Sea King, the Osprey, with its folding wings and blades, would take up very little more space than the helicopter or the folded S-3A Viking. For the ASW role the Osprey could be armed with some 10,000lb (4.5 tonnes) of ordnance, including the Mk 50 Advanced Light Weight Torpedo, depth charges and nuclear depth bombs. Bell-Boeing expects initial funding in Fiscal Year 1988 and puts flyaway unit cost at $16.2 million. Shipboard trials have already been carried out by Bell with its XV-15 experimental aircraft.

Current and future anti-submarine warfare helicopters include the Aérospatiale AS.332F Super Puma and the Anglo-Italian EH101, both described by their manufacturers as unique in the 9 and 13-tonne classes respectively. Agusta and Westland expect to have flown the first EH101 pre-production aircraft in time to show it at the Paris Salon in June 1987, by which time the British and Italian governments should have confirmed the types selection as a Sea King replacement for their navies. The Royal Navy is due to order 50 single-pilot-operable, passive sonar-equipped EH101s, while the Marina Militare Italiana requires some 38 active sonar-fitted examples for operation from ship and shore bases. The Italians are believed to have selected the British Aerospace/Bendix/FIAR HELRAS long-range sonar for their EH101s. Although by late 1986 no British requirement had been issued, it was expected that the British version will be similarly equipped in due course.

The naval Super Puma (licence-built by IPIN as the NAS 332) has been sold to the Indonesian Navy – the first navy to take an Exocet-armed version to sea – and to Brazil for aircraft carrier use. The type seems unlikely to enter service with the French Navy but, by way of compensation, has good export prospects in Canada. Four manufacturers have responded to a Canadian Government request for proposals for a Sea King replacement, the New Shipborne Aircraft (NSA), issued in September 1986. Significant Canadian participation, if not an actual licence-building agreement with Canadair, will be essential to success in the competition.

Aérospatiale's contender is a re-bladed Super Puma with new avionics, currently known as the Mk 2. EH Industries is pushing hard for a Canadian order, which, in a depressed market, represents the best

export chance for the EH101. Sikorsky is offering the enlarged S-70F Oceanhawk, nicknamed the "GrossHawk," and McDonnell Douglas Helicopter Company (MDHC) is making an ambitious bid with a new model based on the Apache attack helicopter's dynamics and rotor system. MDHC, in its earlier Hughes Helicopters incarnation, already has some maritime helicopter experience, though only with a naval version of the Model 500 Defender. Three of the competing companies are thought to be offering the new Rolls-Royce/Turboméca RTM322 engine as an alternative to the proven General Electric T700. The RTM322 has the advantage of an existing licence agreement with Pratt & Whitney of Canada, while the GE powerplant has been in service for some years.

The type eventually selected will carry the Plessey Cormorant lightweight dipping sonar and two Canadian avionics packages, the Helicopter Integrated Navigation System (HINS) and Helicopter Acoustic Processing System (HAPS). Supplementing Cormorant will be a CAE onboard magnetic anomaly detector (MAD). Although anti-submarine warfare will be the primary role, OTHT, SAR, medical evacuation and vertical replenishment capabilities will also be required. The NSA winner will also have to be capable of meeting potential battlefield support and land-based search and rescue requirements without major airframe changes. The total Canadian order could therefore exceed 130 airframes, which is why the major manufacturers are showing such interest in what otherwise seems to be a small procurement.

France's contender in the medium multi-role naval helicopter market is the AS.332F Super Puma. Seen here carrying two AM.39 Exocet anti-shipping missiles, the AS.332F can also be armed with the Murène lightweight ASW torpedo.

Moving down a weight class, several nations are expected to update their Lynxes with 360° radar, passive identification systems, onboard processors and integral MAD. The French Navy has Lynx as its sole ASW helicopter type and plans an improvement programme covering new engines, improved avionics and Crouzet/Dowty MAD. The Dutch and the Germans are thought to be planning an update similar to that intended for the Royal Navy's 80 or so aircraft. To be designated Lynx HAS8, the aircraft to the new standard will have anti-submarine warfare as a secondary role, concentrating instead on anti-shipping and surface search operations. Westland will carry out the upgrade, which comprises the installation of a new 360° radar, GEC Avionics Sea Owl passive-identification thermal-imaging system and the Racal Avionics Management System (RAMS), and modifications to permit carriage of the full range of anti-ship and anti-submarine weapons, including the Marconi Stingray lightweight torpedo.

Other helicopters in this category are also being updated. Turkey's Italian-built AB.212ASW helicopters, until now used primarily for anti-submarine duties, are being given dual-role capability. Turkey is one of three NATO customers for the British Aerospace Sea Skua anti-shipping missile, so convincingly demonstrated during the 1982 Falklands War. The missile system is being integrated with the Ferranti Seaspray radar, which has also been bought by the Federal German Navy to give its Sea Kings an offensive capability, especially in the narrow waters of the Baltic Sea.

Sea Skua is at present the main anti-shipping weapon of the Royal Navy's Lynx force, which has anti-surface vessel warfare as its primary role. The Super Lynx, now on offer from Westland, can also carry the Kongsberg Penguin Mk 3 anti-shipping missile. This weapon has been selected to arm the LAMPS III helicopters of the US Navy and is being offered to Spain and Australia for their S-70B Seahawks.

There is a growing trend towards the arming of larger naval helicopters of Sea King size with long-range missiles. India's order for Advanced Sea Kings armed with the British Aerospace Sea Eagle (also destined for the Royal Navy's Sea Harrier force in 1988), and Italian and South American interest in the Marte anti-shipping missile, are the leading developments in this area. Certainly, there is a tactical need for an addition to the surface action group's over-the-horizon capability that is more flexible than long-range ship-launched missiles.

Although the Soviets cannot be said to have neglected naval helicopters, they have not paid as much attention to them as the NATO and other Western nations, preferring to concentrate on battlefield helicopters.

The Kamov design bureau has developed a family of helicopters for both small and large anti-submarine warships. Distinguished by its co-axial rotors, the first of these, the Ka-25 Hormone, was first seen by Western observers in 1967 aboard Soviet Navy anti-submarine ships. An over-the-horizon targetting and radar reconnaissance version was later identified. The type has since been deployed aboard every Soviet helicopter-capable warship and many from the Warsaw Pact. Hormone was developed into the Ka-27 Helix, with an advanced flight control system, better engines and increased payload-range. It will eventually replace Hormone across the board.

Right: **Older naval helicopters like these Boeing-Kawasaki KV107s of the Royal Swedish Navy** *(left)* **and Air Force are being re-engined and otherwise improved.** *(Rolls-Royce)*

Shore-based ASW protection of naval anchorages and submarine bases was originally entrusted to a naval version of the Mil Mi-4 transport helicopter. In 1974 it began to give way to the Mi-14 Haze, a development of the Mi-8 battlefield transport. Unlike Hormone, it can operate autonomously as a submarine hunter-killer, carrying MAD, sonobuoys and a dipping sonar, and is night-capable. Exports have been limited to Poland, Libya and Bulgaria.

One aspect of naval helicopter operations of small but growing importance is airborne mine counter-measures (MCM). In the last 15 years MCM-equipped helicopters have been deployed in the Gulf of Tonkin, the Suez Canal and, most recently, the Red Sea. The United States is the only Western nation to have developed the idea fully, although Japan has an AMCM squadron equipped with the Boeing-Kawasaki KV-107, which is shortly to be replaced. In the American system unmanned MCM sledges are towed by helicopter, thereby reducing the hazard from mine detonations.

The US Navy is now taking delivery of the three-engined MH-53E Sea Dragon as a replacement for the RH-53D Sea Stallion, which has seen service around the world, including the Iranian desert during the ill-fated attempt to rescue the Tehran hostages. Before the fall of the Shah, Iran was in fact a customer for the RH-53D, but it is thought that the surviving Iranian aircraft no longer have the ability to operate against mines. Recent sightings suggest that the Mi-14 Haze is being developed for airborne mine countermeasures work.

Newest role for the naval helicopter is airborne early warning. Britain leads the way, spurred on by the South Atlantic conflict, equipping the Westland Sea King with the Thorn EMI Electronics Searchwater maritime radar and various passive electronic warfare systems such as the Racal Avionics MIR-2 Orange Crop. The Spanish Navy received its first Searchwaters in October 1986, and India and Italy are said to be interested in similar systems, also to be fitted to carrierborne Sea Kings.

Thorn-EMI Electronics is busy developing the Skyguard lightweight airborne early-warning and surface search radar for use in Lynx and Dauphin-class helicopters, seeing a market among the many non-carrier navies which would be attracted by the tactical advantages of organic AEW. Not only are such helicopter-mounted systems cheaper than long-range, land-based solutions, but they are more flexible and, being ship-based, are available to the task group commander at much shorter notice.

Advances in radar technology continue to be made, resulting in better displays and processing for naval helicopters. Competition is tough in this area, with highly competent companies like MEL, Ferranti, Thomson-CSF and Texas Instruments investing heavily. Generally each radar manufacturer links up with an airframe manufacturer of the same nationality: Thomson-CSF with Aérospatiale, Ferranti/MEL with Westland, and Texas Instruments with Sikorsky. In one instance a third contractor, the system integrator, has been appointed to combine the work of the first two. This was IBM Federal Systems Division,

appointed to oversee the LAMPS III programme. But although no announcement has been made about the integration of the forthcoming Oceanhawk programme – using the same airframe and engines and some of the LAMPS III avionics – it seems that the experiment is not to be repeated and the airframe manufacturer is in the driving seat again.

In Europe, simulation technology is being used to help with integration of the EH101's complex mission equipment with the crew controls and displays, permitting workload and other important human

factors to be assessed. A Singer Link-Miles simulator with dusk/night visuals has been installed at Westland's Yeovil factory and, according to the company, by the time of the first flight some 200hr of development flying will have been eliminated by the use of the simulator, much of it relating to the new automatic flight control system.

As the complexity of naval helicopter missions increases, so does the sophistication of the necessary training aids. Simulation of naval helicopters has now become big business for the six or so major contractors in the field, and every major type entering service is supported by a simulator. The major navies make everyday use of helicopter simulators, and most of the major manufacturers have now designed, built and commissioned rotary-wing systems. The Royal Navy's Portland air station has an advanced Lynx simulator on which complete missions can be flown, including

the visual identification of Warsaw Pact warships and the engagement of targets with Sea Skua missiles. Other systems fully simulated include the Ferranti Seaspray Mk 1 radar and Racal Avionics Orange Crop ECM system. So fine is the detail which Rediffusion modelled into the system that it is possible to fly alongside a surface contact in dark night conditions and illuminate it with the helicopter's landing light for positive identification. The same company has just delivered a Sea King HAS5 simulator to RNAS Culdrose, and this is now being linked to the three new Ferranti observer's stations for fully integrated mission training.

In France, Thomson-CSF's simulation division delivered two Lynx systems during 1986. Although the visual databases are limited, the French Navy is delighted to have a safe and cost-effective method of training and retraining Lynx aircrew.

Naval helicopters are on the increase in both numbers and complexity. The integration of roles in one airframe is proving very mission-effective. But development costs are high and, as in the warship business, numbers are shrinking as capability and price increase.

Left: **Amongst the more unusual uses of naval helicopters, pioneered by the US Navy, is airborne mine countermeasures. The latest type to be employed in this role is the MH-53E Sea Dragon.**

Below left: **A worldwide Sea King replacement market appears to await the Anglo–Italian EH101 helicopter, which first flew in early 1987. This is a model of the British version with chin-mounted Ferranti Kestrel radar.**

Below: **A child of the Falklands conflict, the Sea King AEW2, with its prominent Thorn EMI Electronics Searchwater radar, is now in squadron service with the Royal Navy. Spain has ordered the system and two other nations are thought to be close to buying the radar.** *(Rolls-Royce)*

Overleaf: **The Agusta A129 Naval could be the first of a completely new breed, the light anti-ship helicopter.** *(Augusta)*

Commerce before commonality in NATO communications

John Williamson and Bob Raggett

AS WITH the other arms of NATO, the naval forces have had to devote a great deal of effort simply to overcoming their basic differences in history, hardware and hopes for the future. Although substantial progress is evident when 1949 is compared with 1987, there is still much ground to be covered before the ideal of a truly coherent seagoing deterrent is achieved.

While the theory of non-partisan collaboration for the greater good of the alliance attracts widespread lip service, local political expediency and the lure of commercial advantage often prevent the theory from being turned into practice. The current NFR90 frigate project illustrates some of the pitfalls. This is

Artist's impression of the US Navy's LHD-1 amphibious assault ship in action. This class of ship will be fitted with the Marconi ICS-3 HF communications system. *(Ingalls Shipbuilding)*

an international co-operative effort to design, build and procure ships for the NATO navies in the 1990s. Feasibility studies have been completed and project definition has now begun. In theory, individual countries will ultimately build their own hulls and, in equipping them, use a percentage of standard hardware procured internationally. Each country's access to this

145

equipment market will be determined by how many frigates it procures.

It is difficult to see how in practice particular governments can limit the participation of their domestic industries to the agreed percentages in the case of their own frigates. Some observers doubt that the original NFR90 procurement scheme will ever be realised. Others argue that a more feasible alternative would have been for each of the allies to build its own, while making absolutely sure that they could operate together.

The lack of interoperability and compatibility in communications equipment is an area of major concern for all NATO forces. As a measure of the problem, it is reported that in an exercise in 1986 48hr was considered to be a reasonable time for a flash message to get from one of the allies to the submarine of another. In the future, the more active participation of the Portuguese Navy, and the new involvement of Spain, could compound the difficulty.

In one regard, however, the NATO naval communications sector is quite different from its counterparts on land or in the air. This is due to the fact that the US made what many now consider to be an unwise wholesale commitment to satellite systems and is, for the present at least, unable to compete effectively in high-frequency radio technology. There is thus a greater opportunity for European manufacturers in this market than in many others.

A ship's requirement for long-haul communications depends on its role and theatre of operations. The needs of a Belgian minesweeper or a Turkish fast patrol boat are different from those of a British destroyer operating in the Atlantic. In some cases, UHF provides enough geographic coverage. Non-NATO Sweden, for example, is at present setting up a UHF system to cover the Baltic, using a chain of radio stations sited on high ground all along its eastern coast. However, in the normal course of events a range of long-distance capabilities based on HF, satellites or both is essential for NATO's fighting ships. Sheer communications "reach" is not the whole answer, though. As the Italian Navy recently discovered, its communications system could not cope with the demands of the *Achille Lauro* hijack.

From the early 1900s until quite recently, HF radio was the primary means of long-distance naval communications. But it has a number of disadvantages which, though tolerated by earlier generations of military users, were by the 1960s becoming increasingly unacceptable for modern applications. In particular, HF propagation is subject to ionospheric disturbance and distortion, and graphic coverage is variable. While this is of no great consequence for routine communications, it is less than satisfactory for many military applications. At the same time, some traffic types – such as high-speed data communications – are possible only at high cost, if at all. Meanwhile, since it was being used extensively by military and non-military operators alike, HF was becoming very congested.

Just as HF seemed to be running out of steam, long-haul communications via satellite were demonstrated to be a practical proposition. The US Navy promptly began to put most of its communications eggs into the satellite basket, relegating HF to a minor fall-back role. At the same time, the European NATO nations, initially lacking the financial and technical resources to create their own military satellite capability, continued to develop and refine HF techniques.

A number of factors have subsequently combined to reverse the US commitment to satellites as the only way to go for long-haul, non-wired naval communications. Even before the suspension of the Shuttle programme and the latest failure of Europe's Ariane rocket, the business of actually launching satellites was rather uncertain. There was also the related difficulty of repairing faults in situ.

More critical, though, was the recognition that satellites in geosynchronous orbit were highly vulnerable to attack. Since it was possible to destroy an incoming high-speed missile at near-orbital height, the reasoning went, the destruction of a virtually stationary object such as a communications satellite was also achievable. Growing unease came to a head in the late 1970s following a US exercise which assumed that all friendly satellites had been knocked out by enemy action. The Chiefs of Staff were alarmed by the 1950s-vintage HF technology which remained at their

VHF and UHF are the primary means of communication for light craft like this 14-tonner operated by the Italian Corps of Port Commanders.

Above: **SCOT shipboard satellite terminals aboard HMS *Invincible*. The fortunes of naval satellite communications are reviving.** *(Marconi)*

Below: **HF shipboard antennae on the superstructure of a Royal Navy carrier.**

disposal. Such developments were instrumental in the revival of US interest in HF, and spawned such Navy-sponsored initiatives as the High-Frequency Improvement Program (HFIP) and, later, the High-Frequency Anti-Jam (HFAJ) project.

In 1987 there is much less hostility to satellite communications than was evident earlier in the decade. The argument is now that an enemy would not incapacitate western satellites since this would be an unequivocal indication of its future intentions. Moreover, the vulnerability of satellites is not confined to one side or the other, and in a tit-for-tat offensive against satellites the enemy would probably be inconvenienced in the same measure as the friendly forces.

Meanwhile, not all HF initiatives have come to fruition. HFIP, for instance, has been shelved. Although many of those who participated judged it to be unrealistically ambitious, there are grounds for believing that the failure of such programmes is rooted in hostility on Capitol Hill to offshore procurement. In this context, the delays in the new US Navy shipbuilding programme are viewed by some as a tactic designed to allow the US communications industry to close the gap opened up by its European competitors. This is currently put at as much as five years. Indeed, the HF improvements pioneered in Europe have been substantial. Basic gains have resulted from the use of system diversity and new modulation techniques to overcome the worst effects of ionospheric variations. Under the first approach, the signal is sent two or more times simultaneously; then, at the receiving end, the information most likely to be correct is selected. For their part, the new modulation techniques optimise the use of the available channel while circumventing the worst effects of multi-path delay distortion, additive noise, man-made interference and so on.

Work on automated management systems has also borne fruit. The prediction of ionospheric behaviour is a means of achieving maximum usable frequency (MUF). Early attempts to do this involved maps and tables built up from data produced by vertical-incidence ionospheric sounders. A more modern approach is to use a simple computer program built into terminal equipment to achieve the same result. More sophisticated still are interactive systems which passively obtain information from a shore station and then transmit on the best channel.

There have also been major improvements in terminal equipment itself and, in particular, in the achievement of fast-tuning transmitters. The latter eliminate the former requirement for a separate equipment for each part of the band, and can make the most of the new frequency-prediction techniques by allowing instantaneous frequency and power level adjustments in line with changing conditions.

There are two different approaches to HF communication for large capital ships. One, as exemplified by the ICS-3 system manufactured by UK company Marconi Communication Systems, is to use a non-tuned broadband architecture. Inside NATO, ICS-3 has been sold to the Royal Navy, the Royal Netherlands Navy, the Hellenic Navy, and to the US Navy for installation on its LHD-1 class of combined assault ships. The second approach – typified by systems like the ASYM 3000 manufactured by Aeromaritime Systembau of FR Germany, SINCOS from Hollandse Signaalapparaten of the Netherlands, and a variety of systems from Italy's Elmer – is essentially tuned. Such systems are in service with, respectively, the German Navy, the Royal Netherlands Navy and the Italian Navy (including *Maestrale*-class frigates). Other manufacturers of narrowband naval HF systems are France's TRT, and Rockwell and Litton of the USA. Equipment supplied by the first is in service with the tripartite minehunters of France, Belgium and the Netherlands.

ICS-3 comprises three primary subsystems: VLF to HF receiving, MF/HF transmitting, and control and distribution. Other subsystems, such as VHF, UHF, satellite communications, sonar and message-handling can be incorporated as required. Its architecture enables all transmissions to be amplified and radiated simultaneously using a single power bank of amplifiers and broadband antennae. This arrangement eliminates the need for RF mechanical units. The net result is that frequency changes are very fast, and can be made

Above left: **ICS-3 central supervisory control panel.** *(Marconi)*

Above: **ICS-3 H1250 transceiver aboard the Royal Navy frigate HMS *Broadsword*.**

Above right: **ICS-3 broadband antenna.** *(Marconi)*

in rapid succession. In addition, the radiated HF power can be adjusted instantly and independently for each frequency, and the separation between adjacent HF channels can be reduced to as little as 50kHz. Moreover, narrowband HF and MF channels can be incorporated to suit particular users' requirements. ICS-3 is designated AN/URC-109 in the USA.

Although there is a trend towards broadband systems, other manufacturers' equipment tends to operate without a power bank and with dedicated channels whose outputs are combined using multi-couplers and then fed to a broadband antenna. Elmer's communications system for frigate-type ships, for example, includes a variety of broadband and tunable antennae for transmission and reception over the LF and UHF frequency range. Features include the use of HF/UHF multicouplers and antenna filters, and automatic antenna/equipment switching. This system offers HF/UHF operation with NTDS, TADIL-A (Link II) and other specialised networks.

In some regards NATO navies get only what they pay for. A non-tuned system like ICS-3 is more expensive than a tuned one, but undoubtedly has the

edge in terms of performance. For their part, lower-priced tuned systems are more flexible in that they can be used in much smaller vessels. Rediffusion's ICS-25 system for example is playing a leading part in the Minor War Vessels Programme (MWVP), covering re-equipment of Royal Navy vessels of up to 2,500 tons.

Marconi argues that its system's true broadband architecture has advantages when it comes to the development of anti-jamming or frequency-hopping HF systems. The truth of this argument may be of some commercial consequence in the future. Among the survivors of the recent US enthusiasm for HF is the HFAJ programme. This US Navy-inspired initiative now has multi-service applications and could be worth an initial $2 billion to an equipment supplier. The technology requirement has so far proven so

Left: **Rediffusion's R500-series MF/HF receivers are used in both ICS-25 and the Royal Navy's CJA refit programme.**

Below: **Tuned signals tend to be used in ships of frigate size and above. This is the Royal Navy Type 22 frigate HMS** *Battleaxe*. *(Royal Navy)*

complex that only proposals submitted by a joint Rockwell/Marconi Communication Systems venture have received serious attention. Although this flies in the face of US competitive procurement practices, the partners are optimistic that they will get the go-ahead. The first HFAJ contracts should be placed in early 1987.

In a parallel development, a frequency-hopping standardisation agreement (STANAG) is being promoted within NATO. This is believed to be a UK-led initiative. The principle of frequency-hopping is well established in military radio communications, the basic notion being that if the frequency of synchronised transceivers operating on a link or in a net is changed sufficiently often throughout the duration of a message, detection and interception become extremely difficult. To complicate the task of the eavesdropper it is also usual to encrypt frequency-hopped messages. To date, though, most frequency-hopping work has been done with land-based mobile radio systems operating at VHF.

At HF and over long distances, frequency-hopping faces a number of limitations. The higher the hop rate required, the more energy needed. This energy is residual, and can produce problems with sidelobes, interference and noise. Optimum operating frequencies and power levels, along with channel quality, are much more important considerations in the hopping mode. At the same time, narrowband systems are limited to a frequency-hopping rate of roughly 300 per second. A broadband system may be able to hop an order of magnitude faster, but there is still a lot of work to be done on the use of frequency-hopping at HF for anything other than groundwave communication. Although slow hopping is possible at much greater distances, at the fast hop rates currently favoured by some NATO strategists communication cannot be achieved beyond about 300 miles.

The US and the UK are currently the champions of fast hopping, with most of the other alliance navies favouring slower rates. Marconi has already delivered fast-hopping equipment. The first batch was designed to prove the technique, and trials have been successfully completed. In the future the US Navy and the Royal Navy may use high-speed hopping for mutual communications, with downgraded facilities for links with their other allies.

The relationship between hop rate and the defensive and operational requirements of particular navies and ships is complicated. In simple terms, an enemy would find it useful to intercept and analyse opposing signal traffic at some times, and shut communications down by jamming on spot frequencies at others. To circumvent this, the force under attack would frequency-hop its communications, obliging the hostiles to replicate the hop sequence and rate to gain access to messages. At very high hop rates, the propagation times of signals would make it impossible for an enemy receiver to change frequency quickly enough. So far as jamming is concerned, frequency-hopping can be countered by either using a follower-jammer or spreading power over a wide frequency band. In both cases, the amount of power available to the jammer on any one frequency will probably be lower than that originally transmitted. This means that, to succeed in its task, the jamming platform must move closer to its target, thereby providing some opportunity for cat-and-mouse manoeuvring on the part of the friendly force until the hostile platform is brought within range of a ship's missile defences.

VHF and UHF, which include satellite communications, represent a somewhat controversial area so far as NATO thinking on frequency-hopping is concerned. The US Navy made an early decision to back frequency-hopping at UHF. But for a number of reasons the officially sponsored development programme failed to bear fruit. The involvement of US industry subsequently resulted in Magnavox selling its proprietary PV system for use in US Navy frequency-hopping at UHF. This was the basis of the "Have Quick" programme. In the interim, the Royal Navy has also elected to implement Have Quick-based UHF frequency-hopping. The current position is that any manufacturer supplying UHF electronic counter-countermeasures equipment to NATO navies or would-be Have Quick navies must have a US Government licence to use derivatives of the Magnavox system. A number of observers argue that this underscores one of the drawbacks of standardisation: the lowest common denominator may be preferred to the optimum technical solution.

Communications for submarines present problems significantly different from those encountered on surface vessels. When operating in concert with a surface fleet, submarines need the same sorts of communications facilities, but broadband systems

---

Have Quick frequency-hopping facilities are available on Marconi's Swordfish VHF/UHF transceiver, which is being evaluated by the British Ministry of Defence as part of Naval Staff Requirement 7297. *(Marconi)*

The E-6A is being developed to provide a survivable airborne communications system for the US Navy's ballistic missile submarine force.

cannot be used. A submarine normally only has one HF antenna, and to communicate it has to raise its mast above the water for the shortest possible time. Signals have to be passed up through the mast and through antenna matching units whose design is constrained by the size and shape of the mast and by pressure. Until a very fast frequency-hopping tuner capable of handling power levels above those available at present is developed, frequency-hopping at HF will not be possible.

A submarine commander operating alone and not wishing to reveal his position has even greater problems. A great variety of technologies – including VLF and laser communication – have been tried by many of the world's navies. Most experiments are classified, but some idea of the Royal Navy's general thinking may be available in early 1987, when feasibility study contracts for the SSN20 new-generation submarine are let.

Sonar: seeing more clearly now

Bernard Blake

The angular structure on the bow of Royal Navy submarine HMS *Trafalgar* houses the transducer for the Type 2020 hull-mounted sonar. *(Vickers)*

SONAR has been called the radar of the ocean. But this is a misnomer, so different are the environments in which the two types of system operate. While the air allows radar almost complete freedom, water is an extremely difficult medium for a sound-based system, for a number of reasons. Sound waves travel through water at only several hundred metres a second, as opposed to 3,000km/sec for radio signals in the atmosphere. This low velocity of propagation means that data acquisition is slow, leading to lengthy reaction times. In addition, refraction and attenuation of the sonar signal decrease the range markedly.

These factors detract from sonar performance and make it that much more difficult to detect and track with speed and accuracy. Complicating the problem still further, the sea is filled with natural and man-made noise which must be filtered out. Noise from naval and commercial shipping is increasing year by year, making the collection and analysis of sonar information ever more complex.

Water salinity, temperature, depth and pressure all add to the problems of the sonar operator. Active sonar also gives returns from larger marine creatures such as whales, dolphins and sharks. Anti-sonar defensive techniques include acoustic countermeasures and the cladding of submarines and surface vessels with sound-absorbing anechoic materials (although these are directed primarily at homing torpedoes rather than surveillance sonar, which operates on much lower frequencies). All this means that the modern sonar system must incorporate the most advanced technology, including sophisticated data-processing.

Sonar is used for a variety of purposes, both military and civil. These include the detection and tracking of submarines and other submersibles, free-swimming divers and mines; the guidance of underwater weapons such as torpedoes; and mapping of the sea bed and charting wrecks and other underwater objects.

Sonar sensors can be hull-mounted on both surface ships and submarines, towed behind the vessel, used from aircraft in the form of dipping sonar or sonobuoys, moored on the ocean bed as part of a static detection system, fitted on remotely controlled submersibles, or even hand-held. Systems can be active – transmitting signals and picking up any returns – or completely passive, capable only of listening for noise.

Mounting an active or passive sonar on the underside of a ship's hull, with the transducer installed in a protective dome, is the easiest solution. But this can affect detection performance, since the ship's movement creates noise which is picked up by the sonar receivers. The faster the ship goes, the more noise is generated, with rough weather making the problem worse. Hull-mounted sonar also picks up propeller, engine and other machinery noises from the parent ship. Submarines, which can spend much of their time cruising slowly in still water, are less prone to this kind of interference.

One way of improving reception is to tow a transducer behind the ship in a streamlined container, and to vary the depth at which it operates. Such variable-depth sonars (VDS) also have the advantage of being able to avoid the boundaries between water layers at different temperatures, which mask the noise of the submarine being hunted. The best depth at which to tow the VDS can be determined by the use of bathythermographs.

The main drawbacks to VDS are the drag generated by the "fish" and its cable, noise pick-up from the ship's propellers, and the fact that submarines can dive much deeper than the depth at which VDS can be deployed. In an effort to overcome the limitations of hull-mounted and VDS systems, many manufacturers now link the two with common processing electronics.

The tarpaulin-draped bulb visible on *Mobile Bay*, a *Ticonderoga*-class cruiser of the US Navy, contains the ship's main anti-submarine sensor, the SQS-53A sonar. *(Litton/Ingalls Shipbuilding)*

A third way of deploying sonar is the towed array, which can be used by both surface ships and submarines. Comprising a line of low-frequency hydrophones in a flexible neutrally buoyant mounting, the array is far enough from the vessel to be well clear of self-generated noise. The array can be up to several hundred metres in length, depending on the frequency

Above: **VDS "fish" of the Thomson-Sinta Diodon system.**
(Thomson-CSF)

Below: **Launch of a towed array.** *(Thomson-CSF)*

coverage required. It offers a receiving aperture much larger than is possible on board a ship, and is much more suitable for picking up lower frequencies.

Towed arrays are entirely passive in operation, picking up noise from the target so that an estimate of range and bearing can be made. Under normal circumstances they are used mainly for area surveillance, particularly in the self-protection role.

The interpretation of data from towed-array systems is more complicated than in the case of hull-mounted sonars, range and bearing accuracies being significantly lower. They do however have a much longer range than hull-mounted passive sensors. Their chief drawback is the drag on the ship, development work being concentrated largely on making them lighter and more manoeuvrable.

There are two types of airborne sonar: sonobuoys, dropped in patterns to radiate signals and relay target returns to the aircraft; and dipping sonars, which lower a sensor into the sea at the end of a cable, with the signals received being transmitted up the cable to the receiver in the aircraft.

Dipping sonars are largely confined to helicopters, although one or two streamlined sensors are available for use at low towing speeds. Sonobuoy systems are widely used, tens of thousands of expendable buoys being manufactured each year.

Hull-mounted systems

Most modern frigates and destroyers are fitted with a hull-mounted sonar, as are many submarines. Hull-mounted systems are also fitted to remotely piloted submersibles and used for tasks such as mine detection and location of wrecks. Data are transmitted up the control cable for processing in the mother ship.

The most modern systems fitted to US Navy surface vessels are the General Electric AN/SQS-53 and the Raytheon AN/SQS-56, the former derived from the highly successful AN/SQS-26. One or other of these systems is fitted to most recently commissioned US destroyers and frigates. AN/SQS-56 is fitted to the US Navy's *Oliver Hazard Perry* (FFG-7) class frigates, and versions have been sold to a number of other navies.

The USN's nuclear attack submarines are fitted with the AN/BQQ-5, a digital multi-beam system employing both hull-mounted and towed arrays. A later version, AN/BQQ-6, equips the *Ohio*-class Trident missile submarines. The older American SSBNs and certain SSNs are equipped with the AN/BQR-21 DIMUS, a hull-mounted preformed-beam passive sonar. Other US systems include Edo's range of sonars for both surface ship and submarine use.

Principle among these are the 780 series for surface ships and the 1102/1105 for submarines.

In the UK a range of new sonars is being developed for the Royal Navy's surface vessels and submarines. The Plessey Type 2016 fleet escort sonar and the Type 2020 submarine system are the current hull-mounted standard. New systems include the Ferranti Type 2050 (combining the 2016 array with new processing and displays) for the *Norfolk*, *Birmingham* and *Broadsword*-class ships, the Plessey Type 2051 for the updated *Oberon*-class submarines, and the Plessey Type 2054 for the RN's *Vanguard*-class Trident missile submarines.

The Marconi company is involved in the design and manufacture of hull-mounted systems, as well as being a prime subcontractor to both Plessey and Ferranti on most of the latest systems. Graseby Marine also makes hull-mounted systems. Between them these four companies meet virtually all the RN's sonar requirements.

France has a highly developed sonar industry headed by Thomson-Sintra, formed a few years ago by amalgamating the underwater interests of the two largest French companies in this field, Thomson-CSF and Sintra-Alcatel.

Eledone is a family of hull-mounted submarine sonars in service with several navies. Its DUUA-2A and 2B systems are installed in submarines of the French Navy, and Argonaute has been ordered by the RN as the Type 2040 for use in its new *Upholder*-class (Type 2400) submarines. The Diodon, Tarpon and Salmon active/passive sonars are fitted to surface ships, in either hull-mounted or VDS form. The SS12 panoramic sonar operates at medium frequencies and is designed for use by small and medium-tonnage ships. A version has been developed for helicopter applications. Most of the Thomson-Sintra systems have standardised processing equipment, the array and handling methods being varied according to role.

Krupp-Atlas Elektronik has developed a range of active/passive sonars for the Federal German Navy. They are designed for both surface ship and submarine use, in hull-mounted and VDS forms, and are installed in a number of export warships built in West German yards or under West German guidance.

Most of Italy's sonar activity is in the hands of the Selenia-Elsag Consortium for Naval Systems. Its latest submarine sonar is the IPD70/S, now in service with the Italian Navy.

In the Netherlands, Signaal has developed the HSS-15, PHS-32 and SIASS surveillance sonars. The Royal Australian Navy uses Mulloka, a lightweight active-scanning system developed by Honeywell and now manufactured by Plessey Australia. Westinghouse (Canada) has designed a number of systems for use by the Canadian Navy.

The Soviet Union is known to have a wide range of

Above: **The AN/BQQ-6 sonar of the *Ohio*-class ballistic missile submarines is mounted just behind the bow dome.** *(US Navy)*

Below: **Bow antenna of an Eledone submarine sonar.** *(Thomson-CSF)*

Aboard the Soviet Kara-class cruisers the variable-depth sonar is mounted just below the helicopter deck. *(US Navy)*

systems, both hull-mounted and VDS. The Petya and Mirka-class ASW frigates have hull-mounted sonars, and some of the earlier Petya class have been retrofitted with VDS sonar in place of their aft torpedo tubes. The Kresta and Kynda-class cruisers have hull-mounted active systems, and can also carry Ka-25 Hormone helicopters equipped with dipping sonar and a magnetic anomaly detector. A bow-mounted sonar is fitted in the later Kresta II class and the Kara-class cruisers have VDS mounted beneath the helicopter pad to complement the hull-mounted system. This combination has been continued in the more modern *Udaloy*-class ASW destroyers, which also carry two helicopters, and developed still further in the largest Soviet surface ships. The *Kirov*-class battlecruisers carry three helicopters and both forms of sensor, while the *Kiev* carriers support a similar sonar suite and up to 17 helicopters each.

Many of the Soviet Navy's 76 nuclear attack submarines, 68 cruise missile boats and some 135 diesel attack submarines (SSKs) feature large sonar arrays. In addition, the large classes of nuclear and diesel ballistic missile submarines all have sonar installations.

Towed-array systems

A number of navies employ towed-array systems in addition to hull-mounted sonars, the foremost being those of the USA, UK, France and the Netherlands.

In the USA, Edo's AN/SQR-18A TACTASS is in

service aboard surface ships, as well as being used by the Netherlands and Japan. The Gould AN/SQR-19 has now passed operational evaluation tests and is entering service. The Western Electric AN/BQR-15 is used in SSBNs, and both the IBM AN/BQQ-5 and AN/BQQ-6 have towed arrays in addition to their hull-mounted transducers.

The Surveillance Towed Array Sensor System (SURTASS) was introduced into the US fleet in 1984. It is a mobile surveillance system intended to complement the fixed networks (described later) by extending coverage to remote ocean areas not monitored by static systems. It will also act as an emergency reserve if the fixed systems are disabled. The long arrays are towed by specially built small surface ships designated T-AGOS. The first ships have been delivered and the US Congress has authorised funds for 12 vessels, to be delivered at a rate of two per year. Acoustic target information gathered by the towed arrays is relayed to two processing centres, one on the east coast and one on the west coast of the USA, and processed data are transmitted back to ships at sea.

The latest British towed-array systems include the Waverley Type 2031Z, to be fitted to all new Royal Navy ASW frigates, and the Ferranti Type 2046 passive system, under development for submarines. Both embody the advanced Curtis electronic architecture, developed at the Admiralty Research Establishment, in their processing systems. Curtis techniques allow the on-board hardware to be made much smaller and cheaper.

GEC Avionics has designed and supplied two towed arrays, the Type 2026 for submarines and the Type 2031(I) for surface ships.

The Thomson-Sintra DSBV 61A represents France's entry into the field of surface-ship towed arrays. The system has completed trials and is now entering service in the French Navy's *Georges Leygues*-class ASW corvettes.

The AN/SQR-501 Critical Angle Towed Array Surveillance System (CANTASS) is under development by Computing Devices Company for the new Canadian *Halifax*-class patrol frigates, and is due to enter service in 1989. It was the "wet end" of SQR-19.

Airborne sonar

Sonobuoy-based sonars comprise an airborne receiver, processing and display system, and active or passive sonobuoys. Some of the best known systems of this kind are produced by GEC Avionics in the UK. AQS-901, claimed to be the most powerful acoustic processing system in service in the world, is fitted to the RAF's Nimrod MR2s and the RAAF's P-3C

The whole stern area of *Georges Leygues* is given over to the DSBV 61A VDS fish and its massive winching gear.

Orions. It is designed to exploit the advantages of the more sophisticated directional and range-indicating sonobuoys such as Barra, CAMBS and VLAD.

AQS-902 was developed for use in helicopters and maritime patrol aircraft. It is fitted to Royal Swedish Navy's Sea Kings, and ordered for the Indian Navy's Sea Kings and the Italian Navy's Atlantic Mk 1s. The latest GEC system is AQS-903, under development for the EH101 Anglo-Italian ASW helicopter.

In the USA, the EDMAC AN/ARR-72 is in service on the P-3C, in conjunction with acoustic signal-processors and computers. A later version, the AN/ARR-75 sonobuoy receiver, is in production. A variant probably forms part of the Update III for the P-3C, in combination with the General Electric AN/AYA-8B data-processing system and the new IBM AN/UYS-1 signal processor, which will replace the directional frequency and recording (DIFAR) system, employed in the P-3C for the last 15 years.

Below left: **A DIFAR sonobuoy is loaded into a launcher aboard an RAF anti-submarine aircraft.** *(Plessey)*

Below: **The Fokker Maritime Enforcer's sensor suite includes the GEC Avionics AQS-902 sonobuoy processor and Tactical Processing System.** *(GEC Avionics)*

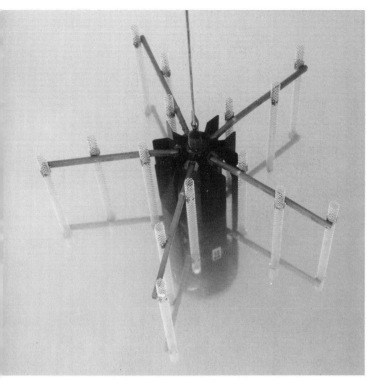

The AN/UY-1 is the USN's first acoustic signal processor and is understood to be capable of handling sensor inputs at a rate of 20 million computational operations per second. Over 1,000 units are due to be delivered by the end of 1987 for use with the LAMPS Mk III helicopter as well as the P-3C Update III.

The Thomson-Sintra TSM 8200 is the primary processing system currently in service with French naval aircraft. Derived from it are the TSM 8210 and 8220 (Lamparo) lightweight sonobuoy processing systems, which are suitable for both fixed-wing aircraft and helicopters.

HS/DUAV-4 is an active/passive equipment for use on board light helicopters of the Lynx type, and HS12 is a helicopter-borne version of the shipborne SS12. HS312S is an integrated ASW system for helicopters, comprising HS12 and the Lamparo processor.

Dipping sonar is used by several countries in a variety of helicopters. The current British system is the Plessey Type 195M, in service on the Royal Navy's Sea Kings. Two new systems, Cormorant and Guillemot, are under development by the same company.

The Bendix AN/AQS-13 and AN/AQS-18 are widely used by the USN and a number of other navies, and in France the current standards are the Thomson-Sintra HS12 and HS312S.

The Soviet Union employs both sonobuoy systems and dipping sonar, deployed from helicopters and fixed-wing aircraft. The ASW version of the Tu-142 Bear-F employs sonobuoys and onboard processing techniques for submarine detection, and naval helicopters such as the Ka-25 Hormone-A use both sonobuoys and dipping sonar. A variant of the Hormone, the Ka-27 Helix-A, is carried for ASW work by the new *Sovremenny* class of guided missile destroyers. The Mi-14 Haze-A is a dedicated ASW helicopter employing a retractable sonar unit and sonobuoys. The Haze-B variant is equipped for mine countermeasures.

Minehunting sonar

The General Electric AN/SQQ-14 minehunting sonar is in widespread service with the USN and a number of other forces. The latest US system, AN/SQQ-30, is fitted to the new minehunters. Under development by Raytheon in collaboration with Thomson-Sintra, AN/AQQ-32 is currently on freshwater trials and is due for sea trials in the near future.

The AN/AQS-14 airborne system, combined with a towed sonar vehicle, equips USN RH-53D helicopters.

A new variable-depth sonar, the Plessey Type 2093, is under development for the Royal Navy's Single Role Minehunter. Deliveries are due to start at the

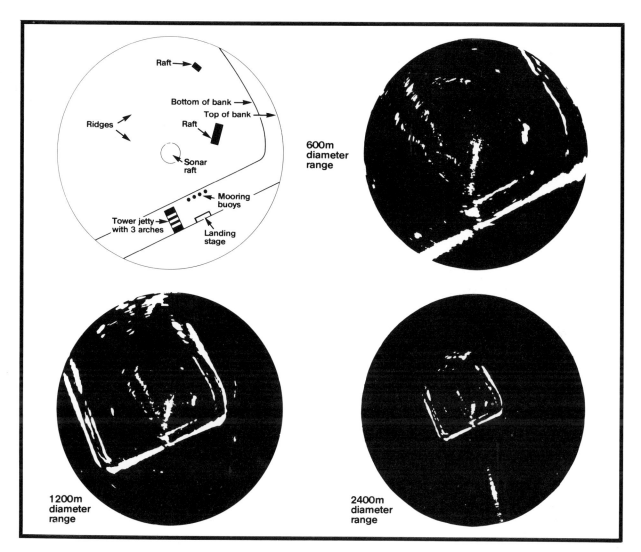

Raft →

Bottom of bank →
Top of bank →
Ridges →
Raft
→ Sonar raft
→ Mooring buoys
Tower jetty → with 3 arches
Landing stage

600m diameter range

1200m diameter range

2400m diameter range

Below: **US Navy RH-53D minehunting helicopter lowers its AQS-14 sonar during operations at Suez.**

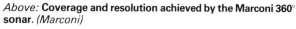

Above: **Coverage and resolution achieved by the Marconi 360° sonar.** *(Marconi)*

end of 1986, and the system will eventually replace the present Type 193M, also manufactured by Plessey.

In France, Thomson-Sintra is again the prime supplier, with its TSM 2021B and 2022 systems.

Static underwater systems

Static underwater surveillance systems have played a large part in submarine detection for a number of years. The USA continues to lead in this area. The original American system, SOSUS (Sound Surveillance System), is still in operational use, although vastly expanded since its beginnings in the 1950s. It consists of undersea networks of passive hydrophone detectors deployed in the Atlantic and Pacific oceans.

SOSUS AN/FQQ-10(V) hydrophones are located at 8–24km intervals along a linking cable connected to shore stations on the USA and the Aleutian Islands, Canada, Denmark, Iceland, Italy, Japan, Korea, the Philippines, Spain, Turkey and the UK. Data collected by these sites are transmitted by military communications satellites to the USN central computer complex, which analyses them for noise produced by submarines. The constantly changing nature of the threat has resulted in a two-stage update programme.

The US Navy has also been working on a system designed to extend surveillance into areas unsuitable for SOSUS or SURTASS. The Rapid Deployable Surveillance System (RDSS) is based on air-deployable, bottom-moored, long-life passive acoustic buoys. Moored at any depth from the shallows to about 6,000m below the surface, the buoys can be emplaced rapidly by aircraft in areas of special interest, from which they transmit data to maritime patrol aircraft. The RDSS programme is currently being reassessed by the USN, and could be replaced by an alternative solution.

Harbour surveillance and the protection of vulnerable underwater installations is another application of fixed systems. One example of this kind of system is the Marconi 360° sonar. Versions are in service for use against submarines, submersibles, divers and free swimmers. The system normally consists of one or more static sensors which supply target information by cable to a land-based processing and control centre.

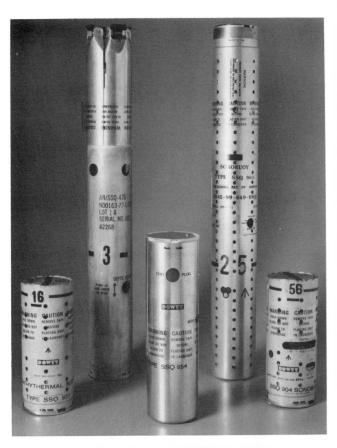

Sonobuoys

The original sonobuoys were large and cumbersome and usually indicated nothing more than the fact that a submarine was within range. Current designs can be either omni-directional passive; of the DIFAR type, providing target bearing information; or of the DICASS type, detecting the range and bearing of the target by transmitting sonar pulses under command from an ASW aircraft and receiving echoes for transmission back to the aircraft.

All three types are normally dropped by parachute and, after hitting the water surface, deploy the sensor unit to a preselected depth while remaining on the surface to permit transmission of data back to the aircraft.

Large quantities of sonobuoys are produced by all the major naval powers. Manufacturers such as Sparton and Magnavox in the USA, Sparton of Canada, Dowty and Plessey in the UK, Thomson-Sintra in France, and AWA in Australia have been designing and producing them for many years.

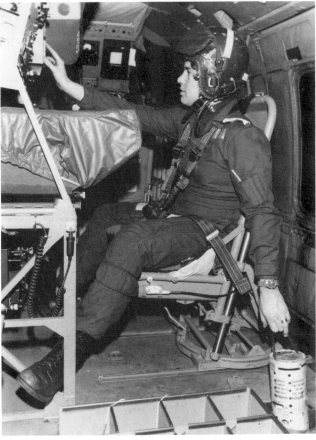

Ancillary systems

There are large numbers of ancillary products for use with sonar-based equipment. Foremost amongst these are underwater acoustic ranges and calibration systems, needed to monitor the performance of torpedoes and other underwater missiles and vehicles. Thorn-EMI in the UK has designed and sold a number of static and mobile ranges, as have Thomson-Sintra and Sippican Ocean Systems in the USA.

Also available are mobile targets to simulate the dynamic and acoustic characteristics of submarines, and noise and vibration monitoring systems, used to prevent ship's noise from affecting sensor performance.

Bathythermograph sonobuoys are used extensively to monitor temperature variations in the ocean. This information is needed to determine the optimum depth for VDS towing.

Handheld sonars are used by divers and free swimmers to detect mines and other underwater objects.

The future of sonar

The days when submarines presented a threat to ships only have long gone. Their ability to launch strategic nuclear missiles over long distances makes their detection of paramount importance. Many programmes to improve both the hardware and the software of sonar systems are currently under way.

The USN is spending $16 billion on a five-year programme up to the end of 1988 in an effort to improve its ability to detect, track and destroy underwater threats. This includes the updating of many of its seaborne, airborne and static sonar systems, as well as developing new technology. The RN has completely overhauled its sonar requirements, and a number of new systems are due to come into service in the near future. The French Navy is working along the same lines, as are those of Italy, West Germany and the other NATO nations.

The most critical area of development is that of signal and data-processing, and information display. The most advanced technology is being exploited to secure improvements on those sectors. The advent of Very-Large-Scale Integration (VLSI) techniques, for example, has revolutionised onboard equipment and provided opportunities for more efficient operation and much more compact packaging. High-speed reprogrammable processors are coming into general use, giving the operator the means to analyse the vast amount of information supplied by modern sensors. Modular concepts are being applied to nearly all the latest systems, permitting common electronics and display consoles to be used by a variety of different systems. Digital processing, carefully designed man-machine interfaces, co-ordinated displays in both colour and monochrome, and keyboard panels make it possible for one operator to control a complete system.

When it comes to hardware, much attention has been focused on improvements in sensor systems, particularly those of towed arrays. STC Defence Systems achieved a recent breakthrough by successfully incorporating both optical fibre and electrical conductors in a tow cable. Several manufacturers are working on an "active" towed-array system, combining a hull-mounted or VDS transmitter and a towed-array receiver. Sometimes known as an "active adjunct" system, this is an attempt to combine the best features of the two techniques. When operating against modern, quiet-running submarines, it is difficult for a passive towed array to pick up sound at any distance.

Typical of the advanced displays currently available is the Ferranti Compact Sonar Console. *(Ferranti)*

The active towed array is designed to operate at a frequency of about 1kHz, giving extended range. Production of an operational system is about five years away.

The USN is carrying out a vast and complex programme known as Undersea Target Surveillance. This consists of 10 individual projects covering the detection, localisation, classification and tracking of underwater targets, including submarines, mines, divers and free swimmers. One of the projects, F11-121, is concerned with the detection of acoustic signals by various configurations of static, mobile and airborne sensors. It also covers methods of relaying data for processing and analysis, and the use of fibre-optic cabling.

Australia's Defence Research Centre has reduced a towed-array sonar for surface ships or submarines to what is claimed to be the smallest size available. Code-named Karrawarra, the array is only 19mm thick, with sensors the size of a cigarette spaced along it. The programme is still in the early development stage but could well lead to towed arrays suitable for small vessels such as fast patrol boats.

Another interesting programme is the USN's Sonobuoy Thinned Random Array Project (STRAP), combining sonobuoys with the collective-processing,

beam-forming techniques of normal sonar systems. Large numbers of buoys, probably around 15 to 20, are deployed randomly over the search area. Since it is essential to know the exact position of each buoy, four would be fitted with a low-power transmitter and deployed in different areas of the pattern. Each would then receive two sets of signals, one from the water and the other from the four emitting buoys. The acoustic processor in the ASW aircraft would correlate these signals and use the information for beam-forming purposes.

In the sonobuoy field, the US Expendable Reliable Acoustic Path Sonobuoy (ERAPS) programme is well under way. A long-range active search sensor designed to exploit the long-range direct-propagation mode known as the "reliable acoustic path", ERAPS can actively search for a submarine that is passively undetectable. An increase in range is gained by using low-frequency, high-power pulses and a volumetric array of hydrophones.

Sonars are now achieving radar-like resolutions. This active undersea volcano was detected and imaged by the Marconi Gloria sidescan system. *(Marconi)*

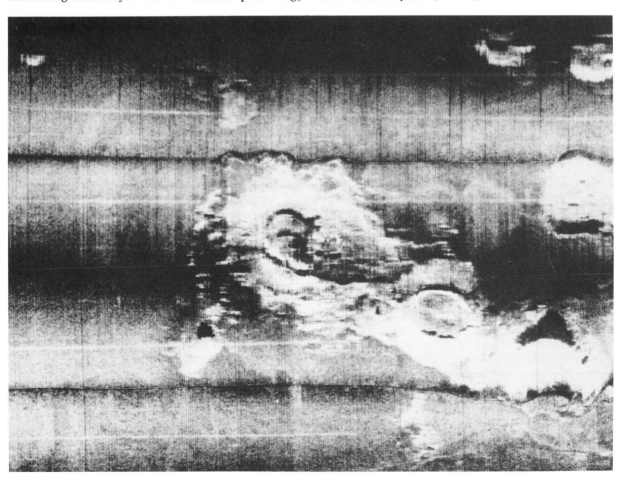

Can Italy solve the V/STOL conundrum?

Antonio Ciampi

Giuseppe Garibaldi at speed, with a single SH-3D anti-submarine helicopter on deck. *(Milpress)*

For the first time in its history the Italian Navy has its own aircraft carrier, the 13,000-ton through-deck cruiser *Giuseppe Garibaldi*. But despite being classified as an *incrociatore portaeromobili*, or aircraft-carrying cruiser, and having a 174m full-length flight deck with ski-jump, she can currently operate only AB.212 and SH-3D Sea King helicopters for ASW anti-ship and electronic warfare duties. In the words of Italian Navy Chief of Staff Adm Giasone Piccioni, *Garibaldi* is still only half a ship, a situation that will persist until the Navy wins the right to operate its own real air wing comprising both fixed and rotary-wing aircraft.

Historical background

The Italian Navy was amongst the first to recognise the value of aviation: the first Italian military pilot, Navy 2nd Lt Mario Calderara, qualified on September 12, 1909. By the last year of the First World War the total of Navy land-based aircraft, airships and seaplanes (operating as bombers, fighters and reconnaissance aircraft), had reached 1,200.

In 1919 Admiral Thaon de Revel, Navy Chief of Staff during the war, tried to found a properly constituted naval air force. But in 1923 the Italian Government finally succumbed to the arguments of the Air Force, which subscribed to the conventional wisdom of the 1920s, as enunciated in the doctrines of Giulio Douhet and Billy Mitchell. The result was the Air Force Law (the first of four such, the others following in 1925, 1931 and 1937), which gave the Air Force responsibility for all aviation. All criticism was deflected with the maxim: "The air is indivisible". When challenged in the 1930s on the need for aircraft carriers, Mussolini replied: "Italy is our aircraft carrier".

Events showed how wrong were the exponents of Douhet/Mitchell-style air power. The hard lessons of the first months of the Second World War quickly convinced the Italian High Command of the need for aircraft carriers. Accordingly work began on the conversion of the passenger liners *Roma* and *Augustus* into the carriers *Aquila* and *Sparviero*, an undertaking which was never to be completed.

After the end of the war the Italian Navy tried again to acquire its own air arm, but the existing laws and the fierce opposition of the Air Force ensured that this would never be anything more than a helicopter force. Indeed, the concented opposition to the concept of fixed-wing aviation for the Navy went to extraordinary lengths. The first two ASW aircraft to be operated by Navy personnel, a pair of helicopters, were stopped by the police when they arrived in Italy in December 1952, ostensibly probably because their Navy markings were not officially recognised. The following summer they were taken on charge by the Air Force.

In summer 1953 the Navy carried out its first shipboard helicopter landing, flying a Bell 47G to the old cruiser *Garibaldi*. The following year the first three AB.47Gs were ordered, and in April 1955 the training school for Army and Navy pilots was inaugurated at Frosinone.

At about this time the Navy and Air Force were at loggerheads over responsibility for airborne anti-submarine warfare, urgently needed to counter the increasing threat posed by modern submarines. The Law for Antisubmarine Aviation, finally approved on October 7, 1957, gave the operational direction of ASW aviation to the Navy, while the Air Force handled

administration and technical and logistical support. Thus, from the administrative point of view, Italian ASW aviation was a part of the Air Force. The result was a succession of misunderstandings and wrangles which ceased only after the Defence Ministry decreed on June 20, 1986, that operations by the Breguet Atlantic ASW aircraft of the 30th and 41st Squadrons should be co-ordinated and directed by the Navy Chief of Staff and the operational commands.

The present

The new concept for Italian military operations, as published in the MoD White Book of 1985, is based on a number of "interforce missions," to be accomplished by integrated and co-ordinated action on the part of the three armed services. This has transformed the needs and tasks of the Italian Navy. The six main missions are:
- North-eastern defence.
- Southern defence and protection of maritime lines of communication.
- Air defence.
- Territorial defence.
- Civil protection, security and peacetime operations.
- Technical and logistical support.

The Italian Navy is mainly concerned with the first two, air support being of paramount importance to their successful accomplishment. The main current Navy programmes relating to these missions are:
- The building of two DDGs, *Animoso* and *Ardimentoso*, at a cost of about 700 billion lire each; the modernisation of the *Audace*-class destroyers and *Lupo* frigates; and acquisition of the aircraft for the *Garibaldi*.
- The EH.101 ASW helicopter programme in collaboration with Britain.

- Building of four 1,300-ton corvettes of the *Minerva* class and modernisation of the coastal radar network.
- Building of three new submarines for the 1990s. They will probably be of an improved version of the *Nazario Sauro* third series (*Prini* and *Pelosi*, currently under construction).

In the near future the Navy will be composed of two major task groups, each based on a cruiser (*Vittorio Veneto* and *Garibaldi*) capable of operating aircraft – in the former case helicopters only – and containing a mix of ASW and anti-ship units. During the 1990s the cruiser *Andrea Doria* will be deleted and replaced with another *Veneto*-class or a further *Garibaldi*. The latter

Above left: **Although at present the Italian Navy is restricted to helicopter operations, the distant upward sweep of *Garibaldi*'s ski-jump betrays a firm intention to acquire fixed-wing V/STOL aircraft.** *(Milpress)*

Below: **When the Italian Navy is finally freed to buy V/STOL aircraft for its carrier air wing, it will have a choice of two types: the McDonnell Douglas/BAe AV-8B *(inset)* or the BAe Sea Harrier FRS1 *(below)*.** *(MDC/BAe)*

Above right: **The Spanish Navy has successfully operated AV-8A Harriers from its small carrier *Dedalo* for a number of years and plans to acquire AV-8Bs for the new *Principe de Asturias*, which is in many ways comparable with Italy's *Garibaldi*.** *(BAe)*

has proven herself to be a relatively cheap ship at about £340 million without embarked aircraft or helicopters, and is regarded by the Navy as well suited to its tasks.

The Navy Staff believes that *Garibaldi*'s helicopters will greatly enhance their ability to carry out naval operations in the Mediterranean. But if she could also operate STOVL (short take-off/vertical landing) aircraft she would be able to interdict hostile aerial reconnaissance, protect warships and convoys from air attack, and undertake defensive missions against hostile surface forces.

Recent events in the Mediterranean have shown that at distances of more than 200nm from their bases shore-based aircraft would usually be unable to give timely support, if any. For example, the bases at Trapani-Birgi and Catania-Sigonella, where the Italian Air Force's Tornados are based, are about 150nm from the island of Lampedusa, scene of a recent air-defence alarm. Even in the event of an alert, the aircraft need about five minutes to take off and at least 12min at 500kt to reach the island. "During the Lampedusa alert," former Chief of Naval Staff Adm Marulli said, recently, "the air cover gave us great problems. It is enough to say that from our request for air cover to take-off, 10–12min were needed. Though the threat was subsequently identified as an Italian

G.222 tactical transport flying on the wrong route our interceptors arrived too late to be able to operate. In addition, on the total of 45 days on which two of our recent task forces were exercising – one south of Capo Passero and the other south-east of Lampedusa – real air cover was assured for some hours only to that operating south-east of Lampedusa. Nothing more."

All studies carried out by NATO and the Italian Navy indicate that the escort of convoys through the Mediterranean would be extremely difficult without air cover. Moreover, according to Adm Marulli, shore-based air cover for a task force costs about ten times as much as comparable protection from embarked aircraft, and cannot be guaranteed at all times and in all conditions.

The Italian Naval Staff claims that the argument for effective naval aviation does not rule out co-operation between the Air Force and the Navy. "To think that the Navy seeks to operate 'against' the Air Force or to replace it is a nonsense," says Adm Piccioni, Navy Chief of Staff. "On the contrary, such is the increasing importance of air power in naval warfare, the Navy will have more and more need of the close co-operation of the Air Force. In the same way, the air defence of national territory, specifically an Air Force mission, will benefit indirectly from the forward defence that the Navy, with its surface-to-air missiles and, potentially, embarked aircraft could contribute on the sea approaches."

"In recent years," Adm Piccioni observes, "co-operation between the Navy and Air Force in the co-ordinated operation of naval units and aircraft has increased, as shown by recent events in the Southern Mediterranean. But to raise our Navy's capabilities to the level of those of other NATO navies we need to be able to protect our ships and merchant convoys with fast-reacting air cover, to cope with attacks lasting no longer than two or three minutes."

But before it can do this, the Italian Navy has to face the problem that in the opinion of many Italian taxpayers *Garibaldi* is little more than a luxury. "This is quite wrong," Adm Piccioni says, "The *Garibaldi*'s

great dimensions are needed to give the embarked aircraft a stable platform in all sea conditions."

The Italian Navy Staff rejects comparisons of *Garibaldi* with other aircraft carriers. The *Nimitz* class and other carriers, nuclear or conventional, are no more, they say, than a vehicle for the embarked squadrons, which supply the real combat power. *Garibaldi* is however a true combatant unit, her embarked aircraft being just one more weapon system, to be used for anti-aircraft and anti-ship defence at medium to long range.

The Navy's proposals and the Air Force response

The problem for the Italian Navy stems from Royal Decree No 645 of March 28, 1923, that unified all existing air arms under Air Force command. The subsequent Aeronautical Act of 1931 prohibited the Navy from training pilots. The result is that today the Navy finds itself facing the threats of the mid-1980s while constrained by constitutional directives dating back over 60 years.

The Air Force point of view is that naval officers should be allowed to fly only the Navy's helicopters and maritime patrol aircraft, and no others. The Air Force keeps fixed-wing aviation to itself, fearing that the creation of naval fixed-wing aviation will eventually erode its own budgets.

The Navy solution, proposed in a study prepared in December 1981 by Adm Mario Angelozzi and Adm Ubaldo Bernini, is the creation of a naval air arm, the acquisition and maintenance cost of which would have borne directly and exclusively by the Navy budget. This would free the Navy to buy and operate both fixed-wing and rotary-wing aircraft, according to its own priorities. Training and procurement would take place within the MoD framework.

Today the Italian Navy has a force of 108 helicopters, more than 300 pilots (many of them already flying

shoulder to shoulder with Air Force colleagues on the ASW aircraft of the 30th and 41st Squadrons at Cagliari/Elmas and Catania), more than 1,200 flight specialists and technicians, and many ground installations. According to naval officials, this force would allow the new fixed-wing element to be absorbed without the problems and costs that would normally be associated with the creation of a new air capability.

A solution in sight?

In September 1985 a bill which would enable the Navy to create its own air arm was presented to the Italian Parliament by Defence Minister Giovanni Spadolini. This has been examined and was approved early this year by the Senate defence committee. It was due to go to Parliament for final approval in February. Its provisions include independent control, organisation and operation of naval aircraft by the Navy, although the Air Force can request their use for the air defence of Italy. The Navy would provide pilots, although some Air Force pilots could also serve. Some technical evaluation of candidate aircraft and other assistance would come from the Air Force.

The auguries for a smooth passage through Parliament are good. Last November Defence Minister Spadolini met Defence Chief of Staff Gen Bisogniero and the Chiefs of Staff of the Navy and the Air Force, Gen Pisano. Afterwards the Ministry of Defence announced that the meeting "underlined the spirit of co-operation between the two forces," and revealed "the importance that both Staffs attach to the legislative initiatives on Defence that are currently under evaluation by Parliament." Without doubt a new spirit has entered the relationship between the Air Force and Navy, and that can only bode well for the future of Italian naval aviation. After the personal collisions between former Chiefs of Staff Adm Marulli and Gen Cottone, whose positions were firmly opposed, the debate now seems to be much less bitter, with plenty of space for a compromise.

The Royal Navy's front line *

Antony Preston and Nick Childs

The Trafalgar-*class attack submarines and* Broadsword-*class frigates are the most advanced vessels of their type currently in service with the Royal Navy. They would also be among the first RN units to engage the enemy in* war. **ANTONY PRESTON** *describes how the crew of HMS* Turbulent *live and operate.* **NICK CHILDS** *explains the developments that make HMS* Brave *a significant improvement on her earlier Type 22 sisters.*

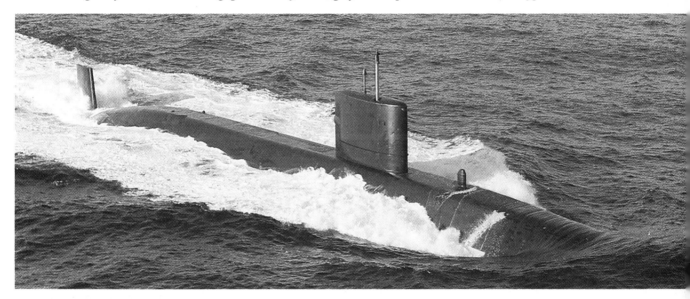

HMS Turbulent

HER MAJESTY'S Submarine *Turbulent* is the second of the *Trafalgar*-class nuclear hunter-killer submarines (SSNs), the Royal Navy's most modern design. She was commissioned in April 1984 and has since been followed into service by *Tireless* and *Torbay*; three more boats – *Trenchant* (launched in November), *Talent* and *Triumph* – are at various stages of construction.

In general the design of the *Trafalgar*s resembles that of the previous *Swiftsure* class, but with major improvements to silencing and some detailed internal changes. In fact, with an interval of at least a year

HMS *Turbulent*'s surface wake suggests a noisy boat, but submerged she is quieter than an *Oberon*-class patrol submarine.

between each SSN order, no two boats are alike; each one shows minor improvements over her predecessors. *Turbulent*'s commanding officer, Cdr David Tall, believes the "Ts" to be the quietest and most effective SSNs yet built, but admits that *Tireless* will be significantly quieter than his boat, with *Torbay* showing a further improvement.

Although the *Trafalgar*s are driven by the same PWR1 pressurised water reactor as the *Swiftsure* class and have a hull of almost identical dimensions, the special measures taken to reduce radiated noise and propeller cavitation have resulted in numerous differences. In 1984 it was revealed that *Trafalgar* had

* Taken from *At sea with Turbulent* and *On board HMS Brave*, published in *Jane's Defence Weekly* for February 21, 1987, and January 17, 1987, respectively.

Above: Turbulent arrives at Portsmouth at the end of a patrol. (*L. & L. van Ginderen*)

Below: Turbulent ties up at Groton US Navy base at the start of a 1986 visit to this East Coast submarine facility.

been tried over an acoustic range in Scotland and had achieved noise levels lower than those of the classic *Oberon* diesel boats. That was achieved with a conventional seven-bladed propeller, whereas *Turbulent* has the quieter shrouded pump-jet propulsor. The latest SSKs are of course even quieter, but the *Oberons* have long been considered a benchmark for quiet running, and the *Trafalgar* class shows what huge strides have been made in submarine propulsion.

The PWR1 reactor is a development of the Westinghouse S5W *Skipjack* type, supplied by the US Navy, via the British Dounreay reactor developed for the *Valiant* class in the late 1950s and early 1960s. It generates steam to drive two English Electric geared steam turbines. As with previous UK SSNs and SSBNs, the plant develops 15,000shp, equivalent to a submerged speed of about 30kt. A Paxman 400bhp diesel generating current to drive an electric motor acts as an emergency "get you home" unit. An accumulator battery is also provided.

Accommodation

A *Trafalgar*-class submarine has two continuous decks, an arrangement which minimises fore-and-aft movement through the control room. This is located amidships on 1 Deck, and flanked by the navigation console to starboard and the DCB fire-control and action information organisation console to port. Forward are the sound room, radar office, and senior rates' bunk spaces. Immediately abaft the control room are the CO's cabin to starboard and the W/T office to port. Further aft is the bulkhead isolating the nuclear reactor compartment, forbidden to unauthorised personnel.

2 Deck, reached by a ladder from the control room, supports the rest of the accommodation. A central passageway provides access. The wardroom, pantry and officers' cabins are grouped together on the port side, with sonar cabinets ahead and the junior rates' bunk spaces aft. The junior rates' mess is aft on the starboard side, with the galley, senior rates' mess, laundry and bathrooms ahead.

Two escape hatches are provided, one right forward and the other in the machinery spaces.

Although SSNs and SSBNs are much larger than SSKs, they are not spacious. Every inch of space aboard *Turbulent* is taken up with equipment, and spare bodies are advised to "rack out" – get into a bunk and read a book or catch a short nap – whenever possible. All sense of night and day disappears, even when the boat is running on the surface, and the desire to know what is going on "up top" becomes all-consuming, with weather reports from Northwood seized upon eagerly and passed from hand to hand in the wardroom.

As in the USN's latest SSNs, the amount of equipment packed in leads to the practice of "hot bunking". This means that a small number of ratings must use bunks vacated by men going on watch.

Weapon systems

The Flag Officer Submarines has publicly expressed his faith in the latest Mod 2 variant of the Tigerfish Mk 24 torpedo, which will shortly replace the Mod 1 in *Turbulent* and other SSNs. The UGM-84B2 Sub-Harpoon is also a potent weapon against surface targets, with its ability to strike at ranges of up to 60km. In time the Tigerfish Mod 2 will be replaced by the Spearfish.

One of the minor casualties of progress in the RN's submarines is the disappearance of the term "torpedo room"; it is now the weapons storage compartment and contains five torpedo tubes. The Sub-Harpoons and Tigerfish are stowed in horizontal racks and loaded automatically into the five tubes. Loading time is counted in minutes, such is the precision needed to guide heavy objects such as torpedoes or missile canisters into snugly fitting tubes.

Even when running on the surface, *Turbulent*'s crew constantly practice techniques and evolutions. The drill for loss of nuclear power is practised frequently, and "watershots" simulate the firing of weapons from the tubes. A watershot not only exercises the firing procedure but also tests the water ballasting which compensates for each firing, and gives the DCB operator a simulated engagement.

Control

The control room is a very crowded place, with the attack and search periscopes and other masts taking up much of the free space. This problem is being tackled in the latest "T" boats by a more integrated arrangement of the equipment, but the long-term solution in future SSN design may be to use non-penetrating masts wherever possible.

In any submarine space is always at a premium, but sometimes the solution is merely a matter of rearrangement: in *Turbulent*, for example, the sound room is too cramped while the radar office on the opposite side of the passageway has room to spare.

One criticism of the diving controls in *Turbulent* is the lack of a central point of reference for the planesman.

Turbulent at speed on the surface. Underwater speed is believed to be 30kt.

The next-generation Submarine Control System will use improved display techniques and more powerful processing to reduce the workload on the attack team.

Operations

Until more Royal Navy SSNs are in service the operating cycle of boats like *Turbulent* will continue to be arduous. Each deployment lasts about 85 days, as part of a normal running time of 17 weeks.

The Royal Navy remains tight-lipped about submarine operations, but the wartime mission for its SSNs is no mystery. The first line of defence against Soviet attack submarines is the chokepoint represented by the deep channel in the Greenland-Iceland-UK

Gap, through which they must pass to reach the shipping routes in the North Atlantic. For more than 25 years NATO has maintained barriers of underwater sensors (SOSUS) to get the range and bearing of any hostile contact. NATO SSNs are deployed behind these barriers, to act as "pouncers", catching those Soviet submarines which escape destruction by maritime patrol aircraft, ships and seabed mines.

In recent years the development of ultra-long-range missiles, capable of being fired from within defended "bastions" close to Soviet bases, has reduced the effectiveness of the SOSUS barriers. NATO submarines would thus have to operate inside the bastions in order to inflict significant losses on Soviet SSNs and SSBNs. To make the problem harder, Soviet submarines are quieter than they used to be.

Conclusion

A modern nuclear attack submarine costs about £200 million, most of which is accounted for by propulsion and weapon systems. A brief look at an SSN such as HMS *Turbulent* leaves no doubt about whether that money is being spent wisely.

When the last "T" boat joins the fleet in 1990 there will be a total of 18 SSNs in Royal Navy service. By then the *Valiant* and *Churchill* classes will be nearing the end of their useful lives, and the successor to the *Trafalgar*s, the SSN-20 design, will be under construction.

HMS Brave

AT FIRST glance the Royal Navy's newest anti-submarine frigate, HMS *Brave*, might seem to be a rather unremarkable warship. After all, she is merely the seventh Type 22 and only the third of the stretched Batch 2s. But *Brave* is charting the future for the Royal Navy in a number of important areas, and boasts several significant firsts.

She is the first warship to take Rolls Royce's new Marine Spey gas turbines to sea. She is also the first ship to be fitted with the improved lightweight Sea Wolf GWS 25 Mod 3 surface-to-air missile system, the first British warship to carry a full version of the new Sea Gnat decoy system, and the first British frigate designed to operate the new Westland-Agusta EH101 anti-submarine helicopter.

The Type 22 design dates back to 1968. It was initially intended to be an Anglo-Dutch collaborative effort, but the attempt proved unsuccessful and co-operation was gradually abandoned. The first Type 22, HMS *Broadsword*, was ordered in February 1974 and commissioned in May 1979.

Above: **HMS *Brave*, first of a new breed of Type 22 frigates.** *(Rolls-Royce)*

Above right: **Midships section of HMS *Brave*. Note the Indian chief insignia just forward of the funnel.** *(L. & L. van Ginderen)*

Right: **Heart of HMS *Brave*'s powerplant is the Rolls-Royce Spey aero-engine.** *(Rolls-Royce)*

The Type 22s were envisaged as successors to the *Leander*-class frigates, 26 of which were built for the RN, but there were always doubts about the size, sophistication and cost of the design. As it turns out, 14 are to be built, though four of them are replacements for ships lost in the 1982 Falklands War.

Brave was ordered on August 27, 1981, accepted into service on February 21, 1986, and commissioned on July 4. She was due to become fully operational in April 1987, on completion of trials. In common with the other Batch 2s, she has had additional hull sections inserted between the bridge and foremast, and has a much more raked bow than the Batch 1s. These additions mean that at 148.1m *Brave* is 17m longer than *Broadsword*, first of the Type 22s. The extra length yields an improvement on the original Type 22s' already fine seaworthiness. According to one report, the first Batch 2, HMS *Boxer*, has demonstrated an ability to maintain 28kt on a diagonal course into a Force 10 gale. Good seakeeping is of course vital to the Type 22s' primary task.

Brave, like all Batch 1 and 2 Type 22s, is a first-line anti-submarine warfare (ASW) frigate. (The Batch 3s, with an improved gun and anti-ship missile fit, will be classified as general-purpose frigates.) She will thus have to spend lengthy periods as a lone picket, operating ahead of major naval formations. As a result, her primary ASW systems are backed up by a potent self-defence capability.

Brave's new Rolls-Royce Marine Spey SM1A

F94

engines are less powerful than the Olympus TM3Bs of earlier Type 22s. This means that, at just over 28kt, her top speed is at least 2kt less than that of the other Batch 2s. This deficiency may be reduced slightly if, as expected, she receives uprated Spey SM1Cs at her first major refit, in 1989. But in any case studies have suggested that a frigate's typical wartime operating profile would call for speeds in excess of 27kt for only 5% of its time under way. *Brave*'s relatively modest top speed might however prove a handicap when operating with US Navy carrier battle groups, which often employ sprint deployment tactics.

One of the Spey's major advantages is its fuel efficiency, amounting to a 30% improvement on the Olympus at full power. In addition, the lengthening of the late Type 22s means that they can carry substantially more fuel than the Batch 1s. Together, these factors give *Brave* exceptional range. Using one Spey and trailing one shaft, *Brave* could steam from the UK to the Falkland Islands and then return to Ascension Island – a distance of about 12,000nm – without refuelling.

Brave is fitted with water displacement tanks, so there is no loss of stability as fuel is consumed. On the contrary, because seawater is heavier than diesel oil, her displacement actually increases the further she goes.

Royal Navy frigates have been criticised in the past for their relative lack of endurance compared with some of their American counterparts. *Brave*'s impressive range is the result of a major effort to give new British warships far greater endurance.

Brave's electrical power is provided by four 1MW diesel generators. At present her maximum power requirements at action stations total 1.8MW. So there is plenty of redundancy in the system to cope with battle damage or future additional weapon fits.

Brave's main ASW sensors are the Type 2016 hull-mounted sonar (eventually to be replaced by the Type 2050) and the Type 2031Z towed-array passive sonar. The latter is housed on a large drum on the port side of the quarterdeck, below the flight deck. When deployed it is trailed at a distance of more than 1.6km. Typical operating speeds when using the Type 2031 range from 8–10kt down to as little as 2–3kt. Varying the ship's speed changes the depth at which the array operates, allowing it to penetrate thermal layers in the sea.

To minimise noise emissions during ASW operations, most major noise-generating machinery is raft-mounted. Among important exceptions to this are the galley and laundry equipment. The theory behind this is that such equipment would be shut down anyway at action stations. But the nature of the ship's role would inevitably mean long periods at a high state of alert, and it must be almost certain that such equipment would have to be used at some point.

The Type 2031 can detect targets at ranges in excess of 100nm. It gives surface forces a significant detection edge over submarines for the first time.

Processing information from passive arrays is an art still in its infancy. In the Type 22s the processing equipment for the Type 2031 has to be housed in a separate compartment below the main operations room. It will be some years before the system can be fully integrated into a frigate's action information organisation.

The hull stretch in the Batch 2 and 3 Type 22s has permitted a very spacious operations room – comparable in size to those of the *Invincible*-class aircraft carriers – situated immediately below and behind the bridge. In emergencies the Batch 2s can provide limited flag facilities, as demonstrated by HMS *Beaver* before the delayed arrival of HMS *Illustrious* for the Global 86 deployment. The Batch 3s will have further improved flag facilities.

Like the other Batch 2s and 3s, *Brave* is equipped with the new Ferranti Computer Assisted Command System 1 (CACS-1) action information organisation (AIO). The major advantage of CACS over the Royal Navy's previous systems – the Action Data Automation Weapons System (ADAWS) and the Computer Assisted Action Information System (CAAIS) – is its ability to receive instructions in plain language input with light pens, rather than through lengthy keyboard manipulations. This greatly reduces reaction times and the chances of input errors. CACS can also handle much more information than either ADAWS or CAAIS.

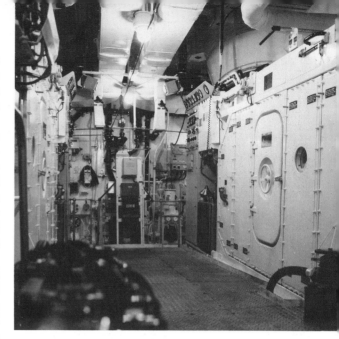

There has been criticism of CACS over the number of teething troubles encountered in trials. But it must be remembered that CACS is the first Royal Navy system of its kind to have all its software development carried out at sea. Originally it was intended that a shore-based CACS test facility would be built at the Admiralty Surface Weapons Establishment near Portsmouth, but this was a victim of the 1981 Defence Review. Nevertheless, *Brave*'s officers regard CACS as a match for any rival system in any other West European navy.

Brave's main ASW weapon system is her helicopter. With a strengthened and enlarged flight deck, chacterised by noticeable overhangs on both the port and starboard quarters, and a bigger hangar, she is the first Royal Navy frigate designed to operate the EH101 helicopter. The main feature of the hangar is its much greater height compared with those of earlier Type 22s.

When it becomes available in the 1990s the EH101 will greatly extend the ASW reach of the Royal Navy's frigates. In the meantime, *Brave* could accommodate the current Westland Sea King, though at present she has a Westland Lynx, with hangar space for a second if necessary.

Brave's other ASW weapon is the Shipborne Torpedo Weapons System 2 (STWS-2). She has two trainable triple torpedo tubes, one on each beam abreast the funnel. These can launch either US Mk 46 or Marconi Stingray torpedoes.

Above left: **The engine room aboard HMS *Brave*. The two Marine Speys are installed in the compartments to right and left. They are backed up by a pair of Marine Tynes, which provide boost and "get you home" power.** *(Rolls-Royce)*

Left: **Stern view of the first Type 22, *Broadsword*. *Brave* has a bigger hangar and extended flight deck to accommodate the EH101 helicopter.** *(Royal Navy)*

Above: ***Brave*'s Lynx comes aboard.** *(Rolls-Royce)*

For self-defence *Brave* has a double-headed Sea Wolf arrangement. She is in fact trials ship for the new lightweight GWS 25 Mod 3 variant of the system. This replaces the original Type 910 tracker with the lighter Type 911 (Marconi 805SW). This is a dual-frequency system, with I-band and millimetric-wave antennae. The millimetric unit is a version of the DN181 Blindfire radar used in the Rapier missile system, and is for use against sea-skimming targets. It eliminates the need for television tracking of such targets, as required by the Type 910.

Mod 3 is also more highly automated than the Mod 0, and engagements can now be carried out fully automatically. According to *Brave*'s officers, the Mod 3 is a substantial technological improvement over the Mod 0.

The forward Type 911 tracker is mounted above and behind the bridge, the aft one above the hangar. The new tracker's lighter weight, and the increased capacity of CACS, could have been further exploited by increasing the number of trackers per ship, and hence its ability to handle a saturation attack. But this would have added significantly to the cost.

The Mod 3 system retains the Vickers six-barrelled launcher of the original GWS 25. This means that each Type 22 has 12 ready-to-fire missiles. But once these have been launched, manual reloading takes about five minutes – a potentially crucial delay. This problem is being dealt with by the vertical launch Sea Wolf GWS 26 system planned for the new Type 23 frigates.

GWS 25 Mod 3 retains the Type 967/968 surveillance radars of the original system, mounted back-to-back in a single stabilised housing on top of the foremast. The Type 967 is used for high-angle air surveillance, while the Type 968 is for low-level air cover and

surface surveillance. *Brave* has the improved Type 967M.

Brave's other defensive armament includes two elderly Bofors 40mm L/60 Mk9 guns. These are no longer effective as anti-aircraft weapons, but they could still prove useful as "junk-busters" if the ship was ever called upon to carry out low-level policing duties.

Like other Royal Navy warships, *Brave* may be fitted with additional light guns when she becomes fully operational. It is also to be hoped that funds will be found to equip her and her Batch 1 and 2 sisters with a modern close-in weapon system (CIWS) like the Dutch Goalkeeper, to be fitted to the Batch 3s. Whatever faith the Royal Navy places in Sea Wolf's ability to stop missiles – and it is considerable – a CIWS would seem to be essential for these vessels, which will be among the Royal Navy's major warships in the future.

Brave's present defensive weapon systems are completed by the first full Sea Gnat decoy system to go to sea in a British frigate. Sea Gnat, a NATO project, can operate in both distraction and confusion modes, and is fully integrated into the ship's command and control system.

The earlier Batch 2s, *Boxer* and *Beaver*, have an interim Sea Gnat. They do however have purpose-designed launchers, whereas *Brave* has to make do with Mk 137 launchers, as used in the US Navy's Super Rapid Blooming Offboard Chaff (SRBOC) system.

Perhaps the weakest element of *Brave*'s weapon fit is her offensive armament. This is limited to four

Brave is the first Type 22 to be equipped to handle the EH101, which is in the weight bracket above Lynx.

Aérospatiale MM.38 Exocet missiles, with no reloads, although the Lynx's Sea Skua air-to-surface missiles provide some additional offensive firepower. It is to be hoped that *Brave* will in due course receive Harpoon, which is to be fitted to the Batch 3 Type 22s.

Brave's damage control organisation incorporates many of the Falklands lessons now applied throughout the fleet. There are smoke curtains across many doorways, and 450 Emergency Life Support Apparatus (ELSA) sets distributed around the ship for use by the complement of 270 or so. In addition, there are five charging points and 32 sets of full breathing apparatus for damage control parties; this compares with a pre-Falklands total of just 12. But other major changes – such as the incorporation of fire-resistant cable cladding, and a significant reduction in cable penetration of major bulkheads – could not be included in the design.

In spite of the British Government's assurances, it seems almost certain that the Royal Navy's destroyer and frigate force will fall well below the desired total of 50 ships in the future. For this reason, *Brave* will inevitably play a significant part in the Royal Navy's operations in years to come. It is thus to be hoped that her motto – *Fortis fortuna adiuvat*, "Fortune favours the brave" – proves to be appropriate.